for the Fairy Godfather

The Lone Pine
PICNIC GUIDE
To Alberta

Nancy Gibson
John Whittaker
with Carolyn Whittaker

Maps & Illustrations
by Diana Gibson

LONE
PINE

The Publisher:
Lone Pine Publishing
#206, 10426-81 Avenue
Edmonton, Alberta, Canada
T6E 1X5

Canadian Cataloguing in Publication Data

Gibson, Nancy.
The Lone Pine picnic guide to Alberta

   Bibliography: p.

   Includes index.

   ISBN 0-919433-60-X

   1. Alberta - Description and travel - 1981-
- Guide-books. 2. Picnicking. 3. Outdoor cookery.
I. Whittaker, John, 1940- II. Title.
FC3657.G52 1989   917.123'043   C89-091092-8

Front cover photo: Douglas Leighton
Cover design: Yuet Chan
Layout and design: Yuet Chan, Jack Lewis, Jane Spalding
Maps and illustrations: Diana Gibson (except p.5, 131-2 & 150)
Editorial: Mary Walters Riskin
Printing: Hignell Printing

Publisher's Acknowledgement
The publisher gratefully acknowledges the assistance of the
Federal Department of Communications, Alberta Culture and
Multiculturalism, the Canada Council, and the Alberta
Foundation for the Literary Arts in the production of this book.

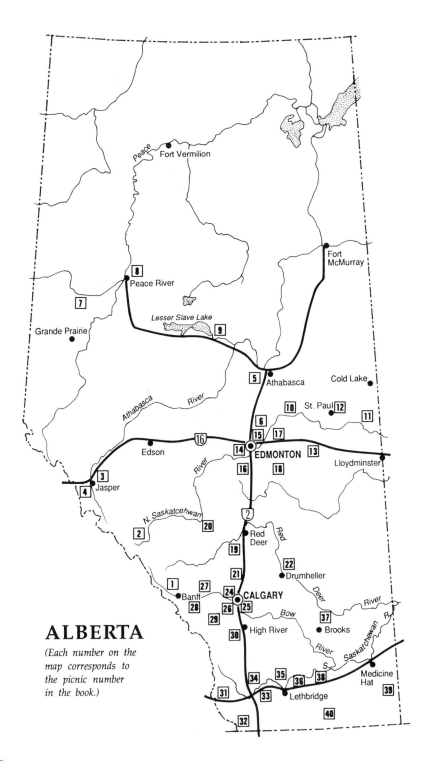

Fort Vermilion

Peace

8 Peace River

7

Grande Prairie

Lesser Slave Lake

9

Fort
McMurray

5 Athabasca

Cold Lake

Athabasca River

10 St. Paul 12

11

6

15 17

16

14 EDMONTON 13

Edson

River

Lloydminster

16

18

2

N. Saskatcehwan

20

2

19

Red
Deer

Red

22 Drumheller

21

1 27

28

Banff

24 CALGARY

26 25

Deer

River

29

37

30 High River

Brooks

Bow

River

S.

Saskatchewan R.

ALBERTA

*(Each number on the
map corresponds to
the picnic number
in the book.)*

34 35

31

33 Lethbridge

36 38

Medicine
Hat

39

32

40

3

4 Jasper

Table of Contents

Acknowledgements

This book reflects the willingness of many people to tell us about their favourite picnic spots, and in several cases, even to take us there, like Mr. Matheson in Dewberry, and Kate and Ian Morrison in Calgary. In response to our usual opening, "We are looking for special places for picnicking. . . . What would you suggest?" people often stopped what they were doing, and took time to describe spots we'd never have found, and to tell us local stories that you would never otherwise be reading.

We would like to thank Ray and Vivian Lowry, whose house served as our Calgary base; Len Bland who gave us the *Atlas of Alberta* which mapped our trail to the past; Terrie Cappello with whom we organized the first annual North Cooking Lake Community Picnic so long ago; Art Clough, Bernie Campbell and Ann Lambert for their help with the photographs; Marion the Librarian, who could always find the missing recipe, poem or place; and her husband, Denis Saffron, who knows a hundred ways to serve rabbit.

Once we had drafted the 40 picnics, we wanted each to be read by someone else who was thoroughly familiar with the area, for, for we do not profess to be experts on all these places. We are grateful to the many people at provincial Travel InfoCentres, national, provincial and municipal park offices, historical associations and chambers of commerce throughout the province who kindly helped us at the research and proof-reading stages. Our thanks to Ervin J. Allen, Duane Barris, Keith Bocking, Vivian Bowman, Mary Craig, Sylvia Gascon, Dan Gaudet, Rod Gray, Jean Harris, Candy Haugen, Eileen Hendy, Les Hurt, Shelby J. MacLeod, Ruth Many Grey Horses, Tony Maxwell, Josephine Mitchell, Lisa E. Oishi, Will Pearce, Pat Scobie, Terry Soldan, R.R. Smith, Bob Tannas, Kevin Van Tighem, Jeff Waugh and Chris Williams. Some picnics reflect the generosity of people who live in the area and who are proud to share their knowledge, people like Greg Kenney in Rosebud, Don Shannon in Blairmore, K.M. Buko and Betty Olson of Markerville, and Farley Wuth in Morley.

Many people have helped us to gather just the right recipes for their favourite picnic, and here we thank Isabel Butler, Barbara Allen, Anna Franklin and Mike Sich.

Grateful acknowledgement goes to Charles E. Tuttle, Company, Inc. for permission to use material from Robert Gard's book, *Johnny Chinook*; to McClelland & Stewart for permission to use the A.A. Milne poem, "Lines and Squares," from *When We Were Very Young*; to

Margaret Gershaw Roche and Ann Mackie for permission to use material from Senator Gershaw's book, *A Brief History of Southern Alberta: The Short Grass Area.*

We are deeply grateful to Uncle Nowell Sadlier-Brown who reviewed the manuscript, giving us the benefit of his extensive knowledge of the English language and of western Canadian history; and to Helen and Hugh Lavender who reviewed the manuscript, took us gold panning, and always had a hot cup of coffee ready when we needed it; and Mary Walters Riskin at Lone Pine Publishing whose enthusiasm, encouragement and incisive editorial eye carried us through to the end.

Despite the willing assistance of so many people, there will be some errors in the text, and these are clearly our own. In some cases facilities change over time, and these changes will conflict with information here. We sincerely regret any inconvenience.

Picnics have always been a family enterprise with us, and so is this book. Although Carolyn and Diana have worked closely with us on the writing and art work, each and every one of our nine children has, over the years, introduced major innovations and refinements to our picnicking. Thank you Michael, Carolyn, Diana, Steven, Ginger, Justin, Jason, Annthea and Katy.

There have been so many friends who have taken us on picnics, lent us their books, and shared their ideas, which we have shamelessly adopted — thank you all.

And finally, we would like to thank Grant Kennedy, president of Lone Pine Publishing, for taking serious picnicking seriously!

Key to Symbols

 Picnic Tables

 Water Source

 Toilets

 Shelter

 No Pets Allowed

 Boat Launch

 Swimming

 Fires Allowed (stoves, or pits, and wood available)

 Telephone

INTRODUCTION

Picnic Preamble

In our family a picnic is a very special thing. It is a delicate blending of the right people, the right setting, a suitable menu, interesting activities and conversation, and nice weather. When all these elements coincide the result is inevitably a delightful memory for the participants. Our picnics are recorded in "memory pictures" by one of our daughters, and in photographs by some of the rest of us. Many a family reunion at Christmas is peppered with each of us remembering a different but splendid picnic, and revitalizing the memories for each other with the full colours of both kinds of pictures.

This book is designed to help you make your picnics memorable occasions, replete with historical anecdotes, legends, adventurous menus and recipes, things to see and do nearby, and a touch of magic here and there. There is no particular logic to the selection of places — we simply followed our whims and instincts. Occasionally we sought the settings for history we already knew; places with strong auras of the past are Turner Valley, for example, or Leduc No. 1 where the Alberta Oil Boom began. Sometimes we were overcome by the natural beauty of a site, like Maligne Canyon or the Blackfoot Grazing Reserve. Often our sense of whimsy led us to a spot to stop and sit and enjoy, and the Vegreville Egg and the St. Paul Flying Saucer Pad are those kinds of places. Several of our picnics reflect the history of Native Canadians, since we are aware that they have been visiting or living in many of the best picnic sites for at least 10,000 years. And sometimes our sense of fun triumphed, and the result is exemplified in the Scotchman's picnic.

A picnic is usually a celebration of some sort. Although most picnics are held outside, indoor picnics should not be overlooked, especially in winter. They require less planning, and transportation is easy — especially if the picnic is on your living room floor, or in the middle of your king-sized bed. A formal picnic, with cold cuts, potato salad and an appropriate libation, served on the floor in front of the fire, can be great fun for the whole family or for a couple (and there are no mosquitoes, either).

Pages of Picnics

Everyone loves a picnic, so we selected spots which are easily reached by car, usually involving no more than a hundred metres of walking so that each picnic would be accessible to most senior citizens and to little kids. Thus, with reluctance we turned down the wonderful site that required 8 kilometres of steep hiking. Most of the picnics are small-scale, meant for friends, couples, and families. We have, however, included a chapter on planning picnics for large groups, and this includes a few recipes for 100, and the rules to some games which we remember playing in our youths. The picnic at Victoria/Pakan includes recipes for 40 people, in case your large groups aren't so large.

Most of our picnic places were discovered as we explored our own region on weekends and in the summer. We found that theme picnics were a great way to educate ourselves and our kids, and the kids quickly became experts in identifying magic picnic places — some of them in the heart of the city.

Each of the forty picnics included in this book has a theme, as do all our picnics. The theme may be suggested by the place, the history, or the name, but sometimes the connection is a bit far-fetched, as you will see.

Picnics in Perspective

Why would any sane person leave all the comforts of a modern home to venture off to a wild, untamed place to eat a meal prepared over a campfire, sitting on an old blanket or a rough bench amid ants and mosquitoes, when the most meticulous preparation may get rained on anyway?

Anthropologists tell us that the human species is driven to interact with the elements, to conquer nature, to reaffirm dominance in the natural order of things. This urge to control the wilderness leads to isolated episodes wherein the human species attempts to "civilize" the wild by using propane stoves, deck chairs, plastic canopies, battery-operated fire starters, and in extreme cases, recreation vehicles, to establish a crude replica of the suburban homestead upon a piece of unsettled land.

The first picnics weren't imitations of anything — people ate out and cooked over campfires on nice days because it got stuffy in the caves. As technology went along, cooking methods became refined, and with the concept of the chimney, moved permanently indoors in most societies, ending forever the annoyance of trying to start a fire in the rain.

But not forever. It has been speculated that the European notion of picnicking crossed the channel to England from France in the 19th century along with the "cult of nature" influence spawned by Jean Jacques Rousseau, and fueled by the Romantic Poets. By then people were living comfortably inside relatively permanent dwellings with such conveniences as indoor plumbing and windows. The simple life of the past was idealized, and living in harmony with nature took on a certain romantic appeal. Romantic idealism is rarely pragmatic, but the adoption of picnicking by the British is either an example of monumental blindness or determined self-deception, given the usual climate of the British Isles. In the never-ending contest between people and nature, it is during the act of picnicking that people are most vulnerable to the elements; to be "rained out" means that nature remains dominant despite technology.

There are several other sociological explanations for the peculiar behaviour displayed by picnickers. These outings can be interpreted as an attempt to escape from the urban industrial environment, an escape from artificiality. Picnic participants may be seeking temporary informality to balance the enforced rigidity of modern daily life. Alternatively, picnics can be seen in a positive light as the reaffirmation of a social unit. For example, making a morose 14-year old son attend a family picnic confirms parental power within the family. (But is it worth it?)

The Spanish carry this to an extreme, collecting 10,000 people for a week once a year on a mountain top, or alternatively in a swamp, and picnicking and dancing day and night for the duration, without even a Port-a-Potty in sight! During this religious picnic, called a *romería*, rain does not diminish the festivities — it is simply ignored. Dancing continues, parades march on, masses are held, and fires miraculously continue to burn. Our equivalent of the romeria is the community picnic or agricultural fair, but unlike the Spaniards, we usually go home at night.

Pique-Niques Past

According to the Oxford English Dictionary the word picnic did not occur in English in literature before 1748. The word is most likely derived from the French *pique-nique*. In England, nineteenth century picnics were a pastime of the rich involving an outing to a pastoral setting and a meal composed of contributions of food from each participant. Hence the rarely used word, *picnickery*, which implies "a collection of things from various sources, like the provisions at a picnic." The Picnic Society in London was a group of people whose gatherings were characterized by dramatic presentations and other social entertainments to which each member of the Society contributed. Finally, a *picnickian* is a person who takes part in a picnic. With this broader sense of the word "picnic," our readers, fellow picnickians all, will understand our concept of the compleat, or in more contemporary terms, the magic picnic, the components of which are not limited to victuals, but must include an appropriate setting, congenial company, and a mystique. This last component is intangible but essential. It provides the theme — and the magic part of the picnic. A magic picnic is one in which all components are in place and are savoured and enjoyed by each picnickian.

The art of picnickery is flexible, limited only by the standards and requirements of the particular picnickians. Some issues may be taken for granted, and remain unspoken, such as clothing. What to wear on a picnic is a personal question. It has been addressed by some of our greatest minds at some length, and here we refer you to the famous painting by Edouard Manet entitled "Déjeuner sur l'herbe" (less elegant in English — "Lunch on the Grass") in which one of the female picnickians elected to wear nothing at all. We leave these delicate issues to the reader.

Particularly Precious Picnics

Our family tradition of picnicking was elevated to an art form one day beneath the ruins of an old Spanish fort as we sat (fully dressed) in the shade of a silvery olive orchard, transported by the beauty of the afternoon, the compelling history of the place, and the wonderful tastes of the Andalusian foods and wines which composed our seven course feast, complete with china and crystal! After our return to Canada we continued to seek out "magic" picnics at home, picnics which had the right combination of elements — and we have discovered many such places.

Some of our picnics are less serious than others. The first of these began when we tried to find Black Forest Cake to eat in the Black Forest. After many stores and bakeries let us down, we finally found a frozen cake in a supermarket . . . and then drove back into the Black Forest from the village to thaw the cake and have our picnic. This sort of theme picnic challenges everyone's imagination, and permits the corny members of the group to display the full range of their talents.

We would be dishonest if we didn't acknowledge a debt to James Michener, who expounded on the art of picnicking before we did in his book on Spain, *Iberia*. He had discovered the Spanish penchant for picnicking, and later so did we, as we meandered through Spain with our five children in an ancient but loyal Volkswagen van called Vincent (see photo on back cover). This van carried all seven of us, our packs and the thirteen boxes of books that always seem to accompany us throughout Europe, at a steady but slowish pace. Vincent took us to many picnics throughout Spain as we read bits of Michener aloud. The van was probably the best-equipped picnic-mobile in Europe — carrying a portable table, a portable propane paella cooker, cutlery, china and linens, and a couple of pretty vases for flowers for table settings.

We have developed and refined our picnic equipment since then, and our suggestions are offered in the next chapter of this book. Many picnic sites are equipped with tables and grills and shelters, but some of the sites that we especially like have no amenities whatsoever other than the magic of the place. You may choose to have an elaborate formal picnic, complete with your own portable table, or you may choose to have a sandwich on a blanket. In some of our picnics we offer both options. We have provided an index of the recipes from all the picnics at the back of the book so that you can mix and match.

Proximate Proportions

Our picnic recipes are expressed sometimes in metric units, sometimes English, and sometimes both. Indeed, it is in the kitchen that Canada's conversion to metric is at its most confusing. Exact conversion produces ridiculous quantities: for example, 1 cup is equal to 236.6 ml. The usual way that a Canadian cook copes is by having measuring devices calibrated in both cups and millilitres. Then it is easy to switch systems to match the recipes. The important thing is to stick to the same system throughout the recipe, as it is generally proportion that is more important than actual quantity. For those who have only one kind of measuring cups, the following approximate conversion table is offered.

Approximate Metric Conversions

1/4 tsp	1 ml
1/2 tsp	2 ml
1 tsp	5 ml
1 Tbsp	15 ml
1/4 cup	50 ml
1/2 cup	125 ml
1 cup	250 ml
4 1/2 cups	1 L

Pursuing Picnic Perfection

We expect our readers to fall into two groups: those who already picnic seriously and want to compare their spots with ours; and those who want to become serious picnickers, and just need a little push.

We must acknowledge the suggestions from friends, many of

whom will recognize elements of their own picnics in these pages. Our friends *did* help us as we went along, although they flatly refused to take us seriously as we described the magnitude of the task of picnic-book-writing facing our family. In fact, the most empathetic comment came from our publisher. "Ah, a tough job," he said. "But someone has to do it!" But was that compassion or envy in his tone?

Everyone has a favourite picnic. As we wandered the province doing our research we found that people who had been strangers to us a moment before had warmed to the word "picnic" and were suddenly confiding intimate family picnic secrets to us in exhaustive detail! There was the family in the pick-up truck who, when we asked them if there were any good picnic spots in the area, turned the truck around, yelled, "Follow us!," and led us along a logging road part way up a mountain to a favourite place. They told us vignettes of local history that wouldn't be found in reference books, but which added the "magic" to the picnic. This wasn't an isolated example. When we asked one man in a small town museum about the local history he quickly telephoned to his wife to ask her to make up a picnic basket, drove us to his farm to pick her up, and took us all on one of the best picnics we've ever had.

We know that we have not seen, discovered nor even heard of all the great picnic places in Alberta. In fact, we would find it very distressing if we had, for much of the fun comes with the joy of discovering a new site, and this is our challenge to our readers. A picnic is an adventure that you share; we invite — nay, we encourage — readers to share their special picnic places for possible future editions of this book. Write to us, care of the publisher. All letters will be answered and suggestions acknowledged.

And now, let's go on a picnic!

Picnic Paraphernalia

In this chapter we provide a checklist which progresses from the very basic kit for the occasional picnicker to the sophisticated gear of the serious dilettante. There is also discussion of the relative merits of different items which reflects our personal biases, but acknowledges other points of view, so that you can make your own informed selections. The following sections are arranged in a progression from a simple picnic kit to a more elaborate set-up.

The Absolute Basics

Also known as the "Boy Scout" or the "Be Prepared" kit, this consists of one Swiss army knife carried at all times in the jacket pocket. This isn't as simple as it seems. Care must be taken when selecting a Swiss army knife because they come with such a delightful array of pop-up gadgets that one is tempted to get the one that does everything including pick teeth, darn socks and yodel. This is unfortunate because knives with all those attachments, if they can still be called knives, weigh so much that they can no longer reside in a pocket but require a belt pouch or pick-up truck to carry them around. Fortunately, the Swiss have priced these knives beyond the reach of most wage-earning picnickers and so, while the temptation may be there, the where-with-all is often not. Our knife, which serves us well, has attachments that:

> flip bottle caps,
> pull corks,
> open cans,
> slice cheese, and
> get the onion pickles from the bottom of the jar.

These are the essential functions, since smacking bottles against rocks to open them is ecologically unsound and potentially dangerous, and an inaccessible can of paté de foie gras can spoil your whole day. These knives are still available for less than $20.

The Basic Picnic Kit

Do you travel much in your car, and do you like the occasional "impromptu" picnic? In that case, in your trunk along with the jumper cables, tire chains, and the half-filled bottle of windshield fluid should be a basic picnic kit. This kit can be kept in a small box, taking up very little space, but permitting spontaneous picnicking without frills. It will do very well for the occasional picnicker, and you can add more equipment if you find you need to.

First there are the basics, the:

can opener,
bottle opener,
cork screw,
knife suitable for cheese.

While the all-purpose Swiss army machine will do, it also may introduce bits of cork into the wine, spray soda pop all over from punctured tops, and leave nasty jagged edges around the lips of tins. Thus we progress to special purpose devices. The cost is truly a function of what you want to spend, with corkscrews and can openers varying in price from $1.98 to $20 each. Electric can-openers are non-functional, of course, at most picnic sites, so purchase one of the more primitive manual models (or reclaim the old one from the back of the kitchen drawer).

Other convenient — and sometimes essential — bits of equipment that can be tucked into your picnic box are:

Bread knife: Although it may be fashionable to tear chunks of French bread from the loaf, there will be times when you want smooth slices, and this requires a knife with a serrated edge and a least an eight inch (20 cm) blade. We prefer a serrated edge to a sharp French or German chef's knife because it tends to stay sharp longer, and is not quite so lethal when you are fishing around in the picnic kit for something else. This knife is also useful for slicing onions and tomatoes.

Insect repellent: Deep Woods Off is among the best.

Sun tan lotion: It doesn't always rain on picnics. Get a high protection lotion, especially if near lakes, glaciers or the ocean.

Band-aids: Place a few in a plastic bag.

Matches: In the old days when smoking was socially acceptable, matches or other forms of fire-starting apparatus, like lighters, were always available. Now they are not, and one must make a special note to remember them. Bring lots, in a water-proof plastic bag or box. If you really want dependability, most camping stores sell waterproof matches.

Toilet paper: In Boy Scout camping days, this used to be referred to as 1001 because it has 1001 different uses. Keep in an old coffee can, with a tightly-fitting plastic lid to keep it dry.

Garbage bags: Always pack out what you bring to any site.

Flashlight: It doesn't matter what time the picnic starts, at some point in the season you may find yourself stumbling around in the dark, possibly looking for something like car keys or a child's tooth retainer. Check the flashlight occasionally to make sure the batteries are not dead.

Binoculars: Whether you prefer the big field glasses, or one of the small but powerful sets, these are invaluable for spotting birds, looking at mountains, and spying on other picnickers.

Although it probably won't fit in your kit box, you will want a *Blanket:* Any old blanket will do, but there are good woolen blankets in matching zipper cases which are sold as car blankets. These have the advantage of doubling as a pillow in the car for tired picnickers.

The final, but essential ingredients of a basic picnic kit are: *Flower, bird and tree identification books:* Invaluable aids when wading through swamps, or wandering mountain meadows. There is something nice about knowing that the fuzzy pink plant is really "Rosy Pussytoes."

Standard Equipment Package

Once you get beyond the impromptu picnic and onto a planned, or at least semi-planned, occasion there are certain items that become standard equipment. These items tend, in our case, to live in a cardboard box in the garage, where they can be quickly found. It is the presence of these items that moves picnicking from rustic ad-hockery to a pleasant art form. Since much of the picnicking takes place in parks, which usually have some of the rudiments of civilization such as toilets and fire pits or grills, the equipment package is directed at making the maximum use of those environments. These items, used in addition to the basic kit outlined above are:

Simple first aid kit: Antiseptic ointment; Lanacaine, to treat a cut, burn or bite; tweezers to remove the sliver or nettle; Dettol to kill the germs; an elastic bandage for the sprained or broken ankle; some Tylenol or Aspirin for pain or headache; and some anti-histamines in case of that unlikely instance where someone stirs up a hornets' nest.

Fire makers: It is possible that someone else always gets to picnic spots just before we do and takes all the good wood; or maybe park staff have never tried to burn the firewood they supply. For whatever reason, our dominant impression of the firewood provided in parks is that it is green, impossible to split, and unwilling to burn. To alleviate the distress we take fire starter: nice little white squares of petroleum product that will eventually ignite the most stubborn of firewoods.

Splitting maul: We were originally of the opinion that little hatchets were a potential disaster, best left in the hardware store window, and that a 3-pound, long-handled axe would look after most eventualities. Several frustrating years of trying to split the wood at parks has changed our minds, and we now carry a 6-pound splitting maul (found in most hardware stores, about $25) which adequately serves the purpose. Although all of us can wield it when necessary, it is best to bring along a son still experiencing his "macho" period. Daughters' boyfriends are a satisfactory substitute.

The kitchen cupboard: A number of things which are always available in the cupboard or the fridge are rarely thought of until you are on a picnic and realize that you don't have them. Our little supply box contains: salt, pepper, soya sauce, Worcestershire sauce, mustard, sugar, ground coffee, a small bottle of cooking oil, and a small bottle of dish washing detergent.

Pots and pans: The absolute minimum implements include: a cast iron frying pan, which will turn an uneven fire into an even heat; a pot for boiling things; a coffee pot; and a large plastic basin which does double duty as a food preparation basin and a washing-up bucket. Other items, woks and double boilers and the like, depend on the menu you propose to use but are not part of the standard equipment. Our coffee pot is an old enamel camp coffee pot into which we throw water and grounds; it sits directly upon the fire. We did experiment for a while with a Melita pot, and one of those fancy Italian jobs that has a spring-mounted plunger to push the grounds to the bottom. These were unsuccessful because you want coffee the most when both you and the weather are cold and miserable. The fancy European jobs have no facility for re-warming the coffee, whereas the old pot can just be set, or left, among the coals. In addition, coffee from the fancy systems just doesn't have that nice chewy texture we associate with campfire coffee.

The kitchen sink: Basic items that make life over the coals more bearable are: an old glove for picking hot pots off the stove; a flipper for turning things in the pan; some tongs for grabbing things; a slotted spoon for fishing, and a serving spoon. Remember also to bring a dish rag, scouring pad, and some dish towels.

Coffee cups: Coffee cups merit a listing of their own since they are still an item that is in dispute in this family. There is a faction that likes the tin or enamel cups like the old miners had. Such a cup has the added appeal that when the coffee is cold, the cup can be placed directly on the grill to reheat. The other faction claims that tin cups burn your hands and lips initially, that the coffee cools down too fast, and finally that there is always a chip in the enamel right where your lips meet the rim. This second faction favors a simple Melmac cup (they are used in hospitals) which the first faction feels are ugly. A third faction has been attempting to introduce earthenware mugs, which are, of course, breakable.

The above list should reduce or eliminate most of the preparation hassles associated with picnics. Planning can then focus directly on the menu and on the central — and usually remembered — items such as the disposable plastic plates, cups and cutlery, the plastic table cloth, and the coffee Thermos.

The Garage Sale Picnic Kit

If you begin to picnic more frequently you may prefer not to use plastic disposable equipment. You may progress to the Garage Sale Picnic Kit, which includes:

Old, hard-sided suitcase: This will be your storage and carrying case, so give some thought to the size you want. It isn't an irrevocable decision, however, since these suitcases cost between about $1 and $5. Your sales resistance should prevent you from spending more than that.

Dishes: Select some that please you from the wide variety available at garage sales and flea markets. You may merely upgrade to a classier set of plastic dishes, or you may choose dinner plates of different, but complementary, antique patterns.

Glasses: Select some good glass or crystal goblets. After extensive research, supplemented by numerous field trials, we have discovered that wine tastes terrible when sipped from plastic glasses.

Table cloth: Linen or cotton, not plastic -- and only occasionally found at garage sales. You may have to buy a length of pretty fabric and hem it.

Table cloth clips: Available in camping supply stores, these hold your table cloth down in a breeze (or even a gale force wind).

Spices: In a small box in your suitcase/picnic kit place small quantities of your favourite fresh spices. Use the little bottles they come in, or save old pill containers or small jars.

Bread board: Picnics often involve slicing and serving cheeses, cucumbers, paté, tomatoes, and chunks of smoked salmon. Picnic tables, although they may contain interesting graffiti, sap drippings, and remnants of previous picnics, are not the most hygienic surfaces on which to work. We suggest that you bring your own bread or cheese cutting board. A slab of wood will likely do, but plastic cutting boards are lighter and easier to clean.

The Abercrombie and Fitch Picnic

We feel that we would be doing our readers an injustice if we did not mention that symbol of Yuppie Splendour, the Abercrombie and Fitch Picnic Basket.

This will cost close to $300 for two, and almost $500 for the set for four. It comes with four dinner plates in an exclusive china pattern, a Thermos, stainless steel cutlery, plastic mugs, glass wine glasses, plastic-covered storage containers, a table cloth, and salt and pepper, all neatly placed in a wicker and leather basket.

Although basically a good idea, with a few first rate features (we especially like the china pattern), the selection has a few flaws which must be overcome if it is to be a truly functional picnic basket. We suggest that you throw out the plastic mugs and replace them with china or pottery mugs; replace the stainless cutlery with silver flatware; and replace the glass wine glasses with crystal.

One final accompaniment, absolutely essential if you expect to achieve recognition commensurate with the Yuppie status, is:

The matching table cloth, picnic blanket and helium filled balloon. The balloon is anchored to your picnic table and enables friends and relatives to locate you on a crowded picnic turf. It also helps if the balloon is coordinated with your sports clothes and to the upholstery of your BMW.

Quest for Fire

The metal grills and firewood provided at parks present a continuing challenge to the patience and resourcefulness of the picnic devotee. These pits can be used to cook the occasional hot dog and marshmallow, but for serious cooking they offer frustration, angst, and burned salmon. Thus, as your picnic menus move beyond hot dogs, we suggest you upgrade your fire sources to include some of the following items.

The coleman naphtha gas stove: It's the sportsman's companion, the traditional camp cooker, the burner that always dies when you are not paying attention to it, and the one which causes you to bang your knuckles when pumping it up. The Coleman is cheap to operate, reliable, and reasonably safe. The problem is that you must love and understand your Coleman, know how much to pump it up, always have the little funnel for filling it, and generally pamper it. If you do, it will give you years of dependable service.

The portable hibachi: Shishkabobs grilling over a bed of coals make a picture postcard picnic. Our problem is that we never seem to be able to get the charcoal going properly and so the meat takes too long, or is still raw at serving time, and the beautiful bed of coals finally appears just about the time we are packing up to go. Also, we have not yet mastered the problems of transporting charcoal so that it doesn't make a mess in the trunk of the car.

Propane appliances: Fuel from a bottle. We must confess that we tend to like the neat, simple, reliable heat that comes from a propane fire. We do not believe that half the fun of a picnic is fiddling with a fire source; we prefer to transport the close control of a modern kitchen stove to our picnic table. The first of these devices we acquired was the single burner propane gas ring which is a little tripod with the propane bottle forming one leg. This works well for one-dish items like stir-frys in a wok, or frittatas, or soups. It's also great for making coffee. It can change from simmer to boil instantly, and as long as you have a spare bottle, the heat goes on. We have been so happy with this little burner that for cooking multipot meals, instead of going to a two- or three-burner stove, we take two or three single-burner units. This is, however, probably the most expensive means of cooking, since the little propane bottles cost about $5 each.

Propane portable barbecue: Recently introduced, this table-top item weighs about 20 pounds (9 kg), sells for about $50, and runs on propane. The control it offers means that steaks and chops can be grilled — not sacrificed — and since the lid closes, baking is now possible at a picnic.

Dutch oven: There is one historic cooking artifact that is great fun, and a source of excellent meals. This is the traditional Dutch oven which is neither Dutch, nor an oven, but rather is a big cast iron pot with a lid like a pie plate. The Dutch oven can be buried in a fire pit, with coals stacked up on the lid, and left to cook bread, casseroles, or stew.

Gilding the Lily

There are some items which may, by some, be judged as frivolous or decadent, but could still find their way into your picnic kit. These include:

Folding lawn chairs: For many these are not an extra, but are rather a basic necessity. The picnic table that is comfortable to sit at for long periods of time has yet to be developed, and a few lawn chairs provide excellent thrones for elders.

The portable picnic table: Plastic folding picnic tables which seat four and can be easily carried are available for approximately $100. Ours folds into a flat case which remains in the trunk of our car and is useful in underdeveloped picnic spots.

Ice bucket: Used for serving chilled wine or champagne. It is also possible to get pottery bottle containers (they look like a plain flower vase) which you supercool in your freezer or in ice. The wine bottle (white or sparkling wine) rests inside the chilled container on the table, and the wine remains cold throughout the meal.

Portable blender: Battery-operated blenders are fairly new on the market and may take a bit of hunting, but they are perfect for mixing margueritas, daquiris, or sauces and salad dressings at the picnic site.

First aid kit: By the time you become a regular picnicker you will need to have a reliable first aid kit. Accidents do happen: ankles get twisted, fingers get cut, wrists get sprained, and people get bitten by all manner of insects. Many such ailments can be treated without spoiling the picnic. We have with us on all picnics a waterproof plastic case containing the following items:

band-aids
3" tensor bandage — extra support for sprains and twisted limbs
Dettol — disinfects wounds
Lanacaine   removes sting from burns and bites

several packages 4 x 4 gauze bandages
several packages 2 x 2 gauze bandages
1 roll 2" gauze bandage
1 roll low-allergy adhesive tape
Scissors
Q-tip swabs
finger splint — to immobilize a sprained or broken finger
butterfly bandages — to pull together the edges of a cut after it
  has been cleaned
Tylenol or Aspirin
A mild antihistamine
A pocket guide to first aid — for the moments when you panic
  and can't remember what to do.

Clothing

Some people wear funny hats, others have a favourite jacket that
is worn only on picnics. Fun and comfort are both important. Picnics
are not to be confused with serious hikes, for which clothing can be
prescribed. Picnics vary widely — what might be right for a city park
picnic might not be right for a ghost town picnic in the mountains.
Still, there are a few general considerations. A light plastic jacket or
poncho that folds up into a tiny pack will be appreciated time and
time again during unexpected showers. Rubber boots are a good idea
if there is a hike near the picnic ground, especially if it passes through
boggy land. Generally we find that on a picnic there is no shortage of
carrying space, as there is on a hike or a longer trip. There is usually
lots of space in the trunk of the car, so the extra pair of boots or
flippers are not a major inconvenience even if they are not used.

Food Storage and Handling

Food storage is an important issue, even if you are only moving
the food a short distance. The danger of food poisoning is serious,
although easily avoided by taking some sensible precautions. The
simplest rule of all is: keep hot foods hot and cold foods cold.

This caution will require a bit of special equipment, and a little
foresight. For example, if you prepare a lasagna at home for the
picnic, cook it just before you leave, wrap it in newspapers or other
insulation material, and transport it in a box or, ideally, in a picnic
cooler with other hot foods. A cooler can be used to transport both hot
and cold foods, but not together. A cooler, after all, is only an
insulated box with handles. The point is to keep the meal as hot as
possible during transfer. Similarly, if a potato salad is included in
your menu, make it the day of the picnic and chill it thoroughly in the

refrigerator. Just before leaving, place it in an ice-filled cooler, or otherwise insulate it to keep it well-chilled all the way to the picnic table. It is a good idea in packing the cooler to place ice blocks or refreezable sacks on top of the food as well as in the bottom of the cooler. Protein foods require special attention; eggs, meat and milk must be kept cold during transfer. This also applies to foods derived from dairy products, such as yogurt, mayonnaise and cheese. Here Thermos or vacuum bottles, long the mainstay of the hot coffee drinker, can also be used to keep milk, yogurt or a cold soup cold.

Foods containing acid should not be stored or transported in metal containers or pans, even if they have been prepared in them. Although the result is not dangerous, it is displeasing, as the acid will react with the metal to discolour the food, and there will be a slight metallic taste. Vinegar is dilute acetic acid, wine contains acid, and most fruits and vegetables contain acid, especially oranges, lemons, tomatoes and rhubarb. Store and transport these foods and their sauces and juices in plastic or glass containers.

Meat is one of the most dangerous sources of bacteria, and deserves a separate discussion. Buy only fresh meats. Keep them cold during transport and processing. Make sure that all meat is well cooked — rare steaks should be served only if the meat was freshly purchased just before the picnic and then transported at 4 °C (40° F) or less. Your control of temperatures is much less accurate on a picnic, so it is easier to estimate doneness on pieces of meat that are about the same size and thickness.

Chicken is especially hard to judge, but as a precaution, ensure that there is no pink meat near the bones, and that all juices are white, before you serve the meat.

Cooking eventually kills the bacteria in meat, but there is a certain range of warmth, 40° to 140 °F (4 °C to 60 °C), during which bacteria flourish. Be very sure that all meat has been cooked until it reaches a higher temperature than this. If you can't measure with a thermometer, carefully examine the meat before serving.

A word about cutting boards. You may have a nice clean piece of wood or plastic in your picnic kit which you then use to prepare the meat for barbecuing. If you later prepare vegetables or anything else on the cutting board, you will contaminate this food with the bacteria from the uncooked meat. There are two solutions: first, have two cutting boards, one for preparing raw meat and the other for everything else; second, carry with you a solution of Javex and water for washing down the cutting board each time it is used for preparation of raw meat.

One way to avoid some of the dangers of bacterial contamination of picnic meats is to use a marinade. The acid in the marinade slows the growth of bacteria. The marinating container (plastic or glass) should still be kept cold in transit.

This completes the summary of the results of our years of experimenting with picnic equipment. Undoubtedly everyone has his or her own personal preferences, and new gadgets continually appear on the market. We are fairly selective because we still want to keep spare tires in the trunk, and occasionally even carry loads of groceries. We only acquire what will fit in our existing picnic suitcase. A picnic kit is an expression of personal taste — give full rein to yours, to make your picnics easy and fun to organize.

ICEFIELDS PARKWAY

1 Cave and Basin
Banff
A CPR Picnic

How to get there

Banff is 128 km (80 mi.) west of Calgary on the Trans-Canada Highway #1. In Banff, drive south down Banff Avenue, across the bridge over the Bow River, and turn right at the T-intersection. The road you are on, Cave Avenue, ends at the Cave and Basin Centennial Centre. From the parking lot, walk through or by the pool buildings to the picnic ground beyond.

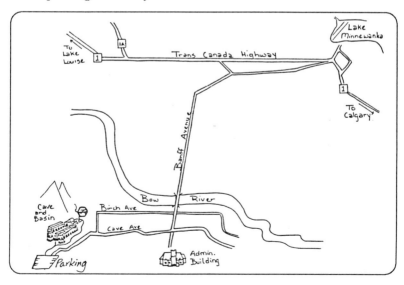

Avarice provides a national heritage

Banff National Park, now regarded as a priceless natural heritage, actually owes its existence more to greed and avarice than to love of beauty or conservationist instincts. The economic development potential of the area was obvious to the very first white explorers. Men like George Simpson saw not only the great natural beauty, but also the potential mineral and timber wealth.

George Simpson was the first recorded visitor to the Banff area. However, for centuries the Indians had visited the hot springs when they were ill, for the waters were thought to have special medicinal properties. The area of the warm waters was also designated as "Peace Grounds" by the tribes who visited the springs, and so here was a place where special trading ceremonies with hostile tribes could be conducted in safety.

In 1883, William Cornelius Van Horne, Construction Manager of the Canadian Pacific Railway (CPR), was impressed by the natural beauty of the Lac Des Arcs area and so proposed to the Government Superintendent of Mines, William Pearce, that the area be designated a National Park. He felt that the extraordinary beauty of the region would be an attraction to tourists, who would travel on his railway to see it. Van Horne proposed that if the government did not want to hold title to the land, the CPR could do so, or that he would even do it personally. William Pearce took Van Horne's suggestion regarding the park, but not the one regarding ownership. He distrusted the CPR's motives and felt that they were possibly more interested in the resource potential of the area than in preserving its natural beauty.

In 1884 Pearce went to explore the lands. There he found Frank McCabe and Tom and William McCardell operating the Cave as a concession for the railroad workers. Pearce explored the area and then, with the support of Thomas White, Minister of the Interior, arranged for an Order in Council that set aside an area of ten square miles around the springs as the Banff Hot Springs Reserve. The justification Pearce and White used for establishing the Reserve was not one of protecting beauty, but rather proposed construction of a sanatorium along the lines of European spas, with the revenue flowing to the government. Economic exploitation, not natural conservation, was the reason for the Reserve.

Pearce found that he was not alone in his interest in the area; as well as McCabe and the McCardells, D. Theodore Siebring, Willard E. Young, and Joseph Healy each laid claim to the area. A legal battle began and was further complicated by claims from squatters and other speculators.

Thus ownership of this special area, an area that the native people regarded as a gift from the Great Spirit, became a subject to be decided in the white man's court. In the final outcome, some of the claimants received some money to compensate them for their development efforts, and the federal government acquired undisputed ownership.

The Banff Hot Springs Reserve became the Rocky Mountains Park, and then Banff National Park, the first Canadian national park. It was followed by Yoho, Glacier, and Revelstoke Parks, also the result of Pearce's action. It is ironic but perhaps fitting that the dreams of personal wealth by the early developers should have produced the lasting legacy of beauty that is Banff National Park.

Things to do

1. Walk through the eerie tunnel to the Cave.

2. Swim in the Cave and Basin pool.

3. Splash in the past by renting a 1914-style bathing suit at the Cave and Basin pool.

4. Ride the gondola to the top of Sulphur Mountain.

5. Join a Park Interpreter for the free one-hour Cave and Basin Discovery Tour.

6. See the National Film Board film, *Steam, Schemes, and National Dreams*, at the Cave & Basin Centennial Centre.

Things to eat

It was the Canadian Pacific Railway that opened the Banff area to exploration and development, and Banff was a CPR town. One of our childhood memories is of interminable train journeys back and forth across Canada each summer which included the elegance of the dining cars with the damask linen tablecloths and napkins, the heavy CPR silverware and always far too many forks for one meal. As best we can recall, the menus read somewhat as follows:

LUNCHEON

Tomato Juice
Cream of Chicken Soup
Heated Bun with Butter
Winnipeg Goldeye
Scalloped Potatoes
Fresh Garden Peas
Ice Cream or Fruit Cocktail or Apple Pie with Cheese
Tea

Unfortunately we cannot duplicate the railway flavour since this would require cooking the peas between Regina and Medicine Hat, and then keeping them warm until Banff, plus having leftover chicken from the night before for soup. But prowl the antique or used furniture stores in any Canadian city, and you are sure to find silverware with the monogram CPR or, in a pinch, CNR. This, together with crisp white linen, should establish the satisfactory ambience. A serving tip: there should be saucers under all glasses, fruit nappies, serving and sauce dishes. The trains did sway a lot and white linen looks quite repulsive with tomato juice slopped over it.

Cream of Chicken Soup

(Serves 6-8)

Prepare a chicken stock by first blanching
   5 lbs. chicken backs, necks, wings and feet
and placing in a pot with
   3 qts. water
   8 white peppercorns
   1 bay leaf
   6 whole cloves
   6 parsley stems
   1 medium onion, diced
   3 stalks celery, diced
   1 medium carrot, diced

Bring slowly to a boil. Simmer for three hours; strain stock into soup pot. Then add:
   2 cups chopped celery
   2 cups cooked rice
   2 cup hot cream
   4 Tbsp. chopped parsley
   salt and paprika to taste

Simmer for five minutes. Pour into a large Thermos for transport to picnic site.

Winnipeg Goldeye

Smoked Winnipeg Goldeye is probably the most famous specialty food produced in Manitoba. It tended to be so much in demand in the railway's dining cars that the CPR took most of the supply, and so it was often not available in Winnipeg. Goldeye is either poached or steamed, and this can be done at the site in a frying pan, or in a closed pot such as a Dutch Oven. Allow one fish for each person.

Poaching — Fill frying pan with water to about 1/4" (1 cm) depth, and bring to a boil. Place goldeye in water and heat through, approximately

4 minutes per side. Remove skin and serve with butter and lemon and garnish with parsley.

Steam — Place fish on a rack in a baking dish with a small amount of water and cover with foil. Steam for 30 minutes; remove the skin and serve with butter and lemon and garnish with parsley.

Scalloped Potatoes

(Serves 4)

Prepare at home and transport to the picnic either in an insulated container, or by placing heated casserole dish directly from oven into a cardboard box lined with newspaper.

Preheat oven to 350 °F.

Grease a 10" casserole dish and place in it, in three layers:
3 cups peeled potatoes, sliced very thinly

Sprinkle each layer with:
1 Tbsp. flour
and dot with
2 Tbsp. butter

Between layers, place onions and sweet peppers, using in all:
1/2 cup onions, thinly sliced
1/4 cup chopped sweet peppers

Heat:
1 1/4 cups milk
Season with:
1 tsp. salt
1/4 tsp. paprika
1/4 tsp. mustard
Pour the milk over the potatoes. Bake uncovered for about 1 1/2hours.

Herbed Pea Salad

(Serves 6-8)

Although CPR chefs were unlikely to serve cold peas deliberately, on a picnic they make a great salad base.

1 kg cooked peas
100 ml French Salad Dressing (See Parkland Picnic)
1 ml dried dillweed
250 ml thinly sliced celery
1 hard boiled egg, sliced
leaves of lettuce

Combine the French salad dressing with the dillweed; pour over the peas and celery; mix well. Chill several hours or overnight, serve in a lettuce-lined bowl and garnish with the egg slices.

Aunt Nell's Pie Crust

(makes 4 pie crusts)

This crust is more appropriate to this picnic than you might think: Aunt Nell was married to a CNR trainman, and her brother-in-law, Nancy's grandfather, was a train conductor.

4 cups flour
1 lb. lard
butter the size of an egg
4 Tbsp. brown sugar
salt
1 Tbsp. vinegar
water

Sift the flour and mix together the dry ingredients. Cut in lard with a pastry cutter until the mixture has the consistency of corn. Place the butter in a measuring cup, add the vinegar, and fill cup to 3/4 full with water. Combine with dry ingredients and mix until moist. Divide into four sections and roll into balls. If not for immediate use store in refrigerator, or freeze.

Apple Pie

Preheat oven to 450 °F.

Mix together:
3 cups diced apples
2/3 cups sugar
1 Tbsp. flour
1/2 tsp. cinnamon or nutmeg

Place mixture in:
2 unbaked 9" pie crusts

Score the second crust to permit steam to escape and place on top of the pie; fasten securely at the edges. Bake in a hot, 450 °F, oven for 10 minutes; then reduce heat to 350 °F and continue baking for 30 minutes or until the crust is nicely browned. Set aside to cool, then refrigerate.

Open Apple Pie

Preheat oven to 350 °F.

Mix together:
1/4 cup brown sugar
1/4 cup flour
and cover the bottom of
1 unbaked 9" pie crust

Peel and slice:
4-5 large cooking apples
and arrange in the shell.

Mix together:
3/4 cup brown sugar
1/2 cup flour
1 tsp. cinnamon
1/4 cup butter
and cover the apples.

Pour over all:
1/2 cup cream

Bake at 350 °F for 30-35 minutes until crust and top are golden brown. Set aside to cool, then refrigerate.

Serve cold with a sharp old cheddar cheese.

2 Saskatchewan Crossing Banff

A David Thompson Picnic

David Thompson, the master map-maker, died in poverty in Montreal in 1857 at the age of 87 years. Despite the fact that he had spent much of his life exploring and creating the maps upon which the expansion of Canada was based, he was forgotten for many years after his death. Only in this century have monuments been raised. One of these memorials is the beautiful highway which leads to Saskatchewan Crossing from the east, the David Thompson Highway. The Howse Pass is one of the many trade routes mapped by Thompson during his long and productive life.

How to get there

Saskatchewan Crossing is towards the north end of Banff National Park at the junction of Highway 11 (The David Thompson Highway) and Highway 93 (the Banff-Jasper Highway, or the Icefields Parkway). The picnic site is on the south-west corner of this intersection. A parking area and a few picnic tables are visible from Highway 93. Pull into the parking lot, and then follow the little hiking trail through the woods. It will bring you out suddenly to a most surprising panorama. A little way along the trail there is a wooden bench at a lookout point. This is where we suggest you have your picnic.

The history

Howse Pass was one of the last passes through the Rockies to be discovered. The Crowsnest, much flatter and easier to travel, had been used both by the Indians and the traders. Until the early nineteenth century there had been little need to cross the mountains. Forts were established along the main trade routes throughout what is now Alberta, and the posts served as depots for various Indian tribes who brought their furs from the mountain areas to places like Fort Edmonton and Fort Carleton. With the increasing competition between the Hudson's Bay Company and the North West Company there was a new incentive to push the chain of forts farther west. David Thompson was instructed by the partners of the North West Company to find the great Columbia River spoken of by Alexander Mackenzie many years before, but never seen since by a European.

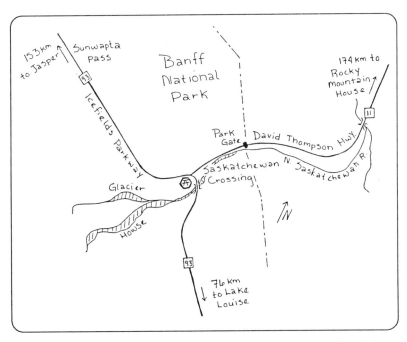

Thompson had tried many times to find this pass. The Peigan Indians who had taught him much over the years, were unwilling to show him the way because they didn't want Thompson to trade with the Kootenay Indians in the interior, and thus supply them with guns. The Peigan were adamant that Thompson should not find the pass to Kootenay country and they deliberately delayed and obstructed him, for as long as they were the only ones with guns, the Peigan could retain their power over a large area. In the spring of 1807, a frustrated Thompson finally managed to sneak one of his voyageurs out from Rocky Mountain House under cover of darkness. This voyageur, Jacob Finlay, followed the course of the Saskatchewan River up into the mountains, and a group of Kootenay Indians guided him across the summit. Finlay blazed this trail, and returned to report to Thompson. Despite the continued warnings of the Peigan, Thompson and a few others left the fort before dawn a few days later, and followed Finlay's trail. On June 25, 1807, David Thompson, his wife, Charlotte, and three voyageurs reached Saskatchewan Crossing. Then Thompson followed the Howse River to the pass and down Blaeberry Creek to where it enters the Columbia River. He established a fort there, but continued his search for Mackenzie's mighty river, not realizing that he was already there as this river flowed north, not south. Because of what is known as the "Big Bend" in the Columbia which takes the river a long way north before it turns south again to reach the Pacific in Washington, Thompson was to find out only years later that he had indeed spent three years on the Columbia without being aware that he had already found — and mapped — the mighty river. The pass was later called Howse Pass after another Hudson's Bay Company trader who followed the trail a few years later.

Things to do

1. Wander along the edge of the valley and see how much of the waterway you can trace below. Howse Pass is off to your left, and Blaeberry Creek begins just beyond it.

Saskatchewan Crossing

2. If you are feeling energetic, take one of the trails down to the valley — and back up. The trails start from a parking area a few kilometres south on Highway 93 toward Banff.

Things to eat

This is a prohibition picnic, because David Thompson disapproved of the rum trade. By the early 19th century, rum had become one of the trade items most sought after by the Indians who supplied furs to the trading posts. Thompson was ordered to carry barrels of rum over the pass to the Kootenay Indians, to encourage them to deal with the North West Company posts rather than the Hudson's Bay. Thompson refused, but was forced to carry two barrels all the way from Rainy River, the company headquarters in the East. Once he reached the rough portage just before Howse Pass he placed the two kegs of rum on an unhappy pack horse, who reacted by trying its best to shed the heavy and awkward load. The horse succeeded in smashing the kegs against the trees, and leaving all of the rum along the portage trail. Thompson reported the event to head office, implying that other shipments of rum would meet a similar fate. He said in his journal, "I had made it a law to myself, that no alcohol should pass the Mountains in my company, and thus be clear of the sad sight of drunkeness, and it's many evils...and for the next six years I had charge of the furr trade on the west side of the Mountains, no further attempt was made to introduce spiritous Liquors." (Tyrrell 1916:396)

The menu for the picnic is barbecued chicken, since game fowl made up much of David Thompson's diet. The meal will include no spiritous beverage — we suggest fresh cranberry juice instead. Fresh buns and a harvest salad accompany the feast, which is completed with rum babas, in keeping with what remained the prime commodity of the trading companies, despite Thompson's personal boycott.

Barbecued Chicken

(allow 1 chicken for four people)

Wash and dry
1 3-pound roasting chicken.
Liberally sprinkle rosemary inside the cavity.

Prepare a sauce of:
1 clove garlic, minced
1/4 cup melted butter
1 tsp. rosemary
coarse ground pepper
Paint the sauce over the chicken.

Bake the chicken on a rack in the oven at 400 °F for 1 hour. Place a pan beneath the rack to catch the sauce drippings, and baste frequently with the sauce. Cool. Chill until serving.

Harvest Salad

(serves 4-6)

4 ripe tomatoes, diced
1 green pepper, diced
1/2 sweet onion, diced, or 4 green onions, chopped fine
1 large cucumber, peeled, seeded and diced
1/2 tsp. ground rosemary

Mix the vegetables together in a bowl, sprinkle with rosemary, and dress with olive oil and red wine vinegar. Add salt and pepper to taste and chill for at least 1 hour before serving.

Rum Babas

(makes 12)

3 3/4 cups flour, sifted
1 1/4 cups butter
1 Tbsp. sugar
2 tsp. dry yeast granules
7 whole eggs
1/3 cup warm milk
6 Tbsp. currants
4 Tbsp. golden sultana raisins
1 tsp. salt

Dissolve yeast in warm milk. Sift flour and salt into a bowl, mix with a fork and make a well in the middle. Into the well gently pour yeast and milk mixture and whole eggs. Mix thoroughly with your hands, creating a paste. Form into a ball, coat with the butter and leave to rise in warm place until double in size. Add sugar, raisins and currants, and knead well. Place in muffin tins, filling each to 1/3 (use paper liners to save mess on picnic). Bake at 375 °F for 40 minutes, or until golden brown on top. Cakes should spring back in centre to touch.

Remove from oven, cool. Pour syrup over top.

Syrup:

Dissolve 2 cups sugar in 1 1/2 cups water. Heat to boiling; let cool and add 1 cup Hudson's Bay Demerara Rum. Stir quickly and pour over cakes. Chill.

3 Maligne Canyon Jasper

A Visitor's Picnic

Jasper, situated at the junction of the Miette and Athabasca rivers, was for many years the entry to the mountains and, through them, to Vancouver. Farther up the Athabasca River is the Athabasca Pass, which leads to the Columbia River which, in turn, flows to the sea. Up the Miette River is the Yellowhead Pass, and the headwaters of the Fraser River. The Hudson's Bay Company Fur Brigades used the Athabasca as the route to Fort Vancouver; the Overlanders used the Yellowhead as the route to the goldfields of the Cariboo; and, for a while in 1873, the Yellowhead was the path by which the Canadian Pacific Railway line was to reach the Pacific Coast.

How to get there

To get to the Maligne Canyon from Jasper, take Highway 16 north out of the Town of Jasper for 2 km (1 1/2 mi.). Signs indicating Maligne Canyon, Maligne Lake, and Jasper Park Lodge will direct you to the right turn across the bridge over the Athabasca River. After the bridge, take the left fork and follow the road for about 9 km (5 mi.). When you cross over the Maligne River and see the Tea Room

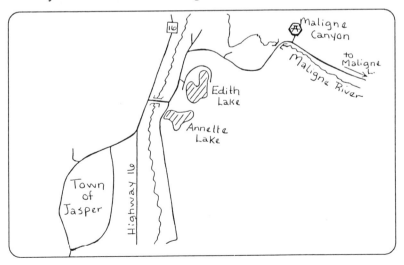

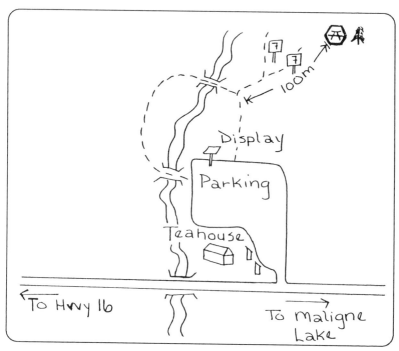

directly on your left, turn left into the parking lot. Drive to the far end of the parking lot and park. Start walking along the trail that leads to the canyon views. (There is only one and it is paved.) Just before the trail turns left and crosses the canyon on a bridge, there is a dirt trail branching off to the right. You will see trail markers, small wooden diamonds painted with the number 7, nailed to the trees. Follow Trail 7, and when it forks, which it does in about 10 m (30 ft.), take the high (right) trail. Follow it along the ridge for about 90 m (250 ft.) and you will be rewarded with a spectacular view of the valley and the mountains. Here, high above the Maligne Canyon and looking out over the town of Jasper, is where we like to picnic.

Some visitors from the past

There is a tendency, especially augmented by the last few decades of conspicuous consumption tourism, to regard Jasper as a little sister, or a scaled down version, of Banff. The facts however, are quite the opposite. Whereas Banff only appeared on the maps in 1883, and then as Siding 29 on the Canadian Pacific Railway, Jasper had since 1801 been a centre of commerce and a major way station on the route to the Pacific. Jasper was named after Jasper Hawes who was in charge of the Trading Post in 1817 (and not, as is commonly supposed, after the bear). The original Jasper House was on the north end of Jasper Lake, about 12 miles north of the current town. Over the years Jasper House had many strange and sometime famous guests and residents. Two of the more interesting were Father Pierre-Jean De Smet, and Colin Fraser — official piper to the "Little Emperor," Sir George Simpson.

Father De Smet, known as Black Gown, was a Belgian Jesuit missionary stationed in Fort Vancouver. In 1845 he set out on a journey that took him up the Columbia River, and on to Radium Hotsprings, Rocky Mountain House and Edmonton. His return journey was via Jasper and the Athabasca Pass down the Columbia to Fort Vancouver. When he left for the journey his sister provided him with 200 shirts. By the time he reached Rocky Mountain House he had only one. He had met many people whose need was greater that his, and so he gave them away. The stories of Father De Smet's devotion and charity are legendary.

In Jasper he encountered an old Iroquois Indian named Travelling Sun, who had originally come west with the fur traders and had settled in the area. Travelling Sun had been baptized a Catholic, but had been living in the bush with no contact with a priest for forty years. The priest held a mass, and baptized the thirty-six immediate members of Travelling Sun's family. This so delighted the Indians that they held a celebration in the priest's honour, and named the mountain immediately behind Jasper House after him. Roche De Smet is the 2,539 metre (8,330 foot) mountain in the shape of a sugar loaf, immediately north-east of Jasper Lake. De Smet was a great correspondent and it is from his letters that we know of much of the life and times of this era. It is worth noting that De Smet first called this river "Maligne" (French for bad). He didn't know that he could cross easily above the canyon, and so he crossed the raging torrent below.

Sir George Simpson, governor of the Hudson's Bay Company, absolute ruler of that vast area from Hudson's Bay to the Pacific Coast, was a man who appreciated a bit of showmanship. On his tours of inspection, when he would visit the forts of his far flung empire, he would always arrive in full Highland costume, accompanied by the banshee wail of bagpipes from his personal piper. The Indians, who were having enough trouble trying to figure out the strange pale-faces that occupied the forts, were astounded by the spectacle of a man with kilt and sporran. The piper, Colin Fraser, chose to settle in Jasper and lived there for a decade. When the Black Gown De Smet baptized all the members of Travelling Sun's Family, he also baptized Mrs. Fraser, her four children, and two servants.

Maligne River at Fifth Bridge

Things to do

1. Tour the Maligne Canyon. The short interpretive trail links back to the teahouse and crosses the canyon at some of the most spectacular points. The more adventuresome may continue on Trail 7 which follows the canyon down to the Fifth Bridge picnic area and parking lot. There your friends can pick you up, although it is not a very strenuous walk back to the top.

2. Drive up the Maligne Lake Road. On the way you will see Medicine Lake, the famous disappearing lake. It was so-named by the Indians because the water drains out underground and reappears in Maligne Canyon and in other springs and lakes along the Athabasca valley (including Lac Beauvert). Maligne Lake, 21 km (13 mi.) up the valley from the canyon, is the largest glacier-fed lake in the Rockies. A two hour boat cruise will take you past peaks and glaciers, halfway up the lake to Spirit Island: the picture-perfect peninsula, or point (for it isn't truly an island), that has graced Jasper and CNR tour literature and calendars for the last eighty years.

3. Splash in the hottest natural water in the Canadian Rockies. The Miette Hot Springs are 48 km (30 mi.) east of Jasper on Highway 16, and then 13 km (8 mi.) up the Miette Hot Springs Road. The Springs are closed from early September to late May.

4. Drop into the Jasper Park Lodge for tea. Take the right fork when you come over the bridge from Jasper and you will come to the

DOs AND DON'Ts OF BEARS

Whenever I walk in a London street,
I'm ever so careful to watch my feet;
And I keep in the squares,
And the masses of bears,
Who wait at the corner all ready to eat
The sillies who tread on the lines of the street,
Go back to their lairs,
And I say to them, "Bears,
Just look how I'm walking in all of the squares!"
And the little bears growl to each other, "He's
mine,
As soon as he's silly and steps on a line."
And some of the bigger bears try to pretend
That they came round the corner to look for a
friend;
And they try to pretend that nobody cares
Whether you walk on the lines or squares.
But only the sillies believe their talk;
It's ever so portant how you walk.
And it's ever so jolly to call out, "Bears,
Just watch me walking in all the squares!"

-A.A.Milne

The poem contains some good advice for avoiding bears — follow the safety rules: if you are in London, walk only in the squares; if you are in the Alberta wilderness, follow the rules listed below. We always call out to the bears when we are in the woods, so that we don't inadvertently interrupt a teddy bears' picnic. Perhaps it works — we have never encountered a bear in all our time in the wilderness!

Do not ever feed a bear, whether it be from your car, or at a picnic site. They are quick to acquire a taste for human food, and will come searching for more.

Avoid bear cubs. They are curious and playful, but Mom is always nearby. A protective mother bear may attack in response to a threat to her young. Steer well clear of a cub or cubs, do not stop and play, or take photographs, but make a wide circle around where they may be feeding or playing.

Don't take your dog for a walk in bear country. Dogs are safer in the car — accidents happen when people try to protect their dogs from bears who are trying to protect their young from dogs.

Make plenty of noise to warn an approaching bear that you are there. We wear bear bells and sing as we walk, if we think we are in bear country. There is safety in numbers as two people make more noise and smell than one does. Remember that a stream may drown out your noise, and that a wind may obscure your scent.

If you come upon a bear by surprise, don't panic. In an encounter the animal is generally as shocked and frightened as you are. Stand your ground, make noise and slowly back up; more often than not, the bear will turn and bolt.

Make sure that your food is in airtight containers, leaving no odours to attract the bears. If your food is all in one place in your pack, you can take off your pack, and drop it to distract the bear while you slowly make a retreat.

If you take the above precautions, you should be able to avoid any confrontations with angry, frightened bears.

beautiful Jasper Park Lodge on Lac Beauvert. The hotel, as you will see, is really a large central lodge with a collection of log cabins scattered throughout the woods on the banks of the lake. Two of the cabins, named Point and Outlook, have housed royalty, presidents and movie stars.

Things to eat

We like to park at Sixth Bridge and hike up the canyon to the picnic spot. Therefore this picnic is meant to be easy to carry on the short hike. All of it will fit into your day pack, and the more you eat, the less you will have to carry down (in your back pack, at least). The menu includes a Thermos of chilled cucumber soup — filling, but refreshing — an eclectic selection of deli meats, cheeses and pickles, and fresh onion buns for the sandwich base. There is a great bakery kitty-corner from the Athabasca Hotel. Bring an onion, a tomato, mustard, salt and pepper, and a sharp knife. Back Pack Squares, a concentrated source of energy, should be munched while exploring the upper part of the canyon trail.

Cold Cucumber Soup

(Serves 6)

This is our favourite cold picnic soup — we have been making it for years, and it is often requested by our friends.

2 Tbsp. butter
1 small onion, finely chopped

1 *clove garlic, finely chopped*
3 *large cucumbers, peeled, seeded and chopped*
3 *Tbsp. flour*
2 *cups chicken broth*
1 *tsp. sea salt*
1 *cup yogurt*
1 *Tbsp. fresh dill weed or 1 tsp. dried dill seed, ground*
1 *tsp. grated lemon rind*
1/8 *tsp. mace*

Heat the butter in a heavy skillet and sauté the onion, garlic and cucumbers until the onion is tender, about 10 minutes. Sprinkle with flour, stirring well. Gradually stir in the broth. Add the salt and bring to a boil. Cover and simmer until the cucumber is tender. Cool. Puree the mixture in batches through an electric blender. Stir in the yogurt, dill, lemon rind and mace. Chill several hours, and pack in a wide-mouthed Thermos for transport to the picnic site.

Mrs. Ellison's Back Pack Squares

Mix together:
1 *6-ounce can frozen orange juice concentrate*
1/2 *cup quick oats*
1/2 *cup dried apricots, chopped*
1/2 *cup pitted prunes, chopped*
1/2 *cup raisins*
1/2 *cup chopped nuts*
1/4 *cup chopped dates*
1/4 *cup wheat germ*
1 *tsp. sesame seeds*

Cream together
1/2 *cup shortening*
1/2 *cup brown sugar*
1/2 *cup table molasses*
1 *egg*

Sift together
2 *cups whole wheat flour*
1/4 *tsp. salt*
1 *tsp. baking soda*
1 *tsp. cinnamon*
1 *tsp. powdered ginger*

Stir dry ingredients into molasses mixture. Add fruit mixture and blend well. Turn into a 13 x 9-inch greased pan and bake at 325 °F for 35 minutes. Cool thoroughly. Cut into bars, wrap in waxed paper to store. Can be frozen, if this stops your children from eating them ahead of the picnic. (It never stopped ours.)

4 Pyramid Lake Jasper

An Artist's Picnic

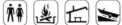

In September, 1846, a company of voyageurs set out from Fort Edmonton to travel through Jasper, over the Athabasca Pass, and on to Vancouver Island. The voyageurs were carrying 5,250 superfine otter skins, the annual rent that the Hudson's Bay Company paid to the Czar of Russia for the privilege of trading in the Russian territories of North America. Accompanying the voyageurs was Paul Kane, a Toronto artist who wanted to paint the Indians and the Canadian West. Since the view in every direction merits a picture postcard, Jasper is a great place for an artist's picnic.

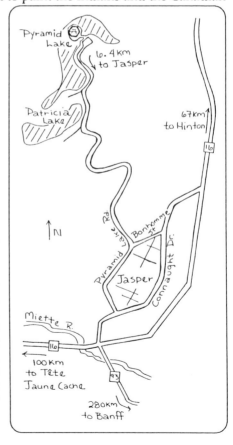

How to get there

The most westerly road in the town of Jasper is the Pyramid Lake Road. The most direct route from the centre of Jasper is to go west on Cedar, which becomes Pyramid Avenue, which becomes the Pyramid Lake Road. The distance from Jasper to the Pyramid Lake Picnic site is 6 1/2 km (4 mi.). The picnic site is on an island. Park your car at the space by the road and walk across the foot bridge. All the sites on the island are spectacular so we suggest you first wander around and then choose which of the many panoramas you want to watch while you eat your picnic.

Paul Kane: Artist, Writer, Explorer

In the 1840s, the people of settled eastern North America became interested in the West. American President Polk's election cry of "Fifty-four-forty or Fight," laying claim to the entire Pacific west coast, had resulted in the British losing Oregon to the Americans. Eastern Canadians came to realize that, unless they started to pay more attention to the British possessions to the west, they would lose them. One of the contributing factors that helped and reinforced this interest was the work of the artist Paul Kane.

From 1845 until 1848, Kane travelled through the west. He visited most of the Hudson's Bay forts, witnessed a great buffalo hunt, and twice journeyed through the Athabasca Pass in the Rocky Mountains in the wintertime. He returned with over 700 sketches of Indians and western scenes, and a journal which he subsequently published with the title, *Wanderings of an Artist Among the Indians of North America*. The journal was translated into several languages and became an international best seller, an unusual circumstance for a Canadian book.

It had been Kane's intention to document the West. This he did admirably and he is acknowledged as Canada's most famous artist-explorer. Although his work reflects his classical training — the Indians seem a bit formal, and his grass a bit manicured — Kane has given us an accurate rendering of the people and costumes of the period.

In 1850 Kane petitioned the Canadian legislature for financial help so he could complete his work and translate the sketches into paintings. The legislature refused his request for assistance, but did vote the sum of 500 pounds Sterling to be used to purchase twelve of his paintings. Eleven of these survive today in the National Gallery of Canada.

Things to do

1. Rent a boat or canoe and cruise on the lake.

2. The area immediately around Pyramid and Patricia Lakes is a maze of hiking trails. These provide the opportunity for many pleasant walks or, if you prefer, horseback rides. Horses can be rented from the stable you passed on the way up. *Day Hikes of Jasper National Park*, a free brochure available from the Information Centre in the town, describes all these trails.

3. The Jasper Tramway, south of Jasper on Highway 93, lifts you to an altitude of 2,285 m (7,500 ft.). From the upper Tea House, now called the Eagle's Nest, the trail to the summit rises another 185 m (600 ft.). Remember though, it can get cold on the top of a mountain,

Pyramid Lake

and the altitude transforms a steep walk into a strenuous one.

4. Drive 30 km (19 mi.) south on Highway 93 to Mount Edith Cavell. That's the beautiful snow-covered mountain off to the south. A short easy walk along the Path of the Glacier trail provides spectacular views of the Angel Glacier; a more strenuous walk to the alpine meadow provides even more splendid views of the glacier with, late in July and August, the majesty of a mountain meadow in bloom.

5. Check at the Marmot Lodge, or Chaba Theatre, for scheduled showings of the film, *Challenge — The Canadian Rockies*. In the words of the *New York Times* review, "This film will knock your socks off."

Things to eat

This is such a splendid spot that we decided to have a gourmet picnic here. Spend the whole afternoon, eating and enjoying the mountains. The menu includes chilled avocado soup, barbecued lamb chops Dijon, broccoli and carrots hollandaise, mint potatoes, and cheesecake. Make your own cheesecake or buy some fresh from the Mountain Foods Cafe on the main street across from the railway station.

Avocado Soup
(Serves 6)

3 ripe avocados, peeled and chopped
1 1/2 cucumbers, peeled and sliced
3 cups chicken stock
3/4 cup sour cream
3 Tbsp. lemon juice
1 1/2 tsp. salt
chopped jalapeno peppers to taste
Tabasco sauce to taste
fresh black pepper

Purée avocados and cucumbers in blender. Add remaining ingredients, blend on medium until smooth. Chill thoroughly, transport to picnic in a Thermos, and serve with unsalted corn chips.

Barbecued Lamb Chops Dijon

Allow 4 small lamb chops per person.

Marinate lamb chops for 24 hours in the refrigerator in the following marinade:
1/4 cup red wine vinegar
1/4 cup oil
3 Tbsp. lemon juice
1 Tbsp. oregano
1 Tbsp. minced onion
1 clove garlic, crushed
salt and pepper
1 Tbsp. Dijon mustard

Coat with more Dijon mustard, grill for 7 minutes on each side over coals.

Mint Potatoes

Select small, even-sized potatoes, peel and boil until just tender. Roll in melted butter and fresh, fine chopped mint leaves just before serving.

Carrots and Broccoli Hollandaise

Prepare broccoli and carrots in long strips. Boil or stream until just tender. Arrange on platter and garnish with hollandaise sauce.

Blender Hollandaise Sauce

4 egg yolks
2 Tbsp. lemon juice
1/2 tsp. dry mustard
dash cayenne pepper
1/2 cup melted butter

Put eggs, lemon juice and seasonings into blender. Buzz on medium for 40 seconds. Increase to high speed and add the melted butter in a stream through the hole in the lid of the blender. Blend until smooth. Keep chilled until serving.

NORTHERN ALBERTA

5 Athabasca Landing
Athabasca
A Trail's End Picnic

Near this picnic site beside the Athabasca River is a monument which marks the end of the 97 miles of the Athabasca Landing Trail, once a heavily-used portage corridor linking the Saskatchewan River system at Fort Edmonton to the Athabasca River system. The Athabasca Landing Trail was in use from about 1877 to 1912.

How to get there

The picnic site is where the Tawatinaw Creek enters the Athabasca River. The highlight of the site is the historic connection and the view. Drive through the town until you reach the river, turn east along the street that runs parallel to it, and turn left into the campground just before you cross the bridge over the Tawatinaw. The location is clearly marked.

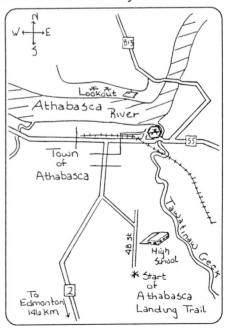

History

The town of Athabasca is at the southernmost point of the Athabasca River. For geographic and consequent economic reasons this site has been an important point of intersection between north-south and east-west trails for several centuries. The Hudson's Bay Company (HBC) built a storage cabin at the landing in 1877. This became an occupied trading post in 1884, and the HBC remained the driving force behind the development of the region for several decades. The Athabasca Landing Trail from Edmonton to the river was improved by the HBC in 1876 so that carts could pass; the HBC built scows for river transport of cargo to the far north from 1881 on, and in 1888 the Company launched the *S.S. Athabasca*, a steamship that carried goods from the Landing to and from Lesser Slave Lake, and up to the Grand Rapids. The trail was the link between the railroad, which ended in Edmonton, and the northern waterway transportation routes. Heavily laden freight wagons pulled by teams of horses or oxen moved regularly up and down the trail.

Because of its importance as a way station — with furs going to Montreal and London, and supplies going to the missions, trading posts and settlements further north — the settlement at the northern end of the trail grew quickly into a supply centre. Athabasca Landing was incorporated as a village in 1905, and as a town in 1911. By 1913 the population had reached about 2,000. The town had been a crossing place for Indian trails en route to and from the fur trading posts, a stopping place for the settlers in the Peace River and Grande Prairie regions, and in due course a way station for the Klondike gold rush: but always it seemed to be a stop on the way to somewhere else.

And then the trains came, carrying goods much faster, and much further north by land, with no need to use the river as a transport route. The first railway train arrived in 1912. Other lines were soon built to the Peace River Country and to Fort McMurray. The Landing continued to play an important role as the place where "rail and water meet," but the days of rapid expansion were over. Athabasca was not destined to become a city. The word "Landing" was officially dropped from its name in 1913 and in 1924 the Hudson's Bay store was finally closed. The town languished for 30 years with a population of between 400 and 600, until the 1950s saw a rebirth. The town has now regained its 1913 level of about 1,900 people, and the economy is firmly established on a broad base.

For you trivia buffs, the word Athabasca is taken from the Cree, and the town was either named for the translated phrase, "place where there are reeds," or because the language that the native people in the region spoke during the years of European exploration was Athapaskan. In any case, the setting has been geographically and economically important for over a century.

Having lunch on the Athabasca River

Things to do

1. Walk along the Athabasca Landing Trail. From the centre of town drive south on Highway 2. Veer left just before the Texaco Station and continue until you reach the parking lot just past the high school. You are on 48th Street. Leave your car in the parking area. From the parking area proceed to the right along the edge of the woods for about 100 metres, watching for a slight break in the bush on your left — part of the Athabasca Landing Trail. Wander along as far as you wish. It is easy to imagine the carts being pulled along 90 years ago. (See the Trail North Picnic).

2. Drive to the viewpoint facing the townsite. From the campsite you can see, on the bluff on the far side of the river, a cross and a welcome sign. It is possible to drive to this spot and enjoy a panoramic view of the townsite and the landing place. Leave the picnic site following the signs for Calling Lake, Highway 813 North. Just across the bridge take the left turn at the sign for overflow camping, but drive on past the entrance and continue up a steep hill to the lookout. There are two picnic tables here and a fine view of the town.

Things to eat

The ideal meal for this picnic is corned beef hash which can be easily prepared over the campfire in a large cast iron frying pan. However, corned beef hash consists of leftovers from a boiled dinner; therefore, to have the leftovers you must first have a boiled corned beef dinner at home.

In the delightful days before refrigeration one of the common ways of preserving meat was by salting, or "corning" it, using a mixture of table salt and saltpetre. Salted meat has nothing to do with corn; the name refers instead to the size of the granules of salt used in the original process which were about the size of a kernel of corn. Corned beef can be bought already prepared in any supermarket or butcher shop, or you can make it yourself.

Corned Beef

To corn beef, rub with salt the surfaces of a 5-pound brisket or rump of beef. Place in plastic or stone crock and cover with a super-saturated solution consisting of:

2 L water
1/2 kg salt
1/4 kg sugar
1 bay leaf
6 peppercorns
10 ml mixed pickling spice

Make sure that the solution covers the meat. It is necessary to keep the meat completely submerged in the solution throughout the corning process. To do this, place a dish inside the crock on top of the meat, with a weight on it. Keep in refrigerator for 4 - 6 weeks, turning beef every 3 to 4 days. Rinse meat before cooking.

Boiled Dinner

5 - 6 lbs. corned beef
6 carrots
6 medium onions
1 turnip or rutabaga
6 potatoes
1 small head cabbage

Put the meat in a large pot and cover with cold water. Bring to a boil. Reduce heat and simmer, covered, for 3-4 hours, or until a fork can penetrate to the centre.

To prepare the vegetables, slice the carrots into chunks, halve the onions, peel the turnip and cut into chunks, peel and quarter the potatoes, and cut the cabbage into wedges. About 1 hour before the meat is cooked, skim off the fat and add the carrots, onions and turnips. About half an hour before the meat is cooked add the potatoes and cabbage.

Serve the meat on a large platter, surrounded by vegetables. Make sure that you make enough that there will be leftovers to make corned beef hash for the picnic!

Corned Beef Hash

Heat oil or margarine in a large frying pan on an open fire or grill. Mix all leftovers from the boiled dinner together and place in the pan, patting down. Allow to cook long enough to form a slight crust on the bottom, then stir and repeat the crust formation on the bottom. When heated through, serve with catsup.

This is plain fare — life on the trail didn't include extras. But we suggest that you serve the main dish with corn relish and a side dish of sweet mixed pickles. You might also include thick slices of whole grain brown bread.

A contemporary dessert is ice cream, made with an old manual ice cream maker. You really earn your dessert — it's hard work, but the ice cream is great! You'll have to bring most of the ingredients from home, and buy the ice locally.

Home Made Almond Ice Cream

Prepare this mixture at home:

Scald
> *1 1/2 cups milk*

Stir in
> *3/4 cup sugar*
> *1/8 tsp. salt*

Beat
> *3 egg yolks*

Pour milk mixture over egg yolks.

Continue cooking in top of double boiler, stirring constantly, until thick and smooth. Chill for several hours.

Add
> *1 tsp. almond extract*
> *1/2 cup almonds, crushed*
> *1 cup whipping cream*
> *1 cup cream*

Keep chilled in transit. At the picnic site place mixture in centre container of ice cream maker. Surround the inner container with ice and sprinkle with rock salt (pickling salt or table salt will do). Turn crank until mixture is well thickened. This is best done in relays — your arm will get tired.

Beverage — Tea! There was many a tea break along the trail. For a while whisky smuggling was a lucrative pursuit at the landing, although the Mounties made it as difficult as they could. You might want to have some whisky with your corned beef hash, but it really should be served from a metal hip flask.

6 Trail North
Bon Accord
The Trail North Picnic

Edmonton is the "Gateway to the North," and indeed the city fills this role as the staging area for supplies for the more northerly communities and industries. The title comes not from today, however, but from the time of the fur traders, settlers and gold seekers to whom Fort Edmonton was the last major supply spot at the start of the Trail North. Steamships on the Saskatchewan River system brought goods from Manitoba to Edmonton; steamships on the Athabasca and Peace systems moved goods on to the north. The Athabasca Landing Trail, the 97 mile long Trail North, was the link between these two systems.

How to get there

Our outing begins with a drive north of Edmonton on Highway 28 or 28A to the Alberta Wildlife Park on Lily Lake (Red Barn). Although this is now a highly commercialized spot, what you see is simply a contemporary use of the trail to the north. The original trail passed by this lake on the opposite shore. We suggest that you stop here to eat before exploring the Trail North.

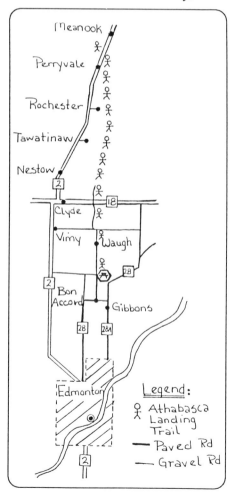

Legend:
Ⳇ Athabasca Landing Trail
— Paved Rd
— Gravel Rd

MOSQUITOES

The term mosquito, meaning little fly, refers to small delicate insects who inhabit diverse environments throughout the world. The 74 species which are found in Canada are dependent for their reproductive capability on a blood meal (often your blood), especially on picnics. The species that commonly seek blood meals from humans are categorized as serious pests, and have been known to drive many a hardy picnicker out of the park.

The anophile species in Canada carried malaria in the early 1800s, but this parasite is now unheard of here. Other viruses can be transmitted by mosquitoes, but they do not commonly afflict humans. The largest threat from mosquitoes in Canada is discomfort from the bites of the females.

Mosquitoes belong to the order *Diptera*, and to the family *Culicidae*. Eggs are laid in moist ground or in standing water. The egg phase is one of seven phases the mosquito passes through before reaching adulthood. Most Canadian species will complete only one generation each year, but some complete two or three; the average life span is three weeks. Males feed on carbohydrates alone, and the common anautogenous female requires a carbohydrate meal — usually nectar — as well as a blood meal to initiate laying of her eggs. Usually females mate once, immediately after reaching adulthood, and then begin the search for a blood meal.

As she approaches a warm-blooded victim, the female will first be attracted by concentrations of carbon-dioxide, then she will sense the body heat. After landing on the host, the female will search the skin for a capillary with her proboscis. She will consume up to three times her body weight and wait 24 to 36 hours for digestion and appropriation of the blood meal. Then she seeks an appropriate spot to lay her batch of eggs. She may subsequently repeat the process of feeding and laying eggs up to five times per generation — unless she is swatted.

History

The route was known to the Indians and was used occasionally by them for centuries. It was the Hudson's Bay Company that finally spent $4,059 in 1876 to develop the trail to Athabasca Landing to transport their own supplies. Although the trail was in heavy use from its inception until its virtual replacement by the railway in 1912, it was almost always a difficult trip. Depending upon the size of the load, the trip from Fort Edmonton to Athabasca Landing could be made in 3 or 4 days. Horses were faster at pulling the freight carts, but oxen could pull heavier loads. The major problems, aside from the unreliable maintenance of the trail itself, were the bugs and the primitive nature of the accommodations. The following account was provided by Warburton Pike who visited Athabasca in June of 1889 and published his remembrances in *The Barren Ground of Northern Canada,* (MacMillan, London 1894).

A fair road some hundred miles in length has been made by the Hudson's Bay Company through a rolling sandy country, crossing several large streams and passing through a good deal of thick pine timber where some heavy chopping must have been necessary. The flies bothered us greatly; the large bulldogs, looking like a cross between a bee and a blue-bottle, drove the horses almost to madness, and after our midday halt it was no easy matter to put the harness on; fortunately we had netting, or the poor beasts would have fared much worse: as it was the blood was streaming from their flanks during the heat of the day. The mosquitoes appeared toward evening, but as the nights were usually chilly they annoyed us only for a few hours. There were no houses along the road, but plenty of firewood and feed for the horses; we had a good camp every night, sleeping in the open air, starting very early and resting long in the middle of the day . . . . Early on the fourth day we came in sight of the Athabasca, running between high pine-clad banks . . . .

There were no stopping houses at first, but by 1892 mention is made of shacks here and there in which there were stoves for meal preparation, amenities especially appreciated during the winter. Prior to this the travellers would eat their food frozen, of necessity. The gold rush in 1898 drastically increased the traffic on the trail to the north. A dozen or so stopping houses sprang up along the way to serve the travellers and to profit from the ready cash of those who dreamed of the riches they were about to discover. The first stopping house was established in 1887 by Johnny Gullion near Bridge Lakes. Some houses could offer bed and board to as many as 40 people. One of the more popular was Egge's Stopping House run by Newton (Bud) Egge and his wife. In the *Alberta Historical Review*, Edmonton author Edna Shore wrote the following account of her 1910 stop at Egge's.

Old St. Mary's Church

When I went inside, the kitchen with its long table of goods, had a delicious smokey smell and the cakes and pies seemed as big as cartwheels ... In a little while the air became warmer and, with the sounds of laughter, more cheerful ... The piano opened its mouth to show its teeth in a pleasant smile and to join in the singing of "Little Red Wing" ...

(A replica of Egge's Stopping House can be visited at Fort Edmonton Park. See Fort Edmonton Picnic.)

Between 1906 and 1912 thousands of homesteaders travelled over the Athabasca Landing Trail headed for the farmland in the Peace Region. They fought the mud, mosquitoes, and muskeg in the last great land rush of the Canadian West. Every year over 100 boats and barges were built and launched at Athabasca, as these hardy pioneers moved on up the Athabasca to Lesser Slave Lake, and then on to the Peace.

For nearly 40 years the trail carried many tons of equipment to the trading posts and settlements. Today parts of the trail have vanished completely, while in some places cart tracks can be found in fields and in the underbrush. It is still possible to travel along portions of the trail on foot or in your car, and to imagine what it must have been like guiding a team of horses along the uneven trail with a wagon-load of supplies, or a boiler for a steamship, strapped to the freight cart. The boilers were also rolled along the trail by placing an axle through them and protecting the outside with wood.

Things to do

1. Visit the Old St. Mary's Church at Waugh, at Mile 42 on the old Athabasca Landing Trail. It has been renovated and is a provincial historic site. It was the first Ukrainian Catholic Church built north of Edmonton and served the area from approximately 1907 to 1940. It is now maintained by the community. The men who have farmed the district for several generations continue to tend the grounds of the old church along with their memories of the weddings and celebrations that took place in their childhood in this tiny but beautiful church. If you are lucky enough to find someone around with the keys, the inside of the church is worth seeing, with its well-preserved murals. It was moved the hundred or so feet to its present site and the larger new church was built on the original site in 1940. Waugh remains a tiny cluster of buildings which gives no indication of the strong rural community on the surrounding farms — the congregation of St. Mary's Ukrainian Catholic Church.

You may choose to wander along the road beside the church as it heads north into a field; this is part of the original Landing Trail, and is marked as such.

2. Drive the Trail. From Waugh it is possible to drive north along sections of the Trail (see map). These are marked with small Trail North signs and the drive is a pleasant change from our normal straight section roads. Watch for a sign that marks the site of another old stopping house, McNelly's.

3. Visit Mile 26 Park at Gibbons. Here you will find a picturesque introduction to the Trail.

Things to eat

Trail suppers consisted of fried dough, reheated beans, condensed milk and occasional sardines. While we don't feel it absolutely necessary to duplicate this, some flavor of the trail must be present in the picnic. As the trail developed so did the stopping houses, and a usual meal was a big bowl of hearty stew loaded with meat and vegetables and fresh sourdough buns. There were lots of desserts, puddings and pies, so bring as many of these as you want. We will give you one dessert recipe, for Saskatoon Pie: this was often served at the stopping houses in July and early August.

Trail Stew

(serves 4-6)

Soak in water overnight
  a handful of navy beans

Brown in hot lard
  2 kg cubed meat
Add
  3 large sliced onions
and continue browning.

Stir in 80 ml flour. Throw in the navy beans, cover with water and simmer for 3 hours.

Add vegetables:
  turnips, cubed
  carrots, chunked
  potatoes, quartered
  parsnips, chunked

Season to taste with:
  Worcestershire sauce
  salt and pepper

Simmer for another 1/2 hour. Transport this in your Dutch oven and reheat on your portable stove.

Sourdough Buns

Mix:
  2 cups sourdough sponge (see Sourdough Starter recipe)
  1/2 cup flour
  1 tsp. baking soda
  1 tsp. salt
  1 Tbsp. cooking oil

Lightly knead, shape or cut into biscuits and place on greased pans. Allow to rise until double. Bake in 350°F oven for 45 minutes.

Saskatoon Pie

For pastry recipe, see Aunt Nell's Pie Crust recipe. You will need enough for a two-crust pie, or more if you are providing a Stopping House selection. We supply one recipe, and you can use some of your own, or select pie recipes from other picnics in this book.

Line a greased pie pan with pastry.

Place in a saucepan
    4 cups Saskatoon berries
(also called service berries in some places), washed and sorted, and
    1/4 cup water
Cover and simmer for 10 minutes.

Add to this
    2 Tbsp. vinegar or lemon juice
    3/4 cup sugar
    3 Tbsp. flour.

Pour berry mixture into the pie crust and cover with top crust, making steam holes in your favourite pattern. Bake at 425 °F for 10 minutes, then reduce heat to 350 °F and continue baking for 30 minutes.

7 Dunvegan Crossing Peace River

A Legendary Picnic

These days, with the population and industry concentrated in the southern half of the province, it is easy to forget that it was to the north that the Europeans first came. The North West Company built a trading post at Fort Vermilion in 1788, another at Fort Chipewyan in 1789, and Archibald Norman McLeod established the trading fort at Dunvegan in 1805. (Dunvegan is the name of the ancestral castle of the McLeods in Scotland).

How to get there

Dunvegan is just north of Rycroft on Highway 2. This is where the highway crosses the Peace River, and the suspension bridge is Alberta's longest clear span bridge. The picnic is in the provincial historic site immediately north of the bridge. The place is called "The Maples" because of the grove of Manitoba maples planted in the 1880s by the Anglican missionary, Reverend Alfred Garrioch. On turning off the main highway, follow the gravel road to the west (right). The Maples are only a short distance away and the place is clearly signed.

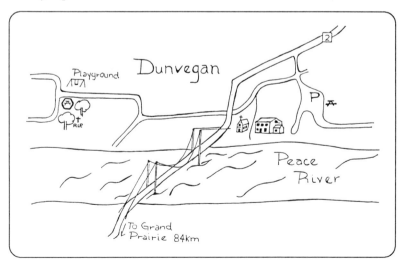

History

The history of Dunvegan is the history of the Europeans coming to the West. Fur traders, Indians, missionaries, free traders, Mounties; starvation, prosperity, fellowship, humour, tall stories and ghost stories — they are all here at the bottom of the hill, on the banks of the mighty river. We encourage you to allow enough time, at least an hour, to tour the historic site and talk to the student interpreters. There are many interesting and exciting stories here at Dunvegan, and we can only touch on a few.

The story of Twelve Foot Davis

Although his statue and his grave are in the Town of Peace River, it was actually in Dunvegan that Henry Fuller Davis spent much of his life. After his famous episode in the Cariboo (see Peace River Picnic), it was to the Peace River as a trader and supplier that Davis came. In about 1870 he established a trading post in the Peace River canyon where the town of Hudson Hope now stands. By 1880 Davis also had a post at Dunvegan, on the south side of the river. He set up a string of trading posts from Peace River to Fort Vermilion. His posts would consist of a log building for the store, and perhaps another building to live in; there were other buildings on the site for the Indians to use. The cabin doors were never locked, and there was dry wood inside for the first fire. A "law of the North" was that when you left a cabin, it was as you found it.

Davis's home at Dunvegan was across the river from the Anglican mission, and the Rev. Garrioch and his family would often cross the river to visit. In his journals, Rev. Garrioch said of Davis, "he did not belong to any church but he was a fine Christian gentleman." It seems that Davis was known the length of the Peace by Indian and white alike for his honesty, his fairness, and his skill in baking pumpkin pies.

Despite his name and reputation, Davis was not a big man. However, he was sturdy and strong and a tireless worker. His ability to pack 200 pounds over the long portages earned him the nickname "The Wolf" from the Indians.

In 1900, he died at the mission at Grouard while on yet another freighting trip. He was in his 80s, blind and an invalid. One of the nursing sisters asked him if he was afraid to die and he replied, "No Miss, I am not afraid to die. I never killed nobody, and I never stole from nobody. I never willfully harmed nobody, and I always kept open house for travellers all my life. No, Miss, I ain't afraid to die."

Reverend Alfred Garrioch

Alfred Garrioch was the second missionary to St. Saviour's Anglican Mission at Dunvegan. He and his family arrived during a period of great scarcity; food was short and many of the Indians were ill with tuberculosis. The second of the Garrioch children, was born at this time and lived only two days. She is buried at the mission site. But the Garrioch family stayed on for five years, and worked with the natives and the traders. Garrioch's journals give us authentic accounts of the times. One of his stories called, "A Hatchet Mark in Duplicate" was published by the Ryerson Press in 1929. We found it retold in an old book about the west called *Johnny Chinook,* and it appears here with permission from the publisher, Charles E. Tuttle.

A Hatchet Mark in Duplicate
by
Reverend Alfred Garrioch

It all apparently began with an Englishman named Armson who panned gold in 1871 at Fort St. John in company with Nigger Dan Williams, Banjo Mike, and Twelve Foot Davis. As fall drew near, Armson was heard to say that he intended going south of the Peace River to trap. This he apparently did, taking with him his beautiful Blackfoot wife.

The wife, so the account goes, had but one imperfection. She had been chopping wood one day and had struck the second toe on her left foot, leaving a scar which extended from the toenail in the form of a ridge.

The Armsons left Fort St. John in a dugout canoe, and Armson stated that in the spring they would return to the Saskatchewan, via Lesser Slave Lake and the Athabasca River. Instead of reappearing, however, the Armsons vanished and were not heard from again.

Less than a year later a Blackfoot Indian named Jean was pad-
dling up the Peace in his dugout looking for beaver. Suddenly he saw
a small raft floating down toward him, and to a stick on the raft was
fastened a red rag. Jean paddled rapidly out and to his profound
surprise discovered a very young baby girl on the raft. He lost no time
in getting the child to shore, and found that she was in the last stages
of starvation. He hurriedly boiled a duck that the had recently shot,
made some soup, and fed the baby a few drops. Fortunately, a camp
of Beaver Indians was close by, and Jean carried the baby to an Indian
mother who nursed the child.

When they were examining the baby the Indians discovered a
curious mark on the second toe of the left foot — a mark which one
of the Indian women said was "older than the child."

Jean left the child with the Beaver Indians, who soon broke camp,
taking the baby with them. That was the last to be heard of this female
Moses of the Peace for a long time.

Some years later the Reverend Garrioch chanced upon a couple
from St. Paul, Minnesota, named Vinning. The couple had with them
an extremely attractive young girl. The Vinnings confided to Garrioch that the child was not their own, but that she had been turned
over to them by a free trader at Edmonton who said he got the child
from some Indians up in the Peace River Country. The Vinnings had
adopted the child and were raising her as their own.

It happened that not long after parting from the Vinnings,
Garrioch encountered the Indian named Jean. In the course of their
travels together, Jean told the missionary about finding the baby girl,
a white child, on the raft. Garrioch immediately began to suspect that
the Vinning's adopted daughter and the raft-baby were one and the
same. He set out to discover where the child had come from.

He enlisted the help of a trapper named Sizerman, who eventually discovered the remains of an old trap-line somewhere south of
the Peace River. He followed the marks of the old line until he came
to the remains of a cabin, across which a large tree had fallen. Digging
in under the tree he discovered two skeletons. One was lying on a
bed. The other was on the floor beside the bed. Hanging on a
projection of the cabin was a small notebook done up in a piece of
skin. On the floor were the remains of a child's rattle, parts of a moss-
bag, and a shattered gun. There was, however, no child's skeleton
present.

Sizerman carried the notebook to Garrioch, and after reading
through it they reconstructed what had probably happened in the
cabin. The Armsons had put up a comfortable cabin in the autumn of
1871 and had spent a profitable winter trapping, for Sizerman found
the moldering skins of many marten and beaver. Probably sometime

in March a child had been born to Mrs. Armson, and soon afterwards Armson had had an accident with his gun, and infection had set in. He became more and more weak, and finally so weak that he could not provide food. The woman was unable to provide, and father, mother, and child were slowly starving to death. When it became apparent that Armson would not recover, Mrs. Armson staggered down to the banks of the river, made a simple raft, placed the child on it, and pushed it out into the current. She then returned to the cabin to die.

One item from Armson's diary explained the mark on the child's toe. "Born this day (March 31), a girl, perfectly formed and with vocal organs in fine working condition. It would seem that when Mrs. Armson's glancing hatchet hit her toe at the mining camp at Fort St. John she inflicted a hatchet mark in duplicate, for on the corresponding toe of her little daughter's foot there is the perfect replica of the scar of hers."

Another item in the diary stated: "May 15, 1872: I am dying — effects of accident. My first wife died in England leaving a son, now five. Write to legal firm Blake and Barstow, London, England. Wife and babe weak from starvation. The Lord will provide."

Garrioch turned the memento of the tragedy over to the couple who had adopted the child — by this time a girl of eighteen. They called her Lily, and she was soon to be married to a handsome young man named Herbert Melvin, fresh over from England. The foster parents immediately cabled the legal firm, stating the facts, and asking for the name and address of the son Mr. Armson mentioned in his diary. The wire was shocking to all concerned. The firm wired back that the son's name was Herbert Melvin, and it was actually established that Melvin was Lily's half-brother!

The Hill — a tall tale

The steep banks at Dunvegan are an traditional source of stories. One relates to a farmer who, when he found himself without a suitable harness, cut some strips of rawhide and used these to fasten his horses to the wagon. As they started up the long hill it began to rain, and the rawhide traces began to stretch and stretch — so much so that just as the horses reached the crest of the hill, the wagon slid back to the bottom. The farmer knew exactly what to do. He un-hitched his horses and tied the traces to a tree. Then he went home. The next day the sun came out, and as the rawhide dried it shrank to its original size, drawing the wagon up the hill.

And a real one

Some of the best yarns about Dunvegan concern the real estate boom. Because it was a fort for such a long time, Dunvegan appeared on every map made of the region. When Europeans and eastern Canadians heard of the great Peace River land boom and wanted to participate, there were real estate people ready to serve them. They surveyed the almost vertical banks of the Peace, marked it off into lots, and proceeded to sell these to the gullible. The story is told of one woman in Scotland who wrote to the Catholic priest at Dunvegan to "please investigate her lot," as she wanted to move to Canada. The priest tactfully replied, "Dear Madam, I regret to inform you that last night my cayuse fell off your property and broke his neck."

Things to eat

We have selected these recipes in accordance with supplies that would have been available to the missionaries and traders. We have rabbit soup, garden vegetable frittata, fried bannock and the dish for which Twelve Foot Davis was famous, pumpkin pie.

Rabbit Soup

(Serves 4-6)

Catch and clean one rabbit. If you haven't caught one lately yourself, rabbit meat is available from specialty butcher shops catering to ethnic tastes.

Cut the rabbit into pieces and remove the bones. Place bones in a pot, cover with water and add
  1 turnip, chopped
  4 carrots, cut in pieces
  1 stalk of celery, chopped
  2 medium onions, chopped

Boil for 1 1/2 hours. Remove the bones, and push the vegetables through a coarse sieve.

Cut the meat into small pieces and add to the pot. Continue cooking for 1 1/2 hours, stirring occasionally.

Mix a seasoning of:
  1/4 cup tomato paste
  1/4 cup flour
  salt and pepper
  1/2 tsp. thyme
  1/2 tsp. marjoram
  water
to make a paste.

Stir into soup, cook for 1/2 hour more, transport in Thermos, or chill and reheat at picnic.

Frittata

(Serves 4-6)

A frittata is an egg dish, easily made and with endless variations. It lends itself to the colour and flavours of a market garden, and picnickers will have noticed that there is one just beyond the historic site. This dish can be made at the picnic site. We use either a cast iron skillet with a lid (use a plate), or what we call "the French Pot," a teflon-lined kettle with a tight-fitting lid which has a steam valve. These pots are made in France, but sold in most housewares departments — a bit pricy, but versatile. In any case, you need a slow fire so as not to burn the eggs, but to cook the vegetables. (The frittata can also be made in advance at home and served cold.)

Heat olive oil in the pan and add a couple of cloves of crushed garlic.

Chop all the vegetables that you plan to use. Saute, in descending order of cooking time, i.e. the quickest last. Some suggested vegetables are: onions, zucchini, peppers of all colours, celery, broccoli, cauliflower, peas, asparagus, mushrooms.

Mix together:
  6 eggs
  freshly ground pepper
  spices from Italy — basil, oregano, rosemary and thyme — fresh, if possible.

Pour over the still-crisp vegetables and stir once. Cover tightly. Cook over low heat for 10 - 15 minutes. To serve, place platter over the skillet and up-end. Serve in pie-shaped wedges.

Fried Bannock

Combine in a bowl:
  3 cups flour
  dash salt
  1 tsp. baking powder
  2 Tbsp. lard

Add enough water to make a thick dough, knead, flatten into frying pan, and cook over hot ashes. Turn and brown on both sides.

Spices and wild berries can be added to the bannock dough.

Twelve Foot Davis Pumpkin Pie

Make up Aunt Nell's Pie Crust or thaw enough for 1 crust for each pie.

To prepare pumpkin:
Wash, cut in half, remove seeds and strings. Bake in 350 °F oven for 1 hour or until tender. Remove the pulp, strain. (If you don't have a pumpkin in your garden, buy a tin of pumpkin and proceed.)

For each pie mix together:
  1 3/4 cups cooked pumpkin
  1 1/2 cups evaporated milk
  2 eggs, beaten
  1/2 cup brown sugar
  1/4 cup white sugar
  1 tsp. cinnamon
  1 tsp. nutmeg
  1/4 tsp. ginger
  1/4 tsp. cloves
  1/2 tsp. salt

Pour into uncooked pie shell. Bake in 400 °F oven for 40 minutes. Cool and transport to picnic.

8 The Grave of Twelve Foot Davis
Peace River Town
A Lookout Picnic

History and beauty conspire here to create the perfect environment for a picnic. A view of the mighty Peace River is essential to a successful picnic in the region. From several vantage points it is possible to see three rivers — the Smoky, the Heart and the Peace, which come together here.

How to get there

Although there are several wonderful picnic spots on the high bluffs above the town, the one that offers the best mix of scenic and historic elements is near the grave of Henry Fuller Davis, remembered now with affection as Twelve Foot Davis. Davis, a gentle and generous man, was buried on top of the bluff by his friend, Peace River Jim. The site, on the east side of the river, is reached from the town by heading east on 98th Avenue. (The Hudson's Bay Company store is on the corner of 98th Avenue and 100th Street. Street signs may be hard to find.) This road winds to the right and becomes the road up the hill — just follow the signs to the grave-site.

At the grave site at the top of the hill, there are picnic tables, but no other amenities. The picnic site at the provincial campsite part way down the hill has additional facilities.

The story of Twelve Foot Davis

H.F. DAVIS
BORN IN VERMONT, 1820
DIED AT SLAVE LAKE, 1893
PATHFINDER, PIONEER
MINER AND TRADER
HE WAS EVERY MAN'S FRIEND
AND NEVER LOCKED
HIS CABIN DOOR

So reads his epitaph. He went to California in 1849 following the gold rush, and came north with the Cariboo gold rush there to British Columbia. Near Barkerville he noticed that two claims, Discovery

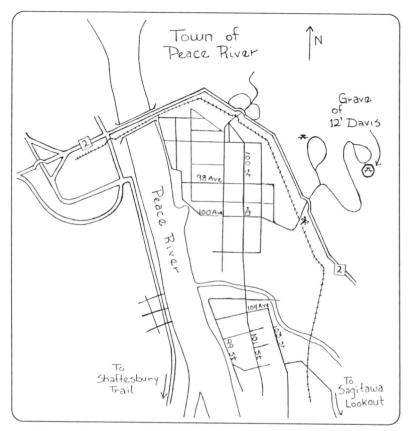

and Claim No. 1, appeared to be larger than the regulation size. Late one night he went out and measured the claims. Finding that they contained twelve feet more than they should have, he staked this extra section as his claim. He subsequently mined between $10,000 and $20,000 from this claim, and gained his nickname.

As Davis could neither read nor write in his early life, it is difficult to fill in its major events. It is known that he prospected and traded in many places until about 1870, when he established a trading post in the Peace River canyon, where the town of Hudson Hope now stands. In 1880 Davis had a post at Dunvegan, on the south side of the present bridge. For more on Davis, see the Peace River-Dunvegan Picnic.

A Stopping Place Between Grouard And Peace River Crossing

Peace River Jim

Davis died in Grouard in 1900 (the date on his epitaph notwithstanding), and in 1910 Peace River Jim arranged for the removal of his body and its reinterment on the top of the hill overlooking the Peace. So who, we wondered, was Peace River Jim? As we attempted to find out, we discovered that Peace River might have overlooked an even more important hero than Twelve Foot Davis.

James Kennedy Cornwall: seaman, miner, trader, war hero, steamboat owner, entrepreneur, mail courier, railway promoter, MLA for Peace River, instigator of Wood Buffalo National Park, trusted friend to the natives, promoter of the North — Peace River Jim.

Born in Brantford, Ontario in 1869, Jim left school at age 14 and went to sea on a freighter. In 1888 his ship docked at Vladivostok, which was abuzz with the excitement of the construction of the Trans-Siberian Railway. Jim left the ship and, together with a friend, hitch-hiked, walked, and rode across Russia.

The year 1894 found Jim working as a miner in the Crowsnest Pass. From there he came north and started trapping, and he quickly learned to converse in Slavey, Chipewyan, and Cree. Jim was at Athabasca Landing when the Klondike gold rush started, and he started building boats for the Klondikers. Soon he was one of the major steamboat owners on the Athabasca River system. He opened packing plants, built trails, convinced the government to institute a mail service, and generally promoted the North.

One interesting story about Jim relates to the establishment of Wood Buffalo National Park. In 1492, when Columbus was sailing the ocean blue, it is estimated that there were about 60 million buffalo on the plains; but by 1889 there were no wild buffalo in the United States, and only a few left in Canada. Those few plus some domesticated buffalo purchased from Americans were put in a reserve at Elk Island National Park where they prospered and multiplied to the extent that by the 1920s the park was overcrowded. Jim convinced the government to establish a northern reserve for the wood buffalo, a larger tougher breed than the plains buffalo, and then he undertook to move all 6,673 of them to their new home. This he accomplished between 1925 and 1928, giving us Wood Buffalo National Park.

In the 1930s when he was in his 60s he was still promoting the north and arranging tours for politicians, artists, and journalists. He died in Calgary in 1955 at the age of 86.

Things to do

1. See the statue of Twelve Foot Davis in the town.

2. Drive to the Sagatawa lookout (see map). You are on a ridge between two river valleys, the Heart and the Peace. Walk across the highway to see both valleys.

3. Drive the historic Shaftesbury Trail along the Peace.

Things to eat

To celebrate Peace River Jim's trip across Russia we suggest a hearty bowl of Russian Borscht (not to be confused with Ukrainian Borscht). Jim opened a packing plant on the Isle of Dogs, and so we will have hot dogs, naturally, as an entree. In recognition of Twelve Foot

Statue of Twelve Foot Davis

Davis, we want foot-long hot dogs, and get the buns to match (loaves of French bread sliced lengthwise work fine). The menu also includes Heart River Salad, and Sagatawa Shortcake.

CANOLA/RAPESEED

Canola is the common name for the Canadian-developed brands of rapeseed which are variations on turnip rape. The most obvious identifying feature of canola in fields of the Canadian prairies is the brilliant yellow colour of the plant in bloom. A flowering field of canola creates an illusion of a sea of yellow.

Canola is becoming a more common crop on the prairies, but it was not introduced until during World War Two. The original variety of rape produced a thick oil that was used to lubricate heavy machinery during the war. With years of experimentation and cross-breeding the Canadian varieties of rape have been much refined. Present varieties contain a reduced amount of erucic acid, and glucosinolates. Today, rapeseed is in demand in North America and Europe as a base for cooking oil, shortening, margarine and salad dressing. The meal that is left over after removing the oil is used to feed livestock.

The popularity of canola on the prairies is readily apparent on a drive in the country in July. One cannot help but notice that, where previously expansive fields of golden wheat covered the land, now brilliant yellow rapeseed crops dot the horizon. Presently more than 2 million hectares of prairie soil is planted with canola, and the grain's popularity continues to grow.

Russian Borscht

(12 servings)

8 med. potatoes
1 cup butter
1/2 cup finely grated carrots
1/2 cup chopped carrots
1 med. beet
1 cup chopped onions (reserve 1/4 cup for garnish)
2 Tbsp. dill
6 cups shredded cabbage
1 1/2 tsp. salt
1 cup sweet cream
4 cups canned tomatoes
1/2 cup chopped green pepper

Pour canned tomatoes into a pan and mash. Add 2 Tbsp. butter and boil until thick.

Place
   1/3 cup butter
   3/4 cup chopped onions
   1/2 cup very fine-grated carrots
into a frying pan and fry, but do not brown.

In a separate frying pan, place
   3 cups shredded cabbage
   1/3 cup butter
and fry until tender.

Boil 3 quarts of water in a large pot. Add
   1 1/2 tsp. salt
   1/2 cup sweet cream
   1/2 cup chopped carrots
   6 medium sized potatoes (quartered to make approximately 2 cups)
   1 medium beet, halved.
Boil until potatoes are tender.

Remove potatoes and mash with 2 Tbsp. butter. Add 1/2 cup sweet cream, set aside.

Place
   2 potatoes, diced
   3 cups shredded cabbage
into potato stock and boil until tender.

Pour the mashed potatoes slowly back into the stock water. Add fried onions, carrots, cabbage and tomato sauce.

Add
   1/2 cup chopped green pepper
   2 Tbsp. dill
Bring to a boil, but DO NOT BOIL. Turn off heat.

Remove and discard beet. Season to taste with black pepper and 1/4 cup onion greens or white onions. Transport to the picnic in a Thermos.

Heart River Salad

hearts of palm (can be bought in tins in most large grocery stores)
celery hearts
strips of pickled pimento

Cut hearts of palm and celery hearts lengthwise and arrange on a plate, with thin strips of red pimento lying across them as if tying them into a sheaf.

Blend together and pour over vegetable arrangement:
4 Tbsp. tarragon vinegar
1/4 cup oil
freshly ground pepper
1/2 tsp. ground tarragon
1 tsp. lemon juice
1 tsp. sugar

Sagatawa Shortcake

Over the coals of your cooking fire, boil the berries you have collected on the hillside (the kind depends on the season and where you were wandering) with some sugar and a bit of water. Pour this syrup over pieces of angel food cake or pound cake.

9 Lesser Slave Lake
Slave Lake
A Boreal Picnic

The boreal forest dominates much of the northern part of the province of Alberta. Some animals that inhabit the boreal forest are the white tail and mule deer, the black bear and the muskrat. Some timber wolves, grizzly bear and woodland caribou also inhabit the area, but are rarely seen. Birds include the sandhill crane, pelican, bald and golden eagles, ruffed grouse, goshawk and great grey owl. You might even catch sight of the rare peregrine falcon on this picnic.

How to get there

This picnic takes place in the North Shore Picnic Area in the Lesser Slave Lake Provincial Park. The site is in the woods near the lake; it is reached from the town of Slave Lake by going north on

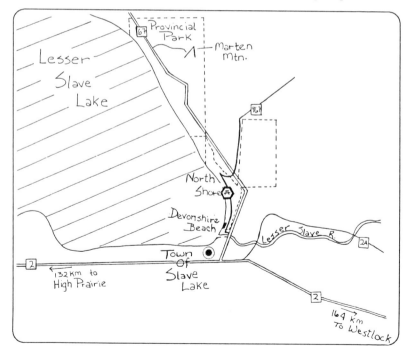

Highway 88 for 9 km (5 1/2 mi.) to the North Shore turn-off. Once you have reached the parking area, walk to your right, past the shelter, to the path leading through the forest to the excellent picnic spots. Depending on the time of year and the weather, you may need to bring insect repellent.

The boreal forest

Lesser Slave Lake lies in the mixed boreal forest zone which covers much of the central part of the province, north of the aspen parkland. It is characterized by both evergreen and deciduous trees growing side by side, mostly trembling aspen, balsam poplar and white spruce. The canopy produced by the poplar permits more light to reach the ground floor than that which filters through the evergreens. When the poplars shed their leaves in the fall even more light and precipitation reach the forest floor, permitting a rich variety of growth and consequently a wide range of wild life. It is much easier to walk beneath the evergreens than through the scrub and bush that grow beneath the poplar stands. After a fire the poplars dominate, but over time give way to spruce and fir. Spruce trees live for about 200 years, and tend to dominate the forest.

The history

For centuries Indian trails passed along the south end of Slave Lake, and one of these was the warpath between the Cree and the Beaver. Conflict between the two mighty tribes formally ended in 1782, on the shores of a river which has been called the Peace River ever since.

David Thompson is considered the first white person to have reached Lesser Slave Lake — in December of 1803, according to his journals. In the late 1800s fur trading forts were established along the trail to the Peace River country, a decade or two after the ones in the south of the province were built, to which the Cree first brought their furs. Intensification of the competition between the Hudson's Bay Company and the North West Company, however, forced the companies to move closer to the source of the furs, and this transition was not made without inter-company violence.

The forts soon attracted missionaries, traders, and native encampments. The settlement of Sawridge, so named because of the saw-toothed edge of the range of hills nearby, was a stop along one of the major routes to the Peace River country. Sawridge, at the east end of Lesser Slave Lake, could be reached by canoe from Athabasca. For a brief period (the summers of 1911-1913) steamboats made parts of the trip to Peace River a little easier, as travellers could take them down the Athabasca River, up the Lesser Slave River, and then make the 60-mile crossing of Lesser Slave Lake. In winter travellers walked across the ice. This era of the trail ended in 1914 when the Edmonton, Dunvegan and British Columbia Railway opened a new route to the Peace country.

The name of the settlement was changed from Sawridge to Lochvale in 1911, and then to Slave Lake in 1938. The name was taken from the Slave River, a derogatory Cree name for enemies who inhabited the area before the Cree moved westward.

The Sawridge Band

The historic name has been preserved, in that the town of Slave Lake is situated on the reserve of the Sawridge Band of the Cree. The band headquarters is in the town, and directs the many industrial operations of the reserve. The band owns lumber mills, hotels, and many other enterprises. The reserve was established in 1899 under Treaty 8, which resulted from native concerns about the increasing pressure from the miners and the settlers on their land, and the government's desire to ensure that land would indeed be available for the settlers. The treaty was signed with much doubt on the part of the native people. Their doubts were well-founded as the treaty — which, they were assured at the time of signing, preserved their right to continue their livelihood as hunters, trappers and fishermen — was altered even before the supposed original was returned to them. A new paragraph regarding regulations and control of hunting and trapping had been inserted, the first of many breaches of the faith of the Indian signatories. Subsequently white trappers have been permitted to encroach upon native lands, and regulations which then became necessary to prevent over-hunting were enforced against white and native people equally. This is in direct in conflict with the promises made so long ago by the Treaty Commissioners, which were to last "as long as this land shall last," and were broken before two moons had passed.

Things to do

1. Wander along the trails in the boreal forest, observing the flowers, trees, underbrush and creatures of the area. If you want to do this more seriously, take *Alberta: A Natural History* (edited by W.G.Hardy), out of your local library and bring it along. It has an excellent section on the boreal forest, with good illustrations of plants, animals and birds.

2. Go swimming on Devonshire Beach, one of Alberta's longest sandy beaches. It was named after a visit in 1920 by the Duke of Devonshire, who was then the Governor General of Canada. He was

North Shore Picnic Area in Lesser Slave Provincial Park

very impressed with the area and the fishing, and stayed for two days. To get to the beach you must drive back along the beach road going south for about 2 km (1 1/4 mi.). Devonshire Beach begins here, and stretches for another 5 km (3 mi.). An after-dinner swim which has you drying off at the beginning of the sunset is good timing: the sunsets across the lake are breath-taking. No pets are allowed on the beach adjacent to the swimming area.

If you manage to time your picnic for the July long weekend, you can participate in the annual Alberta Open Sandcastle Competition on Devonshire Beach, which began in 1987.

3. Drive up to the viewpoint on Marten Mountain. Leaving the town of Slave Lake turn north on Highway 88, and follow the park signs. The viewpoint provides a vista for more than 55 km (35 mi.) from a height of 455 m (1,490 ft.). The ecology of this hill is similar to that of the Swan Hills, from which it was separated some 11,000 years ago by the receding glaciers.

4. Fish from the shore, and catch northern pike and walleye. There is a fish-cleaning table at the North Shore just beside the parking area.

5. Cross-country skiing, snowshoeing, ice-fishing and snow-mobile access to the lake are winter activities available at North Shore.

Things to eat

There's good fishing in the lake, and we'll assume you caught something for the main dish of the picnic, which is grilled whole fish. Along with this you will be serving steamed garden vegetables, so bring along an assortment that pleases your group (Swiss chard, green beans, spinach, snow peas, kale, baby carrots, new potatoes). We'll have Saskatoon muffins for dessert and wash it all down with spruce tea — appropriate in the boreal forest.

Grilled Whole Fish

(Serves 10)

Scale, clean and dry the fish. Sprinkle inside with pepper and lemon juice.

Wait till the fire has burned down to a bed of coals. Grease the grill and place the fish directly on it. Baste frequently with a mixture of melted butter, lemon juice and tarragon. Turn after 15 minutes. A 5-6 pound fish should take about 30 minutes to cook. It is done when the flesh flakes easily with a fork.

If you don't have a grill, the fish can be roasted successfully by wrapping it in a double thickness of aluminum foil and placing it directly on the coals.

Steamed Garden Vegetables

Wash and cut vegetables into attractive slices and chunks of equal size. Place in a steam rack in a pot, and bring to a boil. Check the vegetables often; do not overcook. They should be just tender, not soft. Serve with butter, salt and pepper, and a little vinegar for those who want it.

Saskatoon Muffins

(makes 1 dozen)

Stir together into a bowl:
  1 1/2 cups flour
  1/2 cup sugar
  2 1/2 tsp. baking powder
  1/4 tsp. salt

Add:
  1 cup washed saskatoon berries
And stir.

In a separate bowl mix:
  1 egg
  1/4 cup oil
  3/4 cup milk

Add to dry ingredients and mix only until well-moistened. Spoon batter into paper-lined muffin tins. Bake in 425 °F (220 °C) oven for 15 minutes.

Spruce Tea

Soak half a cup of chopped or broken young spruce twigs and needles in boiling water. Let steep until cool enough to drink. Serve with lemon and/or sweetener.

Note: it doesn't matter if you cannot distinguish between pine, spruce, fir or juniper — they all make good tea.

10 Victoria Settlement / Pakan Smoky Lake

A Church Picnic

In a reverse of the usual sequence of events, the missionaries were the first to settle here, and the Hudson's Bay trading post followed. The mission was called Victoria, and only later, when a settlement was founded, was the name changed to Pakan. The old name hung on, however, as old names tend to do, and the signs direct you to Victoria Settlement. The setting is on the banks of the North Saskatchewan River.

How to get there

(Please note that Victoria Settlement is open only between Victoria Day and Labour Day.)

From Smoky Lake drive south on Highway 855 about 16 km (10 mi.), turning east just before the river. Drive 6 km (3 3/4 mi.) on gravel to the picnic site. The turn is well marked.

From Edmonton, the trip takes about 1 1/2 hours. Drive east on the Sherwood Park Freeway; turn north on Highway 21 just after Sherwood Park. Highway 21 becomes Highway 15, and continues to

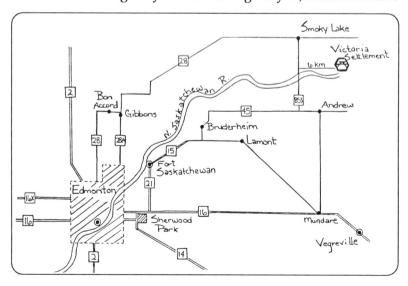

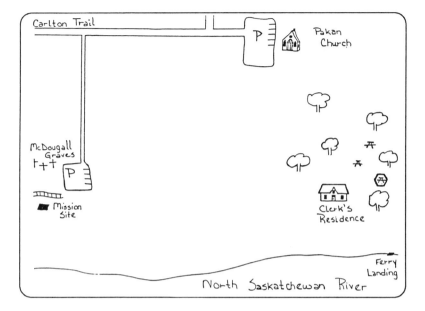

Bruderheim, where you turn north on Highway 45. In 16 km (10 mi.) turn east on Highway 45; continue on to the junction with Highway 855, and turn north, following the signs to Smoky Lake. Just after you cross the river, turn right at the sign for Victoria Settlement, and follow the gravel road for about 6 km (3 3/4 mi.) to the site.

The picnic ground is beyond the church, east of the Clerk's Quarters. (If it rains, move the picnic into the old Methodist church.) The site is suitable for a large picnic.

History

Two old buildings and several huge old trees are the only relics of a settlement established by George McDougall, the man who later established McDougall Church in Edmonton. The Victoria Mission became Fort Victoria, then Victoria Settlement. The name was changed in 1887 to prevent confusion with Victoria, B.C., and the new name, Pakan, honoured the Cree chief James Seenum, also known as Pakannuk who, through his peaceful ways, prevented the ripples of the Riel Rebellion from reaching west to Victoria, and on to Edmonton.

This fascinating site is worthy of an outing during the summer months. The two remaining original buildings are the Hudson's Bay Company Clerks' Quarters and the Methodist Church. Interpreters are on site, and tours are available. An excellent video presentation shown in the church explains the history of the various stages of the settlement.

Clerk's House at Pakan

The Mission

The settlement dates from 1862, when George McDougall and his family arrived to start a Methodist mission to the Indian people of the region. They were quite successful with the Woodland Cree, who occupied the area north of the North Saskatchewan River, but the Blackfoot people on the opposite bank of the river resisted the missionaries, and harassed them in minor ways from time to time over the years.

George McDougall moved away after the terrible smallpox epidemic of 1870 took the lives of his two daughters, Georgiana and Flora, as well as killing many of the Native people. Leaving his son John in charge of the mission, George moved on to Morley.

Fort Victoria

The Hudson's Bay fort was established for fur trading in 1864, and the settlement became home to many Métis people, as well as the Cree. You will notice in the old photographs on the table in the Clerk's Quarters that the land distribution pattern was very much like that of French Canadian settlements farther east, with the properties spread in a line along the river. This pattern was brought west by the Métis settlers. By 1900 these river frontage strips of land stretched for almost 10 km (6 1/4 mi.) east of the settlement. With the ending of the buffalo supply in the 1880s the Hudson's Bay Company decided to close the post in 1883. It was re-opened briefly from 1887 to 1898, but operated at a loss most of the time. With the final closure, the HBC lands were surveyed into long narrow strips favoured by the Métis.

Pakan

In 1885 the Riel Rebellion reached across the Alberta border to Frog Lake, and 9 people were killed by a group of Plains Cree who were wintering on the Frog Lake Reserve (see Frog Lake picnic). Native people were reacting to the events in Manitoba and Saskatchewan with long-suppressed anger, and the Duck Lake and Frog Lake incidents might well have been followed by further incidents in Victoria, and indeed in Edmonton and Calgary. Fear preceded the actual reports, and the settlers in Edmonton and Calgary had already moved into the forts, seeking protection from the anticipated uprising.

In Victoria, however, Chief Pakan was among the first to hear the news of the Frog Lake tragedy. He spoke quietly but strongly to his people, urging them not to repeat the violence, but to let it end there. Had Big Bear retained similar authority in Frog Lake, those lives might also have been saved. Sometime later the Victoria Settlement was renamed Pakan, in honour of this strong and peaceful Cree chief.

The Ukrainian settlers

By the turn of the century the settlement had attracted a group of Ukrainian settlers, and so, in 1901 Dr. Lawford, a Methodist missionary, arrived to convert the Ukrainians. He was successful with only 25 people, but one did become a Methodist missionary himself, which was very helpful, since Lawford spoke no Ukrainian. The mission to the Ukrainians was soon abandoned, but Lawford, also a medical doctor, stayed on and established a hospital in Pakan. It is his medical work among the Indians and the settlers for which he is fondly remembered. Many of the current residents of Smoky Lake entered the world in his clinic.

The present

What is left now is a historic site amidst a scattering of farms. The railway was built in 1918, but it passed through Smoky Lake and not Pakan, and as in so many other hamlets, the fate of the settlement was irrevocably decided. Dr. Lawford even moved the hospital to Smoky Lake. Traffic in the area, however, justified the continuation of the Victoria-Pakan ferry across the North Saskatchewan River until 1972.

Things to do

1. Walk along the river bank to the original mission site, and the graves of the McDougall daughters. Flora and Georgiana lie with their adopted Indian sister, Anna. The other grave, of Abigail McDougall, is that of the first wife of John McDougall. John stayed on in the settlement after his parents and younger brothers and sisters left.

2. Watch the slide/tape presentation in the church.

3. Walk down to the river's edge, to the landing for the river boats and the site of the ferry. It is here that the Blackfoot would come in the night, from across the river, to steal the missionaries' or the settlers' horses.

4. Drive along part of the old Carlton Trail, likely Canada's oldest westward overland trail. It connected Edmonton and Winnipeg, and was in use by Hudson's Bay Company traders from about 1821 until the railway replaced it, early in this century. This section, from Edmonton to Pakan was also known as the Victoria Trail. Several kilometres of the trail still exist, and the drive along the North Saskatchewan River is very pleasant. Leave Victoria/Pakan on the gravel road that leads back to Highway 855, cross the highway and continue straight on.

Things to eat

This is the place for the traditional church picnic. It is a large group gathering. There should be races and balloons, and of course, a big baked ham, potato salad, cucumber salad, buns, and apple pie with cheese. If you are with a smaller group, we suggest that you use the menu from one of the other picnics.

Party Potato Salad for 40

12 pounds potatoes
4 dozen eggs (hard boiled)
2 cups finely chopped onion
1 cup finely chopped dill pickles
1/2 cup chopped pimento
1 cup chopped green pepper

Boil and cool potatoes. Peel and dice into a large bowl. Slice the eggs, and add remaining ingredients. Mix well.

To make the dressing, combine:
2 cups mayonnaise
1 cup hot bouillon
1 cup white vinegar
1/2 cup salad oil
1 Tbsp. dry mustard
salt & pepper to taste
And mix into the salad thoroughly, but gently. Let stand in refrigerator for at least 12 hours. Keep chilled until serving.

Cool-as-a-Cucumber Salad

(serves 40)

Place 16 large or 20 medium cucumbers, peeled and thinly sliced in a bowl with 6 tsp. salt, and let stand for 2 hours.

Make a sauce:
3 cups sour cream
4 Tbsp. sugar
4 Tbsp. vinegar
1/4 cup chopped green onion
pepper to taste
Mix gently with cucumbers and chill.

Baked Ham

Select a whole pre-cooked ham with the bone; or unwrap (thaw) a processed ham and wipe with a damp cloth.

Preheat oven to 325°F.

Bake ham uncovered on a rack. Allow 25 minutes per pound (60 minutes per kilo). The meat is done when the meat thermometer registers 160°F. Take the ham from the oven about one hour before it is done and remove the rind. Cut diagonal slashes across the fat so that the result is about 1" diamonds.

Glaze with a mixture of:
1 cup brown sugar
2 tsp. dry mustard
3 Tbsp. maple syrup

Stud the fat at the intersections of the diamonds with:
whole cloves

Return the ham to the oven for about 45 minutes. Increase the heat to 425°F. Bake for 15 minutes longer.

Garnish with:
Pineapple rings
Maraschino cherries
held in place with toothpicks. Refrigerate and serve with a variety of mustards and relishes.

For the apple pie recipe, see the Banff Cave and Basin Picnic.

11 Frog Lake
St. Paul

The North-West Rebellion Picnic

The Riel Rebellion, the Métis Rebellion, or the North-West Rebellion, as it is variously called by historians, took place in Manitoba and Saskatchewan. Fort Garry, Duck Lake and Batoche are the battle sites commonly recalled. But the hunger, disruption and consequent discontent of the Métis and Indian people of the time were not limited by the new provincial borders, nor curbed by the short-sighted policies of the distant central government. The ripples of the rebellion spread out from the centres of battle to touch the lives of many people in distant places. People were evacuating or taking shelter in forts as far away as Edmonton and Calgary.

How to get there

From Highway 16 turn north on Highway 897 at Kitscoty. At Marwayne, Highway 45 joins 897 for 7 km (4 1/4 mi.), after which 897 continues to the Frog Lake Store. Turn east here, and continue for 3 km (almost 2 mi.). Turn south-east on the road which leads to the historic cairn and the cemetery. The picnic site is 300 metres farther along the road past the cairn; a single cross on the grassy hillside on the left marks the place. Park as far off the road as

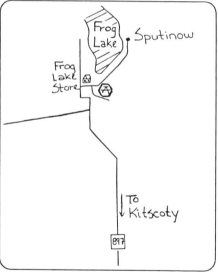

you can, and climb up the rise. The place we choose to spread our blanket is just behind the cross. This is in the settlement proper, as you can see from Bill Cameron's map on one of the markers by the cairn. As you wander on the top of the rise you will find some of the depressions labelled, some not. All of them are the cellars for the houses, barracks, trading post, and offices which once stood here, in the settlement of Frog Lake.

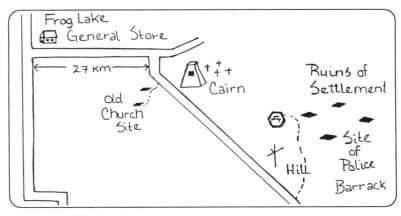

The picnic requires some imagination, but it is a site to which we return often because the events which happened here are not so much glorious as sad in an everyday sense. They involve ordinary people doing their jobs, or caring for their traditions and their people. This was one of the many clashes between two cultures in a time when violence was still hand to hand, and not documented in triplicate.

The shadow of a distant battle

The facts of the deaths at Frog Lake are told on the cairn near the graves of some of those whose lives ended a few metres away. This picnic, however, is concerned with other people; one a survivor of the Frog Lake incident, another the officer in charge of the NWMP at nearby Fort Pitt, and the third a desperate and angry leader of the Plains Cree. The picnic draws from the lives of these people and their time: William Bleasdell Cameron — Hudson's Bay Clerk at Frog Lake, and later writer and journalist; Inspector Francis Jeffrey Dickens — commander of the Mounted Police detachment at Fort Pitt; and Wandering Spirit, war chief of Big Bear's band. First, their stories.

The One-eyed Clerk

Bill Cameron was known as the One-eyed Clerk because he had lost an eye in a childhood misadventure back in Ontario. As soon as he finished school he left for the West, seeking adventure. He was bright and friendly, and willing to work. In a few short years he worked variously as a free trader, a pile driver for the CPR, and a cowboy. He spoke Cree fluently and had many friends among the Native people. By the time he was twenty-three he had become the new Hudson's Bay clerk at Frog Lake. He knew Frog Lake and its Indian, Métis and white residents well — he had been a free trader here a few years before, but had sold out to his rival and joined the Hudson's Bay Company to be trained as a clerk. His return to Frog Lake was his first posting with the Company.

Chicken Stalker

Christened Francis Jeffrey Dickens, the third son of the great novelist was something of a disappointment, an impression to which his stammer undoubtedly contributed. In a rare mo-

Cross at Site of Frog Lake Settlement

ment of pride after a successful grouse hunt, his illustrious father, Charles Dickens, honoured his son with the epithet, Chicken Stalker. It is hard to say whether it was the name or the heritage that turned Chicken Stalker into a truly Dickensian character.

Having completed his education, young Frank asked his father to help him to get established as a gentleman farmer in Canada or Africa. He requested his passage plus 15 pounds, a horse and a rifle. His father replied that he expected that Frank would be robbed of the money, thrown by the horse, and would likely blow his own head off with the gun, and that he consequently felt he must refuse his son's request. Young Francis went off to India for several years in the colonial force, returning to England upon the death of his father. He then came to Canada, and was among the first to enlist with the North West Mounted Police.

Although his unfortunate nickname, Chicken Stalker, might serve to elucidate a character in *Hard Times*, or might even inspire a certain confidence from a character in *David Copperfield*, it brought only derision to the already incompetent leader of the Fort Pitt detachment of the NWMP. To be fair, he was commander of a fort which was a "fort" in name only. There were no stockades, only a small fence on one side to keep the cattle back. It was indeed indefensible. His judgement was poor; he sent scouts at the wrong time, on the wrong path. He had no strategy for defending his detachment in case of attack, nor even a thought about protecting the settlers in his care. He seems truly Dickensian in that although he never did anything right, he carried the double burden of being aware of his own shortcomings. He inherited none of his father's talent, least of all for descriptive writing; nevertheless, we do have Chicken Stalker's diaries of these difficult years on the prairies, as law and order were established among restless Indians, whiskey smugglers and determined settlers and traders. He was in his 43rd year in 1885.

Wandering Spirit

The Frog Lake settlement was on the edge of the Woods Cree reserve, but in the spring of 1885 a group of Plains Cree had been wintering over. They were Big Bear's people, but he was getting old, and his leadership had been informally assumed by his son, Wandering Spirit. These leaders and their people wandered the plains seeking the last remaining buffalo. The people were starving and Big Bear and Wandering Spirit had no means of supplying them with food. Wandering Spirit and many of his followers were tired of the actions of the Great White Mother (Queen Victoria) back in England, who took their lands and furs, giving little in return, and then sent the Mounted Police to enforce an inflexible system of law that made little sense in the frontier West.

Wandering Spirit had a desperate plan. He wanted to kill all the white people at Frog Lake, then kill all the white people at Fort Pitt, especially the Mounties, and move east, killing all the white people in Fort Garry and Winnipeg, Toronto and Montreal, and eventually England. Then he would take back the land from the Great White Mother and return to life as it had been before the traders came. He

ANTS

No picnic book would be complete without the mention of ants. The word "ant" refers to most of the insects of the family of *Formicidae*, order *Hymenoptera*. They are a most numerous, diverse and fascinating insect group. Ants are social insects, and although prehistoric ant colonies contained as few as twelve ants, modern colonies often contain millions. They live in a complex hierarchical society — usually, although not always, dwelling in the ground, and frequently beneath picnic blankets.

Although ants are fascinating to watch, they are not welcome guests at blanket picnics. Their tiny segmented bodies make them easy to recognize, and a few species do bite. Some species even fly — usually the reproductive ants who will mate in the air.

There is no sure way to avoid ants at your picnic, but some techniques work better than others. The first step to take is to scout out your spot very carefully and be sure to avoid setting up on top of — or near to — an ant colony. Avoid dousing yourself with bug repellent; this may repel other picnickers, but it will not deter the ants. Some people believe that ants can be distracted from a picnic by placing a bowl full of sugar and water four paces from the picnic blanket. The idea is that the ants will head for the sticky bowl instead of your iced tea glass. In reality, the ants will still come marching across your salami.

hoped that this action would permit the buffalo herds to increase again, and save the lives of his people. This kind of millenarianist movement occurs in situations such as the desperate one which faced the Native people in the West at the end of the last century: many people were willing to try the most desperate plan in the faint hope of survival. Hope could only be seen in terms of the past, when life was balanced, before the white man came.

The beginning: April 2, 1885

Wandering Spirit and his braves, against Big Bear's express wishes, interrupted the Sunday morning church service at Frog Lake and killed nine white people. Two women, wives of settlers, were taken captive. Bill Cameron, the one-eyed clerk, was saved by a native friend who insisted on buying a hat from the HBC store. This kept him from the church during the shooting. The Indian then counselled Bill to leave with the women, who were being sent to the

Indian camp. By walking with the women he was safe, since the Indians would not shoot a woman. And so Cameron became a prisoner in the Indian camp.

Fort Pitt was 30 miles east of Frog Lake, and on the day of the disaster, Inspector Dickens's diary reads, "Fine morning. Const. Roby left for Onion Lake with team for lumber, returning in afternoon. He reports Indians very excited on reserve." Word of the events reached the inspector a day or so later via another survivor who had hidden in the woods at Frog Lake. Inspector Dickens was totally unprepared for an attack, and Hudson's Bay factor MacLean provided the actual leadership in the days of siege to come. He built a scow, anticipating that the settlers could use it to escape down the river. When word of the Frog Lake disaster reached Ft. Pitt, Inspector Chicken Stalker decided, against the advice of his own staff and MacLean, to send out three scouts to assess the situation. Off went the scouts to Frog Lake, fortunately just missing the 250 Indians riding through the hilly country towards Fort Pitt. The scouts noticed nothing unusual at the Indian encampment near the Frog Lake settlement, so they turned back toward Fort Pitt. Meanwhile, the Indians had reached Fort Pitt, and negotiations were going on between MacLean and Wandering Spirit; progress was being made. But just then Chicken Stalker's scouts returned and, thinking that the Indians were attacking instead of negotiating, tried to rush through the Indians to the Fort. One of them was killed instantly, a second wounded, and the third managed to slip away.

Using his skill to the utmost, MacLean convinced Wandering Spirit to continue negotiations. The most serious animosity was between the Indians and the police; they were less disturbed by the settlers, and held the Hudson's Bay staff in high regard because the clerks were fair, and offered credit. The Indians had no sympathy for the wretched agricultural workers sent out by the government, however, as they were unhappy with the prospect of learning how to farm, an occupation which the government was forcing upon them.

Factor MacLean sensed that Wandering Spirit was anxious to continue his grand plan to rid the world of white people, starting with Inspector Dickens and his Mounted Police. So MacLean arranged for the police and their horses to escape on the small river scow while the Indians were sleeping. Wandering Spirit did indeed notice, but by the time he and his men reached the bank of the river the police scow was on its way to Battleford. Dickens went down in history as the only Mountie who not only didn't get his man, but who also lost the fort. This was an ignominious ending to an unremarkable career for Inspector Chicken Stalker, who marked the event in his diary in his usual understated way: "April 15 — Very cold weather. Travelled."

And after

Bill Cameron was held for several months in the Indian camp, and then released by a friendly Woods Cree. He went on to write several books about his experiences: *Blood Red the Sun* about the Frog Lake incident, and *The Trial of Big Bear*. Cameron had testified at the trial that Big Bear and Wandering Spirit had permitted the Mounties to escape from Fort Pitt. For a while Cameron was popular on the lecture circuit with his frontier stories and lantern slides, and for twelve years he was editor of *Western Field and Stream*. Later he worked at a variety of jobs. He died in Meadow Lake, Saskatchewan in 1951.

Inspector Dickens resigned from the force when he reached Battleford. He went to visit some friends in the United States, and died there the following year of a heart attack. He was a lonely unhappy man, all too aware of his own shortcomings.

Wandering Spirit had permitted the settlers at Fort Pitt to go free; he looted and burned Fort Pitt to the ground, and held the MacLean family prisoners for some weeks. Wandering Spirit eventually surrendered to General Middleton's reinforcements at Fort Pitt, in part because he feared that some of his own men were planning to kill him. Loyalties wavered often with so little left to fight for. Factor MacLean negotiated the surrender, and peace was established, with the usual ambiguity which blurs such triumphs — or defeats. Wandering Spirit attempted to take his own life after the surrender. He was later tried and was hung at Battleford together with several of his followers. Big Bear was tried for the crimes of his band, and was sentenced to three years in prison, which he served in Stoney Mountain Penitentiary in Manitoba. He died soon after his release.

Things to do

1. Read the markers and descriptions of events near the cairn. This site is somewhat neglected, as you can see. The grass around the cairn is mowed now and then by a local person who is paid on an informal basis, as far as we could gather, by the provincial government.

2. Find the mission site. The bush has grown over much of the site, but if you cross the road from the cairn you will notice a little path that winds into the bush. Follow it, and in June, eat the succulent raspberries along the way. The trail quickly brings you to a depression in the ground, which was the mission church. There is a sign low to the ground, if you can find it. Just a little farther on and back is another such place, the rectory for the two fathers.

Cairn and Graves at Frog Lake

3. There is a wonderful array of wild flowers on the hillside here. Some that we identified in June were yellow beard tongue, common blue bell, *Ledysarum* (the purplish variety), prickly rose (Alberta's symbol), Labrador tea, and western wild bergamot (mint).

Things to eat

Amongst the mixed blood population of Western Canada, the predominant group were the French-speaking Métis. Just as the French Métis were the leading force in the North West Rebellion, so also have the French been the leading force in Canadian cooking. Thus, the suitable menu for the Frog Lake Picnic is a French Canadian habitant meal.

MENU

Pork Paté
French Bread
Split Pea Soup
Tourtière
Sugar Pie
Vin Ordinaire

Pork Paté

In a heavy saucepan, cook slowly until brown and crispy:
   1 lb. of diced pork fat

Remove the bits and add:
   1 1/2 lbs. ground pork
   1 cup bread crumbs
   2 medium onions diced
   1 tsp. crushed garlic
   1 cup boiling water
   1 tsp. dried parsley
   1/2 tsp. cinnamon
   1/2 tsp. nutmeg
   1/4 tsp. allspice
   1 tsp. salt
   1/4 tsp. coarse ground pepper

Simmer for two hours stirring occasionally. Cool.

Line a two cup ceramic bowl with plastic wrap. Put mixture in bowl packing it down well. Chill overnight.

Split Pea Soup

(Serves 8-10)

Soak overnight:
   2 cups green or yellow split peas.

Put into a kettle of cold water:
   1 ham bone
and simmer for 2 hours with the lid on. Do not boil.

Add the peas and
   2 carrots diced
   1 onion diced
   1 celery stalk, diced
   savory
   cayenne pepper

Continue to simmer for one hour or until the peas are very soft. Remove the ham bone. Rub the soup through a sieve and return to kettle. Add salt only if necessary.

Tourtière

(Serves 6)

Preheat oven to 500 °F
> 1 lb. chopped pork
> 1 medium onion, diced
> 1 tsp. crushed garlic
> 1/2 tsp. salt
> 1/2 tsp. savory
> 1/2 tsp. celery pepper
> 1/4 tsp. cloves
> 1/2 cup water

Bring to a boil, and cook for 20 minutes. Remove from fire and add:
> 1/2 cup breadcrumbs

spoonful by spoonful until all the fat has disappeared from the top.

Cool the mixture and pour into a pie shell. Cover with more pastry and cook for 25 minutes or until golden brown.

Sugar Pie

Preheat oven to 450 °F.

Sprinkle:
> 1 1/2 cups light brown sugar

over a pie shell.

Cover with
> 1/2 cup milk,

and dot with
> 1/4 cup butter.

Bake at 450 °F for 10 minutes; then reduce the oven temperature to 375 °F and continue baking for another 15-20 minutes. Remove from oven and cool. Protect from domestic vultures — some members of our family have been known to eat a whole pie by themselves, and to do so in a sneaky fashion.

12 The UFO Landing Pad
St. Paul

An Out-Of-This-World Picnic

Bring along some extra food on this picnic, in case you are joined by a party of extraterrestrials while you lunch on the flying saucer landing pad.

How to get there

Highway 28 from Edmonton becomes 50 Ave., or Main Street, in St. Paul. The UFO Landing Pad is at the corner of 53 St. and the highway. You can park along the street, just off the highway.

There are no tables or other amenities here but, since the site is in town, all are available nearby. We think it is worth spreading your picnic blanket on the bit of grass beside the landing pad, and sitting on the steps. Or you can put up a portable picnic table on the landing surface itself, although you should be prepared to move quickly if an unidentified flying object (UFO) appears to want to land.

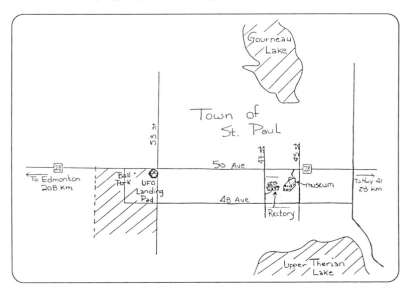

History

The town of St. Paul is known for both its friendliness and its community spirit. As responsible world citizens — or rather, citizens of the universe — the people of St. Paul, Alberta, chose to build a flying saucer landing pad to welcome strangers from other planets to their town, and incidentally to Canada. The project was designed and constructed through voluntary efforts of local professionals, at no cost to the town.

REPUBLIC OF ST. PAUL
(STARGATE ALPHA)
THE AREA UNDER THE WORLDS FIRST U.F.O. LANDING PAD WAS DESIGNATED INTERNATIONAL BY THE TOWN OF ST. PAUL AS A SYMBOL OF OUR FAITH THAT MANKIND WILL MAINTAIN THE OUTER UNIVERSE FREE FROM NATIONAL WARS AND STRIFE. THAT FUTURE TRAVEL IN SPACE WILL BE SAFE FOR ALL INTER GALACTIC BEINGS. ALL VISITORS FROM EARTH OR OTHERWISE ARE WELCOME TO THIS TERRITORY AND TO THE TOWN OF ST. PAUL

The sod was turned by the Honourable Grant MacEwan in 1967, and the site was officially opened in a good-humoured gesture by the Minister of National Defense, the Hon. Paul Hellyer, who arrived in the closest thing he could find to a flying saucer: a helicopter.

A flying saucer is defined as a disk-like object, and some people claim to have seen them flying rapidly over various parts of the earth. Some folks have even seen them land, and photographs of these occurrences exist. There are formal associations of people who have seen flying saucers, or UFOs, as the conservative government agencies prefer to call them. There are people who believe that aliens are among us at this very moment. There is some disagreement about the level of intelligence of these extraterrestrial creatures: some people believe them to have superior intelligence, while others reject the idea of superior beings.

Some more serious history

St. Paul originated as a Métis settlement, first established under the guidance of Father Lacombe in 1896. The settlement failed to develop a momentum of its own, however, since despite the best efforts of the Oblate Fathers, the Métis people had not yet recovered from the blow which the extinction of the buffalo had caused to their traditional economy. They could not convert to farming overnight, and chose instead to continue a subsistence way of life by hunting and fishing. In 1909, the priests recommended that the land be opened up to white settlers, and 500 quickly arrived from Edmonton. From then on the story of St. Paul is much like that of any other agricultural town on the prairies, except that both French and English languages are still spoken here.

Things to do

1. Give everyone on the picnic a pencil and a piece of paper with "extraterrestrial" written on it, and give them 5 minutes to make as many words from the letters as they can. Give an appropriate prize to the winner — a Frisbee!

2. Play with the Frisbee.

3. Visit the St. Paul Historical Museum, in an old school at 4537-50 Avenue. It is open during July and August from Monday to Friday, 10 a.m. to 4 p.m. There are well-arranged displays of events in St. Paul's past, with old photographs, and an intriguing list of the first settlers to homestead in the area.

4. Visit the Old Roman Catholic Rectory just south of Highway 28 on 47th Street. It served as school, residence for the Oblate fathers, and headquarters for the Métis settlement. Tours through the house take place periodically through the day.

What to eat

For a space-age picnic, drop into the snack bar across the street from the landing pad, pick up some fast food, and eat it from styrofoam containers.

13 Elks-Kinsmen Community Park Vegreville
An Egg-ceptional Picnic

Through the years our level of organization for summer holidays has been such that we never get farther from Edmonton than Vegreville on the first night of any trip. We always begin with a night camping beside the world's largest Ukrainian Easter egg, so it is from a base of repeated experience that we recommend this egg-citing picnic.

How to get there

The town of Vegreville is 101 km (63 mi.) east of Edmonton on Highway 16. Take Highway 16A into town to get to the egg which is on the east end of Vegreville. You will easily spot the big egg on the north side of the highway in the Elks-Kinsmen Community Park. There is a turn-off and a parking lot adjacent to the monument.

The Elks-Kinsmen Community Park provides the ideal setting for a picnic, as the gardens surrounding the Pysanka (the Ukrainian word for traditionally decorated eggs) are beautifully maintained, and there are many different picnic sites. You can spread your picnic blanket on the well-kept lawns directly beneath the egg in order to read the placards, and catch the corny jokes of the other tourists. If

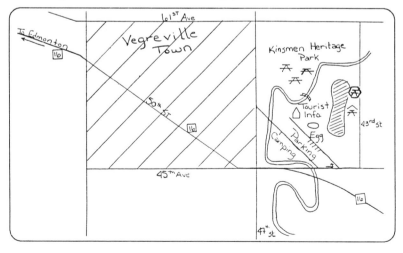

you prefer a table, you will find picnic sites just across the footbridge over the Vermilion River to the west of the egg. There is a large brick barbecue for general use, a gazebo containing several sheltered picnic tables, and also a fire circle for larger groups.

Our favourite spot, however, is on the opposite side of the Elks Pond from the Pysanka, to the east. The view encompasses the monument with the adjacent park and the fountain in the pond. There is a choice of two tables, one under cover, and one in the direct sunlight. This is the last table on the walkway, and you can park directly beside the little covered pavilion if you prefer. The only disadvantage to our spot is that it has no cooking facility. But there are no tourists, either.

Egg-citing facts

The Vegreville Egg is the end-product of one of those rare coincidences in history in which all the right elements come together to result in something unusual like . . . the world's biggest Easter Egg! What came together were: a bundle of provincial government money offered to Alberta communities to create a fitting memorial to the RCMP centennial in 1974; a Ukrainian community with pride in its traditional pysanka; and an engineer who knew how to build an egg that weighs 32,000 pounds!

While you stand below the 31-foot high monument, admiring the design, you will undoubtedly overhear comments such as the following:

"I'd love to see the chicken that laid that one!"

"That would make a heck of an omelette!"

"I wonder how that chicken managed to cross the road!"

"I'll bet the egg came first that time!"

The setting seems to inspire such humour.

But seriously . . .

The towering pysanka monument which dominates the picnic grounds of the Elks-Kinsmen Community Park in Vegreville was created by the most modern technology, but inspired by the Ukrainian traditions of the distant past. The monument was erected by the

Vegreville and District Chamber of Commerce in 1974 to commemo-
rate the one-hundredth anniversary of the Royal Canadian Mounted
Police in Alberta.

The setting of the commemorative statue in Vegreville is not
entirely coincidental. The early community of Vegreville, in the late
nineteenth century, was predominantly settled by Ukrainian peoples,
but the outlying areas and the neighbouring communities were
populated by Native, Irish, French, British, German, Polish and
American settlers. In those days, Canada's West was administered
by the traders and the pioneers, but each group of people tended to
have their own system of justice: hence the term 'the Wild West.' The
coming of the North-West Mounted Police in 1874 meant the coming
of a justice system which would govern the native peoples, the
whiskey runners, and the settlers alike. The new police force was
made responsible for the 'taming of the West', which subsequently
paved the way for the increased settlement and growth of the
Vegreville community. (The history of the formation of the RCMP is
discussed in more detail in the picnic at Fort Macleod.)

The pysanka symbolizes more than the birthdate of the police
force in the west. This egg structure also represents the inherent
interdependence of the present and the past. The astounding structure is 31 feet high, 25.7 feet long, and 18.3 feet in width. It is made of
aluminum coated in permaloyhard anodized colours of bronze,
silver, and gold. These three colours are coordinated into a grid of
patterns made up of triangles. Using ancient themes, Paul Sembaliuk
designed the egg with the aid of a computer.

The tradition of the pysanka in the Ukraine has been an important
part of the preparation for Easter within the Ukrainian Orthodox
religion. The eggs are not painted, but are written upon with time-
honoured designs (pysanka comes from the Ukrainian verb *pysaty*, to
write). Geometric designs such as triangles, bands, stars and crosses
are the most usual.

The pysanka before you is constructed of 1,108 equilateral triangles; the triangle represents air, fire and water, but in the past
century or two has also been taken to stand for the Holy Trinity. The
star symbolizes eternal life and good fortune, the zigzag band encir-
cling the egg symbolizes eternity, but the jagged edge is called the
wolf's tooth, and signifies protection and security. The six-pointed
star symbolizes good harvest. These designs have a long history in
the traditions of the Ukraine, predating Christianity. The significance
of these designs evolved with time, and the monument of the
pysanka is the most modern interpretation of this age-old symbol.
The tradition of the pysanka to the Ukrainian community, and the
most modern graphic designing and engineering of the monument,
reflect the important contribution of the heritage of the Canadian
settlers to their present identity, and to that of the nation.

Egg-zotic facts

Sex test for eggs:
Thread a needle with about 6 inches of thread, doubled. Hold the needle by the knot at the end of the thread, perfectly still over the egg. If the needle begins to swing back and forth, the egg will hatch a male. If it swings in a circle, the egg is female. If it hangs still, the egg is no good.

— Old Wives' Tale

Test for hard-boiled eggs:
Spin the egg. If it wobbles and spins slowly, it is fresh. If it spins fast and smoothly, it is hard boiled.

Egg-scursions

1. Wander around the little lake, resting on the occasional bench, and observe the lovely swans. There were several cygnets on our last visit.

2. Have a real Ukrainian dinner at one of the cafes in downtown Vegreville. Egg-cellent pyrohys!

3. Visit the shops in the town and buy your own pysanka — there are some egg-ceptionally fine egg-samples around.

4. Attend the Ukrainian Cultural Festival on the July 1st long weekend in Vegreville. There are eggs-clusive arts and crafts for sale, and continuous Ukrainian dancing displays.

Egg-zotic things to eat

The subtle theme of this picnic, gentle reader, is eggs.

Egg Salad Sandwiches

We trust you to make these yourself, but you really should use that super-rich egg bread, if you can find it.

The menu also features egg nog, made ahead and brought, well-chilled, in a Thermos container. Our favourite recipe has a thick, pudding-like consistency — use it for dessert rather than a beverage.

Egg Nog

(Serves 4)

6 eggs
6 half eggshells sugar
6 half eggshells full of Marsala or sweet wine

You will need a saucepan, a bowl which can rest comfortably over it, and a whisk. Put the pan of water on to boil. In the bowl, beat the eggs with the sugar until they are light and fluffy. This will take twice as long as you think. Beat in the Marsala.

Rest the bowl over the now-boiling water. Beat until the mixture is firm and holds the mark of the whisk. Serve in tall glasses with a long spoon, if you can — or in cups with a short spoon.

Every Ukrainian community bar (our favourite is in Smoky Lake) has a bottle of pickled eggs on the counter. They are a must on this picnic. We try to keep a jar of them in the fridge, but it is difficult because people keep eating them.

John's Pickled Eggs

1 dozen eggs
3 cups white vinegar
2 cups water
2 Tbsp. salt
1 Tbsp. sugar
1/2 tsp. turmeric
2 Tbsp. mixed pickling spice

Hard-boil, cool and peel the eggs. Place in a crock or glass jar. Mix together the remaining ingredients in a pot, bring to a boil, reduce heat and simmer for 10 minutes, pour over eggs, and refrigerate for at least 24 hours before serving.

For the last course, serve jelly beans or candy Easter eggs, unless you think this is egg-cessive.

EDMONTON AND AREA

14 Fort Edmonton
Edmonton
The Trader's Picnic

For this picnic you move back in time to the days of John Rowand, factor for the Hudson's Bay Company, who lived with his family in the building now called Rowand House. If you plan your picnic for a summer afternoon you will undoubtedly be there when the free trader, Mr. MacKenzie, arrives to trade furs for supplies for his family. Or you may witness the landing of the York boats with the shipment of supplies from Fort Garry and Upper Canada. Scenes such as these are re-enacted several times a day, from Victoria Day to Labour Day, by the well-trained and irrepressible interpretive staff. Much of the action takes place in the square in the centre of the fort, on the lawn in front of Rowand House — our picnic site.

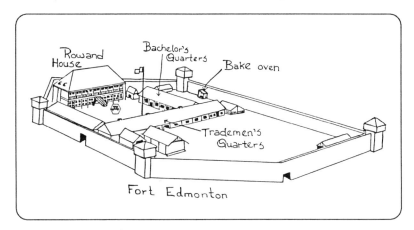

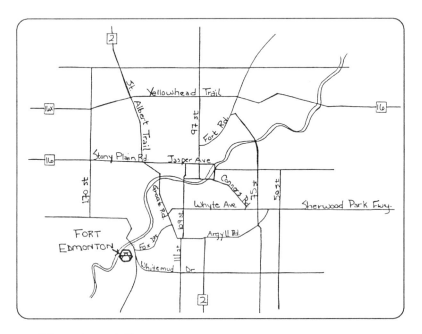

How to get there

Fort Edmonton Park is at the junction of Fox Drive and the Whitemud Drive, beside the North Saskatchewan River. The turn-off is clearly marked with signs on the freeway. The brochure which you receive as you enter the park provides a map with all washrooms, drinking fountains, picnic areas, restaurants, and other facilities clearly marked. Please note that there is an admission charge to this park.

You are welcome to use the tables in the clerks' quarters for your picnic; if it is sunny we suggest a blanket on the grass in front of the factor's house.

History

Fort Edmonton, the most northerly fort on the Saskatchewan River system, became increasingly important to the Hudson's Bay Company in the late nineteenth century as an access point to the northern river systems, and to the Rocky Mountains. The site of the fort was moved several times during the first few years, but was eventually established where the Legislature Grounds are now, in downtown Edmonton. That site was selected for its easily defended position high on the bluffs overlooking the river. It was protected on several sides by steep cliffs, and there was good visibility all around to give adequate warning of attack.

The twentieth century site of the fort was selected with more regard for freeway access and parking space. Traded here now are memories and images of the past, glimpses of the fort as it was in 1846.

Rowand House at Fort Edmonton

John Rowand

Rowand is remembered as a little man with a strong personality. He was born in 1789 in Montreal, the son of an Irish doctor. He spoke Gaelic, English, Blackfoot and Cree. An experienced fur trader, John Rowand was appointed to the position of chief factor at Fort Edmonton in 1826. He was reputed to drive a hard bargain with his traders, but he was well respected. The earlier reputation of the fort as a wild trading post was quickly reversed under the direction of Chief Factor Rowand, and rumours of his courage and justice spread quickly. The fort assumed an increasingly administrative role under Rowand, and he maintained an uneasy peace in the midwest. Within the fort Rowand built the "Big House" for his family. It was somewhat pretentious for the time, with real glass windows: shipped all the way from England in barrels of molasses.

Barrels as shipping containers featured prominently once again for John Rowand in the somewhat bizarre story of his burial. Rowand died of a heart attack in 1854 as he was breaking up a fight between his son and another man. His friend, Sir George Simpson, also of the Hudson's Bay Company, undertook to bring Rowand's remains to Montreal for burial. Transporting bodies was not commonly done in those days, so Simpson engaged a Fort Edmonton resident to boil Rowand's corpse in a cauldron, stirring until only the bones remained. The bones were then packed into a barrel filled with rum,

and labelled salt pork. The barrel was loaded onto a boat bound for
Montreal via the Great Lakes. Somewhere along the way, however,
the barrel was mislaid, and it was later discovered to have reached
London, England, instead of Montreal. The rum had been replaced
by water, which caused no damage to Rowand — whose presence
must have been quite a surprise to the sailors who'd consumed the
rum. The bones were once again sent off to Montreal, and Rowand
was finally buried there two years after his death!

Things to do

1. This picnic can take all day, if you wish, as a visit through the
exhibits can take several hours. A walk around the fort enclosure will
reveal many other activities which contributed to the economy of the
fort when it was in operation. You can watch the blacksmith, the
cooper, the boat builder or the carpenter at work. The traders and
clerks will be bartering with the Indian and Métis hunters for the pelts
they have brought in.

2. Wander down re-creations of Edmonton's history: 1885 Street,
1905 Street, and 1920 Street.

3. Buy a holiday package tour for Hawaii in January or February,
and follow in John Rowand's footsteps. He was undoubtedly the first
Edmontonian to make the now-traditional winter pilgrimage. In 1842
Rowand and Sir George Simpson made the trip from Edmonton to
Hawaii by pack horse and boat. (Purists will walk or ride on horse-
back as far as the International Airport.)

Things to eat

If you venture behind the clerks' quarters you will often find a
volunteer dressed in the costume of the late 1800s, baking bread in the
traditional manner in an outdoor, wood-fired oven. If you ask, you
will find out how difficult it is to maintain a constant heat in such an
oven. And if you wait around till it's done, you will be given a piece
of bread to taste.

Our menu for this picnic includes bread — and we'll supply a
recipe, in case you want to try it — cold sliced meats, dill pickles
(made in a barrel like the one in which John Rowand travelled about
the world), and for dessert an ice cream cone, bought as you wander
through the exhibits.

Bread was made from whatever was on hand. In summer a
handful of ripe saskatoon berries might be added for flavour. Whole
wheat (stone ground, of course) was used. Sifting the flour was
essential, as flour was stored in large barrels, and wood chips were

mixed in with it to absorb the moisture and prevent the flour from spoiling. It makes you wonder why recipes still demand sifting nowadays, when we no longer need to remove the wood chips! The following recipe is adapted from a booklet prepared by the Fort Edmonton Historical Foundation entitled *Old Time Recipes from Fort Edmonton Park*.

Whole Wheat Molasses Bread

(2 loaves)

Dissolve in 1/2 cup warm water:
> *1 Tbsp. yeast*
> *1 tsp. sugar*

Set aside until bubbly.

In a large bowl, measure and combine:
> *2 cups water*
> *2 tsp. salt*
> *2 heaping tsp. lard*
> *3 cups whole wheat flour*
> *1/4 cup molasses*

Stir until all ingredients are well-blended.

Add yeast mixture and mix well.

Gradually add additional flour (about 3 cups) until the mixture is stiff. Turn out on a floured board and knead for 10-15 minutes, adding more flour if necessary.

Grease the dough well, cover and set aside to rise to double. Punch down and knead again for a few minutes. Cut in half, shape into rounded loaves and set on well-floured wooden paddle. Let rise again in warm place, about one hour. Bake for 45 minutes in a stone oven.

Old Fashioned Crock Pickles

Mix together in a one-gallon crock:
   2 quarts vinegar
   1 medium onion, sliced
   2 Tbsp. dry mustard
   3 Tbsp. salt
   1 inch ginger root, grated
   2 Tbsp. whole cloves
   1 Tbsp. ground cloves
   3 cinnamon sticks, broken
   1 Tbsp. peppercorns
   1/2 pound brown sugar
Stir to dissolve dry ingredients.

Add:
   2 quarts pickling cucumbers, washed and drained

Use a plate to hold the cucumbers under the liquid. Cover and let stand in a cool, dark place for at least one month before eating.

The Lazy Picnic

The ubiquitous buffalo burgers and sturdy homemade soup are available for take-out at Jasper House. Bread and saskatoon preserves can be purchased at Lauder's Bakery on 1885 St.

15 Legislature Building
Edmonton
A Bureaucratic Picnic

Here on the original site of Fort Edmonton, where shrewd traders negotiated huge profits from the hides of local animals, now the politicians and bureaucrats devise more advanced methods of skinning Alberta residents. The fountain court was built in the 1970s at the peak of the oil-induced prosperity, during the reign of Premier Peter Lougheed. Historians might recall that the palace and fountains of Versailles were built by Louis XIV during a period of French ascendancy. In fact the Alberta fountains with their stepping stones and wading pools far surpass Versailles as a picnic spot.

Whether you work in one of the government offices nearby, or are just waiting in line in one of them, you will enjoy a picnic by the fountains on a sunny afternoon.

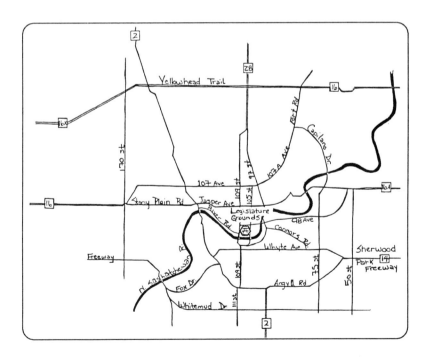

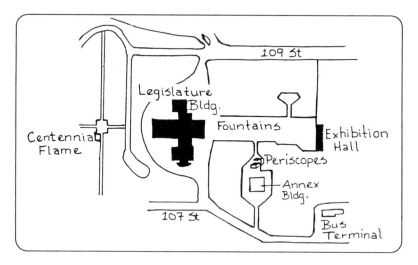

How to get there

The fountains are in front of the Legislature Building on 108th Street directly south of 98th Avenue. They can be reached by bus, light rail transit line or car. Parking can be a problem; most civil servants, however, walk from the nearby buildings.

From Fort Edmonton to "The Leg"

The original Fort Edmonton was built in 1795 on the north bank of the North Saskatchewan River about 1 1/2 miles from the mouth of the Sturgeon River, near the current site of the town of Fort Saskatchewan. The original fort was built by George Sutherland of the Hudson's Bay Company; it was named "Edmonton" as a compliment to the clerk, John Pruden, who came from the town of Edmonton in England. The name, Edmonton, was derived from the Anglo-Saxon Christian name Eadhelm and Tun or ton, meaning field. The fort was rebuilt on the river bank behind the site of the present Legislature Building in 1830, where it stood until 1915, when the city fathers chose to take it down. Then in 1974 a replica of the fort was opened as an historic site, down on the river flood plain, an unlikely spot for a fort. (It is, however, a nice site for a historical park — see Fort Edmonton Park picnic.)

The current boundaries of Alberta were determined on July 1, 1905, when it became a province. Prior to that it had been part of the Canadian North-West Territories. The province was named after Princess Louise Caroline Alberta, fourth daughter of Queen Victoria. The present Legislature Building was constructed from 1907 to 1912, designed by A.M. Jeffers, and constructed with sandstone from Calgary and granite from British Columbia.

The legislature building is nicknamed "The Leg" (pronounced "Ledge") by affectionate Edmontonians.

Things to do and see

1. Tours of the Legislature Building are free, and are conducted daily every half hour: Monday to Friday from 9 a.m. to 4 p.m.; Saturday, Sunday and holidays from 1 p.m. to 4 p.m.. Recorded carillon concerts provide pleasant background music for picnics at 12 noon on weekdays. There is a live concert on Sundays at 1 p.m..

2. Have a look at the large periscopes on the east side of the fountain. They permit a full view of the fountain from the pedway below.

3. Tour the underground pedway. On the east edge of the fountain are covered stairways to the pedway below, where you will find an unexpectedly magic place. Follow the corridor, stopping to look through the periscopes, which give the illusion that people walking past the fountain are walking directly toward you. Admire the many fountains and murals in the corridor, reminiscent of the fountains in the court above.

4. Visit the Pedway Exhibition Hall. These unique exhibits illustrate Alberta's natural wealth and ethnic diversity. Special fun is the

Legislature Grounds

"cityscape," where huge photographs of buildings in Calgary and Edmonton have been arranged to create a composite street. You can peek in the windows of many of the buildings through the astonishing device of many tiny television sets, which serve as windows on the people who live and work in the buildings. Some of them even wave at you as you peek in at them!

5. The stepping stones which descend into the north fountains invite wading, especially on a hot day or a warm summer evening.

6. A walk behind the Legislature Building provides various views of the gardens, and the High Level Bridge through the trees.

Things to eat

The fountains are a favourite spot for civil servants from the surrounding office towers to eat lunch. To adapt to the local customs and traditions, we suggest some typical picnic menus that have been observed in the regulars' lunches.

The Bureaucratic Bagel

Salmon flavoured cream cheese (in these days of government restraint we can't afford real smoked salmon) on a plain bagel, garnished with alfalfa sprouts. For a beverage we suggest Nanton water, followed by a 15 minute power walk around the grounds.

The Secretarial Sandwich

A croissant stuffed with shrimp and avocado on lettuce, with black cherry flavoured seltzer, followed by 15 minutes of serious suntanning.

A Clerk I Basic Brown Bag

Bologna on lettuce with mayo on enriched white bread; coffee from the machine or in a Thermos brought from home. Lunch break is 15 minutes.

A Clerk II Basic Brown Bag

Black forest ham and lettuce on rye bread with Russian honey mustard, with a Coke Classic. Spend the remaining 15 minutes reading the text for an evening course in self-improvement.

A Clerk III Basic Lunch

Steak sandwich and fries with coffee at the cafe — (Clerk IIIs don't eat in the park!)

The Minister's Gourmet Picnic

(Prepared by an ADM and served by an Administrative Assistant)

The starter is a marinated tomato and mushroom salad, followed by a main course of chilled poached salmon steaks with asparagus and French bread. The wine is a light white selected from the offerings of the cellars of Andrew Wolf in Stony Plain, Alberta. Dessert is fresh strawberries and cantaloupe with a bowl of melted chocolate in which to dip the fruit.

Tomato Mushroom Salad

(serves 4)

Make a marinade by mixing together in the blender the following ingredients:

3/4 cup olive oil
1 Tbsp. lemon juice
2 cloves garlic
1 tsp. basil
pinch black pepper
1 Tbsp. chopped fresh parsley

1 tsp. Worcestershire sauce
1 tsp. dry mustard
1/2 tsp. honey
3 Tbsp. red wine vinegar

Pour marinade over:
4 green onions, including tops, chopped
3 large tomatoes, cut into eighths
4 cups of button mushrooms, quartered

Mix well and refrigerate for several hours.

Poached Salmon Steak With Asparagus

(serves four)

1 quart of water
1 medium-sized onion, sliced
6 peppercorns
1 bay leaf
1 tsp. salt
2 pounds fresh asparagus
4 salmon steaks, each about 1" thick
lemon slices, capers, parsley sprigs for garnish

In a pan over a high heat create a stock by combining water, onion, peppercorns, bay leaf and salt. Bring to a boil, cover, reduce heat and simmer for 15 minutes.

Snap off and discard the tough ends of the asparagus. Add the asparagus to the pot and simmer uncovered until tender (6-8 minutes). Remove asparagus, rinse under cold water, let cool, cover and refrigerate.

Place the salmon steaks in the stock pot, ensuring that they are completely covered with liquid. Simmer until pink throughout, 8-10 minutes. Remove and drain, let cool slightly, cover loosely with foil and refrigerate until well-chilled.

Pack lemon slices, capers and parsley in plastic bags for garnishing at the picnic site. Serve with spiced mayonnaise.

Basic Mayonnaise

Mix together in a blender at medium speed for 20 seconds:
1 egg
2 Tbsp. lemon juice
1/2 tsp. salt
1/4 tsp. dry mustard

Then add in a slow steady stream through the opening in the top of the blender cap while the blender is running:

1 cup salad oil

Ingredients will emulsify while the oil is being added. If ingredients fail to emulsify, pour mixture into a cup, rinse out the blender, put a new egg and lemon juice into it and repeat the process using the mixture in place of the oil, and this time pouring in a *slow* steady stream.

Spiced Mayonnaise

To produce spiced mayonnaise add 2 Tbsp. of your favourite spice to the mixture in the blender before adding the oil. Some suggestions:

Parsley
Tarragon
Thyme
Curry powder

16 Leduc #1 Oil Well
Devon
The Tailgate Picnic

Everyone has heard about it, but hardly anyone knows exactly where the Alberta oil boom began. Despite the fact that the well came in in February, the summer is a much nicer time for this picnic.

How to get there

Leave Edmonton driving west on Highway 16. Turn south on Highway #60 to Devon. Just south of Devon you will pass the intersection with Highway #19. Continue for .8 km (1/2 mi.) watching for the sign on the east side of the road which marks the entrance to the lease site of Leduc #1. An alternative route is to leave Edmonton on Highway #2 going south; turn right or west on Highway #19 and proceed 13 km (8 mi.) to the junction with Highway #60. Turn south for .8 km (1/2 mi.), and turn in at the sign for the lease. Follow the road until you come to the pumps. The original well is a monument,

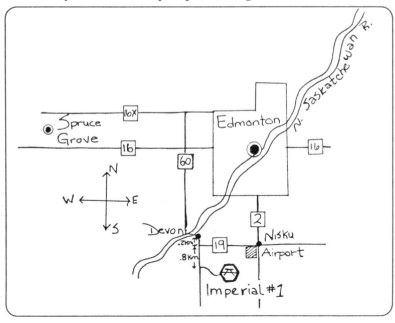

but beside it is a working horsehead pump, a sign that the Leduc field is still supplying us with oil, 40 years after its discovery.

The first oil discovered in Alberta was in Waterton in 1902. The second oil well in the province was at Victoria Settlement, but it was not productive enough to develop. The first major oil field was discovered at Turner Valley, southwest of Calgary in 1913. However, the discovery that initiated the transformation of Alberta's economic base from agriculture to oil was the development of the Leduc oilfield by Imperial Oil. The oilfield roughneck replaced the cowboy as the image of the Alberta workingman, and the pick-up truck replaced the horse.

Roughnecks are the people who work on the oil rigs. If they are lucky, they live within driving distance of the field, but often they drive or fly to the rig site and stay for several weeks at a time. The pickup truck is very much a part of their daily lives. Hence the tailgate picnic. Lunch at the site will be informal. You can set out the sandwiches and the beer on the tailgate of the pickup, and participants can serve themselves.

History: Leduc #1

In November of 1946, Imperial Oil Limited's Vernon Hunter spudded in Leduc #1. By the following February the hole was 5,000 feet deep and there were signs of oil. Vernon was so sure that he would strike oil in this spot that he called the newspaper and radio people, along with various government and company officials, to meet at the site on February 13, 1947. They stood in the cold, waiting for something to happen; many gave up after awhile and went home. But those who stayed witnessed history in the making at 4 in the afternoon, when the oil came in — with a roar and a big black cloud.

The Leduc field had 1,278 wells and contained 200 million barrels of recoverable oil. Its discovery was rapidly followed by discoveries in Woodbend, Redwater and Pembina. By 1980 there were more than 17,000 producing wells distributed across most of the province and Alberta was supplying 80% of the Canadian domestic production. As you stand by the pump today you can see only four or five working horsehead pumps. This is because the recoverable oil, a nonrenewable resource, is nearly depleted in this site.

Things to do

1. On the journey out from Edmonton you can play "Count the Pumps." See how many horsehead pumps you can spot in the fields that you pass — and they have to be pumping as you count them!

2. Play poker like the roughnecks in the northern camps, with matchsticks (unlike the roughnecks!).

3. See the actual Leduc No. 1 rig beside the Edmonton Travel Infocentre on the Calgary Trail just south of the city.

Things to bring

There isn't a picnic table here, so bring a portable one, or bring a blanket: unless you have a tailgate to use for a table.

Things to eat

Starters: either onion rings and root beer;
or potato chips and dip;
or piggy puffs and Labatt's Pilsener.

Chip Dip

Combine one 500 g container of sour cream with half a package of Lipton's Onion Soup mix (we find that substitute brands result in an inferior product — even No Name!) Be sure to mix the soup powder so that you get a good blend of the powder and the onion bits — then add to the sour cream and stir. This gets better if it is made at home, allowing the soup powder to dissolve during the ride to the picnic.

Among generous people this recipe may be enough for four, but if your roughnecks are hungry, multiply the recipe exponentially.

Main Course

It is our observation that oilfield workers like their food fast and flavourful. If the oil industry is the backbone of Alberta, the oil industry workers are the backbone of the province's burgeoning fast food industry. Our main course consists therefore of either a bucket of Kentucky fried chicken; or six Big Macs, 1 quarter-pounder, and a six-pack of Chicken McNuggets.

Note: fast foods can be picked up as you leave Edmonton from any of the following convenient locations: McDonald's is on the Calgary Trail southbound at 51st Avenue; A & W is at 5035 Calgary Trail northbound; for the Kentucky Fried Chicken you make a slight side trip to 3901 106 St.

Should you arrive at Devon without your fast food fix, it is possible to get a take-out pizza. Sausage rolls and pastry are available at the bakery.

Dessert is always something special brought from home. For this occasion we recommend Terrie's Brownies. The appropriate beverage is instant coffee, luke-warm, from an insulated thermos jug.

Terrie's Brownies

If this is a last minute picnic Terrie, our favourite rig wife, might actually buy the brownies at a bakery.

If there is a little more time, she will take one package of Duncan Hines brownie mix from the shelf, and follow instructions.

Terrie's best brownies, however, are made from scratch, as follows (she has been known to make these at 2 in the morning while doing the last load of laundry before the 6 a.m. flight leaves for the north):

> 2 squares unsweetened chocolate
> 100 g butter or margarine
> 250 ml (1 cup) sugar
> 2 eggs, beaten
> 250 ml (1 cup) all-purpose flour
> 1 tsp. salt
> 1 cup chopped nuts
> 1 tsp. vanilla

Melt chocolate and butter together over low heat (microwave is fine); add remaining ingredients and mix thoroughly. Pour into a greased 8" square pan. Bake in 350 °F oven for 30 minutes.

Ice with tinned chocolate icing, or

Fluffy Chocolate Frosting

> 2 Tbsp. butter or margarine
> 2 cups sifted icing sugar
> 4 Tbsp. cocoa
> 1 egg white
> 1/8 tsp. salt
> 1/4 tsp. vanilla

Cream butter, sift together icing sugar and cocoa, add about 1/4 of this mixture to butter, cream until light. Add unbeaten egg white and salt, beat until blended. Gradually add remaining icing sugar mixture, beat until fluffy. Ices an 8" or 9" pan of brownies.

17 Ukrainian Village
Edmonton
A Ukrainian Picnic

It is easy to imagine yourself as a pioneer on the prairies a century ago as you taste the traditional foods of the Ukraine, and wander about this village: an accurate re-creation of the past.

How to get there

The village is on the south side of Highway 16, 50 km (31 mi.) east of Edmonton; the drive from the city limits takes about 25 minutes. The picnic area is just to the left of the main entrance to the historic village.

The special picnic site which we prefer, however, is just beyond the actual picnic ground. It is a few metres farther to walk to, but well worth it. From the parking lot walk across the picnic ground towards the building housing the washrooms. Pass behind this building, and follow the short path which ends abruptly at what looks at first like a wharf. A closer examination reveals it to be an old ferry which has been restored to sit permanently on the edge of the shore. A breeze reduces the number of mosquitoes — they much prefer the picnic tables in the woods, as do most of the people. There is no table here, but your picnic can be spread on the sheltered ledge on the side, and

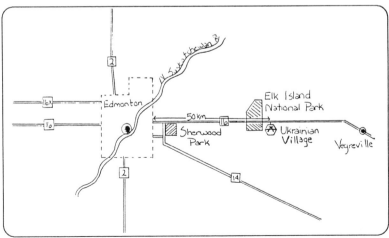

you can sit on the floor of the ferry, or on the substantial railings. Alternatively you can be truly decadent and bring your portable picnic table. A Ukrainian settler might have chopped down a tree and made a rough table, but this sort of activity is now discouraged.

From the old, weathered ferry you have an panoramic view of the whole town from across the slough, from the railway station to the church on the hill, just opposite.

History

The buildings on the site have been collected from a variety of places, and some have required extensive restoration. We suggest a tour of the village before your picnic, so that you catch the flavour of the Ukrainian settlements in Alberta. This was an agricultural society established by hardworking immigrants from what is now western U.S.S.R. The buildings are staffed by interpreters in period costume, and it is possible to observe family and community life as it was eighty years ago. Meals are being cooked, gardens are being weeded, harnesses are being repaired, and bread is being baked.

The first wave of Ukrainian people settled in Canada in the latter part of the last century. They were discouraged with life in the Ukraine, which at that time was part of the Austro-Hungarian Empire. Taxes were very high, and it was difficult to earn enough money to support a family. Land was scarce, as family holdings had been divided and subdivided again over the generations, until inherited plots were no longer large enough to sustain a family. The rumours of vast stretches of fertile land in Western Canada were tempting, and hundreds of people took the difficult boat trip, followed by the long, miserable train journey, to reach their new tracts of prairie, which were freely available to those willing to live and work on the land.

As you walk through the park you will see the various kinds of housing built by these determined people as they adapted to their new surroundings. Anyone who has farmed the prairies has a strong respect for those who broke and cleared this land — before the days of bulldozers and monster tractors!

The Ukrainian people tended to settle in groups, sustaining their cultural traditions, and maintaining a sense of community to ward off the homesickness which sometimes overwhelmed them in the new land. To this day Ukrainian families continue to honour the time-bound traditions of special foods at Christmas, Easter and the New Year. Wedding celebrations in the Ukraine lasted almost a week; Ukrainian weddings in western Canada are legendary even now, although they last only two or three days!

The Legend

The centre of all Ukrainian celebrations is the kolach, a special bread made in a ring shape, and decorated symbolically. It is carefully glazed by painting milk on the surface using goose feathers (or, if necessary, a pastry brush). At Easter it is traditional to have the bread blessed by the priest before it becomes the centrepiece of the dinner table.

The Story of the Magic Goose Feathers

Once upon a time, in a cold and snowy land, long after dinosaurs walked the earth and dragons flew the skies, a little girl and her mother lived with an old, wise man whose name was Uncle Alex.

Now Uncle Alex had been born in a far-off land called Romania and he had learned many wonderful, magic things from his forefathers. As the little girl grew, Uncle Alex shared his magic with her.

When the warm South winds blew he taught her to catch potato bugs on the potato leaves. When the cold North winds blew, he taught her to catch bunnies from old Uncle Nick's wood pile by putting salt on their tails. But best of all, Uncle Alex knew how to make magic bread. The grains, yeast and salt from mother earth seemed quite ordinary. But after they had been mixed together and made into a loaf (that somehow grew to twice its size as if by magic), Uncle Alex did a very special thing. He carefully took an egg, mixed it with a little water and then, from deep inside an old cupboard, he brought forth three beautiful goose feathers. With the feathers, he very gently brushed the egg white onto the lovely, round loaves and placed them in the oven. When these loaves came out again, they were a beautiful golden colour. Now everyone knows that old mother goose laid the golden egg of the sun and that is why we find a golden sun in every egg. So the goose feathers brought the growing power of the sun to every loaf of bread; and the little girl grew healthy and strong from the bread made from the magic of wise, old Uncle Alex and blessed by the sun.

This legend, retold by Charonne Regan in a delightful little booklet sold at the interpretive centre, illustrates the importance of bread to these people. Kolach is a special kind of bread, sweeter than usual bread recipes. The strands of dough are shaped into an interlocking ring to symbolize eternity. Sometimes three rings of bread are placed one on top of the other with a candle in the centre. The three rings represent the Holy Trinity. Additional decorations molded from a slightly different dough may be added. Doves, for example, symbolize peace; they are used at Easter and for wedding cakes. Braids are also sometimes placed on top.

Things to do

1. This "things to do" section is slightly different in that the first activity has to be done a day or two before the picnic. We thought you might enjoy making the legendary magic bread called Kolach for your picnic, so we are including a traditional recipe from the *Ukrainian Daughters' Cookbook*. (Kolach can also be ordered from any Ukrainian bakery, although they will need a few days notice.)

Kolach

Kolach — a braided ring-shaped bread. The name is derived from the Ukrainian word "kolo" meaning a circle.

1 Tbsp. yeast
3/4 cup butter or margarine, melted
1 cup lukewarm water
2 tsp. sugar
1 tsp. salt
1 cup sugar
5 eggs, beaten
4 cups warm water
12 1/2 — 13 cups flour

Dissolve sugar and yeast in water and let stand 10 minutes. Dissolve cup of sugar in 4 cups of warm water. Add melted butter, salt, and beaten eggs. Add yeast mixture. Mix in flour and knead until smooth and elastic. The dough should be just a little stiffer than for bread. Cover, let rise in a warm place until double in bulk. Punch down and let rise again.

Divide the dough into 3 equal pieces. Take 1/3 of the dough and divide into 6 equal pieces. Roll 2 pieces to a length of about 30." Put the 2 lengths side by side, and starting from the centre, entwine dough, thus forming a rope-like twist. Place the entwined dough in a circle along the edge of a well-greased 9" foil pan. Make 2 more twists about 24" long using the remaining 4 lengths of dough. Now take these 2 twists and entwine them in the opposite direction, making a double twist. Form into a circle by

cutting the ends at an angle and pinching together. Place on top of first twist. There should be a small, empty, circular space in the middle of the pan. Let rise to about double in bulk. Be careful not to let the loaves rise too long as the twists will lose their definition.

Brush with beaten egg (using goose feathers, or a pastry brush) and bake at 350 °F for 1 hour. Bake kolach until they sound hollow when bottom is tapped. This recipe makes 3 round kolachi.

Ornamental Doves

> *1 cup boiling water*
> *food colour, yellow*
> *1 tsp. oil*
> *3 cups flour*
> *1 tsp. sugar*
> *1 egg*
> *1 egg, beaten, for glaze*

Combine the first six ingredients. Add one cup of flour. Mix well with a wooden spoon, then add another 2 cups of flour and knead by hand. If more flour is required, add a little at a time. The dough should be thick, like play dough.

Take a piece of dough, and roll on the table to a pencil shape, about 4" long. Tie in a knot. Use the short round end for the dove's head, shape a beak and comb, use poppy seeds for the eyes. Flatten the tail and make

about three slits with a knife. Bake 15-20 minutes, till beak turns brown. Glaze with well-beaten egg, and return to oven for five minutes.

Things to do (continued)

2. Visit the Interpretive Centre, and take time to read the placards in the little exhibition area. It is a superior display, with a mix of old photographs and original oil paintings and carvings, illustrating the experiences of the first settlers from the Ukraine. Unfortunately the artists are not named, but we were able to discover that Dan Bagen painted our favourite painting, the wall-sized gathering of immigrants on the deck of a boat. This was painted from an archival photo.

What to eat

The easy picnic is to buy some of the Ukrainian food from the kiosk at the edge of the picnic area. There is a food kiosk beside the picnic grounds, offering the usual snacks plus some traditional Ukrainian items such as borscht, pyrogys, koubasa on a bun, and the ubiquitous combination platter.

Purists, however, should stop in at the market in downtown

Edmonton on a Saturday morning and buy a coil of Mundare sausage. There is also a store on 124th Street near 107 Avenue called the Mundare Sausage House. True purists will pick up sausages now and then in the town of Mundare. Don't forget to bring your favourite mustard. We like the mustards made in Sherwood Park by Schultz and Radomsky and sold in the gift shop at the Interpretive Centre.

Bring along some buns from a bakery, and a pot of home-made borscht, and complete the meal by eating your kolach — if the cook will let you, after all that work!

Ukrainian Borscht

(Serves 4-6)

450 g soup bones
1.5 L water
2 onions, chopped
2 beets, cut in shoestring strips
1 carrot, also cut in strips
100 g cooked white beans
2 potatoes, cubed small
150 g shredded cabbage, red or green
salt and pepper to taste
125 ml sour cream

Cover the bones with water and simmer for at least an hour. Then add the onions, beets and carrots, and cook slowly for 20 minutes. Add the cabbage, beans, and potato, and boil for another 5 or 10 minutes. Add the sour cream just before serving. You may also wish to have a side dish of sour cream for those who want extra dollops.

(Note: The Ukrainian Daughters' Cookbook is available for $11.95 plus $1.50 postage and handling from: Ukrainian Womens' Association, 1920 Toronto Street, Regina, Sask. S4P 1M8)

18 Blackfoot Grazing Reserve Tofield

A Parkland Picnic

Thirty kilometres east of Edmonton is a picnic spot of unique beauty. The ninety-seven square kilometre Blackfoot Grazing Reserve has been developed as a facility where agriculture, wildlife management, natural gas extraction and recreational activities are integrated.

How to get there

Leave Edmonton heading east on the Sherwood Park Freeway (Highway 630). Continue straight through Sherwood Park on this road, which now becomes the Wye Road. The Wye road heads due east for 16 km (10 mi.) and then bends slightly to the south: parallel to, but not crossing, the railway tracks. Nine km (5 1/2 mi.) after the bend you come to Range Road 210 on your left, and the North Cooking Lake General Store just beyond, on your right.

A quick digression for history buffs: back in about 1910 the store was a resort hotel, serving the people who came out for a day-long excursion on the beach train, a branch line from Strathcona settlement. An abortive make-work project during the Depression — a canal linking the lake to Camrose — caused the water level to drop,

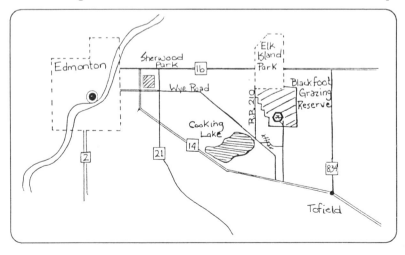

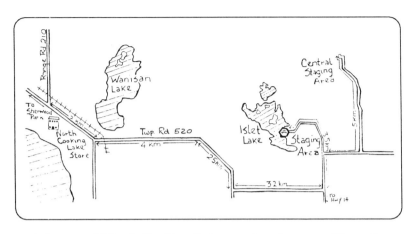

and destroyed North Cooking Lake as a beach resort. The railway station is long gone, but the hotel (now the store) continues to serve the community. The store is your last chance to stock up on things you might have forgotten for the picnic. It also has an excellent supply of penny candy in big old jars.

Our favourite picnic spot is at the Islet Lake Staging area. To get there continue along the Wye Road about 2 kilometres past the store, and turn left onto Twp. Rd. 520. Proceed another 18 km (11 1/4 mi.) to the left turn, clearly marked with a sign, which leads into the staging area. From the store you can also proceed north on Range Road 210 about 6 km (4 mi.) to the Waskehegan Staging Area of the Reserve.

The Aspen Parkland

Listen to the rustle of the wind in the aspen poplar trees; lie on your back in the grass and watch the glittering of the summer sun on the small round leaves. These images are part of the childhood of many western kids, since the aspen parkland extends in a thin strip (maximum width 320 kilometres or 200 miles) all the way from Manitoba to the edge of the Rocky Mountains. The parkland is composed of aspen groves interrupted by prairie grasslands. It is bounded by the prairie to the south and the dense boreal forest to the north.

Parklands have been much reduced over the past century with the introduction of agricultural machinery, and presently the aspen parkland covers 23,000 square miles of Alberta. It is generally described within four basic categories; aspen groves and woodlands; creeks and rivers; fescue prairies; marshes and wet meadows. Because of this variety, the parkland is the preferred habitat of many animals, notably buffalo, beaver and elk. (You may have noticed the

beaver dam on your right on the road into the staging area.)

The beauty of the aspen parkland is derived not only from the diversity of animal and plant life that thrives in this environment, but also from the aspen trees themselves. The flat stems of the aspen leaves catch the wind, and tremble and rustle with the slightest breeze; hence the name, "trembling aspen." This is the dominant tree in the parkland. Aspen poplars usually live about twenty years. In the parkland succession the grasslands become home to the poplars, which then provide shade for the spruce trees, which will eventually dominate the area in their turn. There are occasional groves of birch in the wetter areas, too.

The grazing reserve is situated on land which is a geological part of the great Cooking Lake Moraine, which was a result of the last glaciation.

The story of the reserve

People have been raising cattle in this district since the last century, and the idea of cooperative grazing dates back nearly as far. In 1922 the Blackfoot Stock Association was formed, marking the beginning of northern Alberta's first community pasture. The members grazed their cattle here on what was then part of the Cooking Lake Forest Reserve: established in 1899, it was the first forest reserve in Canada. The land is now leased from the provincial government by a more recent organization, The Blackfoot Grazing Association.

The use of common land for grazing and finishing cattle is efficient and economical. The cattle are turned loose in the early spring, after calving. The cattle rotate among 7 fields in the 7,000 acres of grazing land: about one-third of the park area. In the fall they are rounded up in true western style by cowboys on horseback, and returned to their owners' farms.

Cowboys

The cowboy clothing which has become very fashionable in recent years was — and still is to a cowboy — workin' gear. F.W. Gershaw, a senator from Alberta some years back, explains how it all works:

> The clothing of the cowboy has changed very little in the last century. He seldom wore a coat because it hampered free movement. He wore a vest, usually unbuttoned, and thick underclothing. The active cow man was often kicked and thick clothing protected his body from injury to some extent. He wore chaps — not for their appearance, but to protect his legs from the underbrush and from the bites of insects. He wore high heels on his boots to keep his feet from slipping through the stirrups. He wore gloves to protect his palms from being burned by the lariat which he used constantly. He paid good money for a broad hat to protect him from the sun, the rain and the snow. He did not spare expense on a fancy belt and the bandanna was the non-official flag of the range country. A few of its uses were as follows: To protect the back of the neck from the sun; a dust mask; an ear cover in cold weather; a towel; a blindfold for a skitty horse; for tying calf's legs together while branding; a strainer while drinking muddy water; a dish dryer; a hat tie in windy weather; a sling for broken arms; a bandage; an aid in signalling and for hanging horse thieves.

Things to do and see

1. Bird watching. A serious bird watcher will want to take binoculars along. Robert Lister counted 251 different species of birds in the region, and discusses many of them in his book, *The Birds and Birders of Beaverhills Lake*. Watch for the ruffed grouse, a mottled grayish bird that lives in the underbrush. The male has a large ruff on top of his head, like a rooster's comb. In the spring you are more likely to hear than to see grouse, as they drum out their mating dance while standing on a hollow log. Although this sound is most commonly heard in the spring, the male grouse sometimes drums in the autumn.

2. Hiking. The reserve contains 50 km (32 mi.) of well-maintained nature trails which loop back to the staging areas. (These trails are also excellent for cross-country skiing.) If you are going for a long walk on a hot day remember to carry a water bottle in your day pack, because there is none along the way. The trails abound with trees,

wildflowers and birds. You might want to take along Doug Gilroy's book, *Parkland Portraits*, which will help you to identify the things you are seeing.

3. Visit the other staging areas, the Central and the Waskahegan. You will see where they are from the maps at the picnic site.

4. There is another park nearby, the Strathcona Wilderness Reserve, on the Baseline Road at Range Road 211. During the summer canoes can be rented here for a peaceful ride on a prairie lake. The Centre is open from 9 a.m. to 4:30 p.m. daily — just stop at the office for more information. The lodge is available for hosting group picnics, too, at a nominal charge.

5. If you happen to pick a weekend around the middle of May or the middle of October, you could drive in to the Central Staging Area, one entrance farther east of the Islet Lake Staging Area (see map), and watch the cattle operations. Call ahead to the ranger, at 922-3293, to make sure of the best date and time. In May the cattle are brought into the grazing area and released for the summer. In mid-October the cattle are rounded up. This is especially interesting to those of us who are intrigued by the legends of cattle roaming the range — here they really do!

6. This is a fine place for a winter picnic, too. There are over 90 km (56 mi) of cross-country ski trails, ranging from short beginner's loops to more extensive back-country expert trails.

Things to eat

Since this is cattle country, the appropriate feast is a barbecue, with steaks, baked potatoes, steamed vegetables, and a Parkland Salad.

The best steaks for barbecuing should be selected from the following cuts: sirloin, T-bone, porterhouse, wing, or rib.

Steak Cooking Times (minutes per side):

Thickness	Rare	Medium	Well-done
2.5 cm (1")	5-7	7-9	9-11
4 cm (1 1/2")	8-10	10-12	16-20
5 cm (2")	13-15	15-17	24-30

The flavour and tenderness of a steak is often improved by a marinade.

Marinade

(Enough for 1 kg or 2.2 pounds of meat)

1/2 cup salad oil
1/2 cup lemon juice
1 small onion, chopped
1 clove garlic, crushed
dash of Worcestershire sauce
1/4 cup soy sauce
1 tsp. dry mustard
1 tsp. oregano
coarse ground pepper to taste

Combine all ingredients and blend well. Pour over the meat in a shallow dish and allow to stand at room temperature for 2 hours or in the refrigerator overnight, turning occasionally.

Barbecued Vegetables

Vegetables wrapped in pockets of heavy aluminum foil and baked on a barbecue grill are easy to prepare in advance, and scrumptious to eat.

Vegetable	Preparation	Time
Carrots	Peel and cut to sticks. For each pound of carrots combine a Tbsp. brown sugar, 1 Tbsp. lemon juice, 1 tsp. salt, 2 tsp. powdered ginger 1 Tbsp. melted butter. Mix together in a bowl, divide into four equal portions and wrap each loosely in aluminum foil, sealing the edges tightly.	60 minutes
Mushrooms	Wrap one pound of large mushrooms in foil with butter, salt and pepper.	20-25 min.
Potatoes	Brush each medium sized potato with oil and wrap in foil.	45-60 min.

Parkland Salad

Salads can be boring bowls of lettuce, or they can be fascinating combinations of vegetables served with imagination. To provide you with a little inspiration, the following includes some of our favourite salad things. The worst that can happen is a guest exclaiming, "I never thought of putting pine nuts in a salad before!" This is simply said to cover the fact that the guest has never heard of pine nuts — but what better garnish for a Parkland Salad? So:

Select crisp fresh lettuce — butter, bib, leaf, or the usual iceberg, or a combination of these. For fresh salads it is best to do the final preparation at the picnic table just before announcing dinner. Take along a small cutting board for your last minute salad preparations. At home wash lettuce leaves in cold water, dry in a dish towel (or use one of those magic lettuce drying machines). Place the lettuce in a plastic bag with a piece of paper towelling to absorb any extra moisture, and chill in the fridge for several hours before the picnic.

Other vegetables: Wash well and take along several tomatoes, some green onions, a couple of stalks of celery, a cucumber and a green pepper.

Just before the steaks go on the barbecue, chop the vegetables in the sizes that most please you (large chunks for a picnic which includes one or more teenaged boys who are only impressed by quantity and potential speed of ingestion, or thin slices and diced pieces to suit a more refined group).

Tear the lettuce into bite-sized pieces into the salad bowl, and mix well with the vegetables. A spoon and a fork will work, but it is much easier to toss a salad with the wide-bladed, short-handled salad servers which are part of our picnic kit. Once the salad is mixed, shake the dressing (see below) and pour it over, tossing just a little bit more.

Garnish with a handful of pine nuts (available in the bulk section of large grocery stores, or in health food stores). They add a sweet, woodsy flavour to the salad, plus lots of protein.

French Dressing

Combine the following ingredients in a blender, and when mixed place in a screw-top jar in the picnic basket. Dress the salad just before serving it at the picnic, to prevent wilting.

1/2 cup olive oil
2 Tbsp. red wine vinegar
2 Tbsp. lemon juice
2 tsp. sugar
1/2 tsp. salt
1/2 tsp. dry mustard
1/2 tsp. paprika
dash of cayenne

Garlic Dressing

Make ahead at home, dress at the picnic.
1 cup salad or olive oil
1/4 cup white wine vinegar
1 clove garlic, minced
1 tsp. sugar
1/4 tsp. black pepper
1/2 tsp. salt
3/4 tsp. dry mustard

Miscellaneous notes

Bring your own drinking water on this picnic. There are taps here and there, but the water has a high iron content, and not everyone likes the taste.

Bring a bucket along to carry water to put out your cooking fire.

CENTRAL ALBERTA

19 Markerville Red Deer
An Icelandic Picnic

A weather-beaten
refugee
I find calm
in your green valley
hands
of meadow lake, knoll, pass,
shelterbelt and hollow

On a pale spring
night, northern lights
hover in the high
corner
of a glacier,
and a red wild rose
is covered with rime
this morning

from *A Toast to Alberta*
by Stephan G. Stephansson

How to get there

The beauty and serenity of Markerville, a place on the Red Deer River about 30 km (19 mi.) southwest of Red Deer, has attracted and held people since the first Icelandic homesteaders arrived in 1888.

There are two equally convenient ways to get to Markerville from Red Deer. One is to travel south on Highway 2 to the Penhold turnoff,

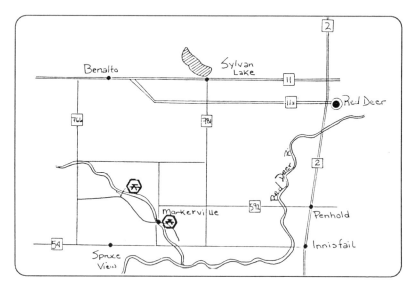

and then west on Highway 42 and 592. The other is to leave Red Deer heading west on Highway 11X for Sylvan Lake, and then turn south on Highway 781.

The picnic site we prefer is by the monument, on the banks of the Medicine River, across the street from the church. Here you can rest and enjoy both the beautiful view and the sense of history. Normally we would be reluctant to choose a site so close to the road, but in the two hours we were there no cars came by so we feel that the proximity of the road is not a problem. There are additional tables by the church, and toilets and water are available at the creamery.

This site is fairly small and if there is a large group of picnickers, an alternative and almost equally desirable site, with picnic tables, toilets and water is at the Stephansson House.

A place to stop and stay

They came.

Recurrent volcanos and bad weather caused a group of Icelandic farmers to seek new homes in North America. In 1873 they journeyed to Wisconsin, and on to the Dakota Territory in 1880. Drought, dust and religious dissension caused them to leave the Dakotas and come to Alberta. Here, by the banks of the Red Deer River, they established Tindastoll, Alberta's first Icelandic community.

. . . The Poet, Stephan G. Stephansson, was one of the early homesteaders. On his land near this settlement, he farmed, fathered eight children, and wrote six volumes of poetry appropriately titled,

Sleepless Nights. Although he was one of Canada's most prolific poets and has been called by some the greatest poet in the western world, he is relatively unknown in Canada, since all his poetry was written in Icelandic. Icelanders however consider him their greatest poet in the past six hundred years. Despite his international fame, Stephansson chose to spend his life in Markerville.

... The Buttermaker, Daniel Morkeberg, came to Markerville in 1897 to operate the newly established creamery. A Dane who had worked briefly in the States, Daniel was on his way to the Klondike to search for gold when he lost all of his possessions in the river. The territories dairy commissioner, C. P. Marker, persuaded Dan to go to Tindastoll for a six month period to set up the creamery. Dan never did get around to hunting for gold; he eventually retired from the creamery in the 1930s, to be replaced by his son Carl who operated it until 1972.

... The Priest, Reverend Pjetur Hjalmsson, was appointed to Markerville in 1905 by the Icelandic Lutheran Synod. He promptly set about constructing a church which was completed and opened in 1907. The services were dominated by Rev. Hjalmsson's three-hour sermons. He was, however, an extremely orthodox Christian, and the community contained a lot of free thinkers and liberal Lutherans. Stephansson, a leader of the liberal thinkers, was denounced as an atheist and Hjalmsson was determined to halt the agnosticism in the settlement. In 1909 the congregation released Hjalmsson from his duties and services were no longer held in the church. Hjalmsson, however, stayed on in the area to homestead, and was always available for weddings and baptisms.

And so they stayed.

Things to do

1. Tour the Markerville Creamery Museum. It is open from 10 a.m. to 6 p.m., May to September. Bright, pleasant guides, whose blond complexions testify to their Icelandic ancestry, will guide you through the workings and explain how, until the creamery was built, there was no basis for a cash economy in the settlement. There is no charge but since the creamery is being restored and run by a private historical trust, donations are much appreciated.

2. Visit the Stephansson House site. Stephansson died in 1927 and his house was allowed to fall into a state of disrepair. A grant from the Icelandic Government initiated the recognition and restoration process and now the house is an Alberta Culture Historic site with an interpretive program.

Markerville Picnic 1921

3. Check with the Creamery Museum (728-3006) for exact dates and try to attend the Icelandic Day Picnic, sometime in mid-June; the Tombola Festival (Icelandic Picnic complete with Icelandic bake sale and sheep shearing contest) at Stephansson House the 2nd Sunday in July; or the Cream Day near the end of August.

Things to eat

The menu for an Icelandic Picnic consists of cured leg of mutton, sliced thinly and wrapped in a soft potato pancake. Dessert is Icelandic cakes and pastries and saskatoon berries in Skyr.

Salt Cured Leg of Lamb

(Serves 6-8)
(to be prepared three months before you need it)

2 kg pickling salt	*4 L water*
15 ml sugar	*1 leg of lamb (about 3 kg)*

Make a brine with the salt, water, and sugar. Put the leg into a crock (ceramic or plastic), cover with the brine, weigh down to keep it submerged, and put in a cool place for two weeks.

Remove leg and rinse thoroughly, wrap in cheesecloth or muslin and hang out to dry in a well-aired, cool pantry. It will be dry, delicious, and ready to eat in 2 to 3 months.

(A roast leg of lamb is an acceptable substitute if you didn't think of this three months ago.)

Potato Pancake Wrappers
(Lompe)

(Serves 4)

This light pancake is used to wrap thin slices of cured mutton for an unusual picnic fare.

6 old potatoes	*1 Tbsp. salt*
1 cup flour	*1 Tbsp. butter*

Boil the potatoes in their skins, cool and peel. Mash with the salt. Add the flour, creating a dough. Form into a long sausage and cut off into 10-12 pieces. Roll these pieces into pancakes about 1/8 inch think. Fry in butter in heavy cast iron frying pan. When just cool enough to handle, place a thin slice of cured mutton in each pancake and roll it up.

Layered Cake with Prune Filling

(Vinarterta- from Stephan G. Stephansson's granddaughter)

1/2 cup butter	*1 cup sugar*
2 eggs	*1/2 tsp. salt*
1/2 cup sweet cream	*1 tsp. baking powder*
1 tsp. vanilla	*Flour — enough to roll out.*

Cream butter and sugar; into this mixture beat the eggs one at a time. Add cream and dry ingredients. Roll out and bake in thin layers in jelly cake tins. When cool put filling on and put together.

Prune Filling:
   1 pound prunes, pitted, chopped or mashed
   1 cup prune juice
   3/4 cup sugar
   1 Tbsp. vanilla
   1 tsp. cinnamon
Boil to consistency of jam. Cool and use filling between layers.

Pastries

(Kleinur)

3 eggs	*1 1/2 cups sugar*
1 cup sour cream	*1 cup sour milk*
1 tsp. baking soda	*1 tsp. cream of tartar*
1/4 tsp. nutmeg	*1 tsp. cardamom*
6 cups flour	

Beat eggs, but not too much. Then add sugar and beat a little more. Dissolve baking soda in sour cream and add to mixture. Sift dry ingredients; then alternately add amounts of wet and dry ingredients to the mixture, blending after each addition. Add more flour if necessary to get a good pastry dough. Roll the dough out to about pie crust thickness and cut into diamond shapes, about two inches on the side. Cut a small slice in the centre of the diamond and pull one corner through.

Deep fry until golden brown, then sprinkle with sugar.

Icelandic Sweet Pancakes

(Ponnukokur)

These can be made at the picnic for a tantalizing hot treat.

2 eggs
1 Tbsp. sugar
1/2 tsp. salt
1 tsp. vanilla
1/4 tsp. soda
1 tsp. baking powder
1/2 tsp. nutmeg
2 1/2 cups milk
2 cups flour

Beat eggs. Add sugar, salt, vanilla and nutmeg. Add 3/4 cup milk and beat well. Add flour, baking powder and soda, sifted together alternately, and remainder of milk. Bake on a hot cast iron pan. Each pancake should take no longer than 1 minute. Roll up with a tsp. of sugar while hot.

Curd Cheese

(K.M. Buko's Skyr Recipe)

Take 4 quarts of sweet milk and bring to a boil. Cool until lukewarm. Take 1/2 cup milk and stir into lukewarm milk. Add 12 drops rennet and stir well.

Set aside in a warm place for about 24 hours. Drain off the liquid through cheese cloth. Remove from the cheese cloth and place in a bowl; beat well and serve with saskatoons, cream and sugar.

20 North West Company Fort Rocky Mountain House

The Voyageur's Picnic

For some time Rocky Mountain House was the most westerly outpost of the fur trade. It wasn't until 1807 that David Thompson eluded the Peigan tribesmen and persuaded the Kootenay Indians to show him the way to the pass at the source of the Saskatchewan River. (See Saskatchewan Crossing Picnic.) Before that time Rocky Mountain House, established by the North West Company in 1799, was the starting point of the spring journey of the voyageurs, carrying the winter harvest of furs to the headquarters of the company in eastern Canada. Hence, Rocky Mountain House is the right place for the Voyageurs' Picnic.

How to get there

The National Historic Site of Rocky Mountain House is on Highway 11A, 7.5 km (4 1/2 mi.) west of the town of Rocky Mountain House.

As you face the Interpretive Centre there are picnic tables off to the right. Alternatively, you might like to spread a blanket on the

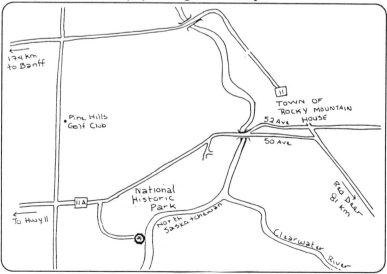

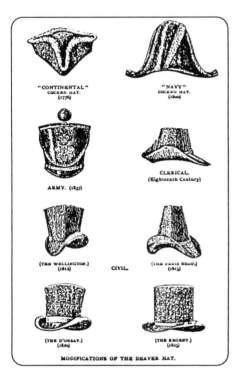

"CONTINENTAL" COCKED HAT. (1779)

"NAVY" COCKED HAT. (1800)

ARMY. (1837)

CLERICAL. (Eighteenth Century)

(THE WELLINGTON.) (1812)

CIVIL.

(THE PARIS BEAU.) (1815)

(THE D'ORSAY.) (1820)

(THE REGENT.) (1825)

MODIFICATIONS OF THE BEAVER HAT.

river bank, near the sites of the early forts. There is also a picnic site by the Brierly Rapids, a short distance upstream. Here you will find fire pits with grates and firewood.

Beaver hats

In the middle of the seventeenth century a new fashion emerged in England: beaver hats were suddenly much in demand, and were to remain so until the 1830s when the silk hat became the new fashion. Although the actual style of beaver hats changed over time, the material remained popular because the felt created from the underhairs of the beaver pelt was very malleable and permitted creative designs. Beaver hair is the easiest hair to "carrot": that is, to curl and interlock with other hair to make felt. Beaver hair made a firm and rigid felt, permitting the wide-brimmed hats worn by the cavaliers to have brims that stayed flat.

The demand for beaver pelts for hats was a major impetus for the fur trade in North America. The felt was made by hatters in England who used mercury to treat, or carrot, the fur. Exposure to this chemical over time caused the appearance of madness: hence, the Mad Hatter in *Alice in Wonderland*.

The voyageurs

The North West Company was started in 1779 by a number of Scottish entrepreneurs, as competition to the Hudson's Bay Company. The Hudson's Bay model had been to establish forts and wait for the Indians to deliver the furs. The North West Company was much more aggressive, hiring French Canadians and Métis people (often referred to as Canadians or Canadiens in the literature of the era) who already knew the Indians and the waterways. Using fast canoes, the voyageurs could traverse the continent relatively quickly. The voyageurs crossed and recrossed the continent carrying carefully wrapped 90-pound packs which fitted into the canoes or strapped onto a voyageur's back during portages. David Thompson often travelled with them to map the new territories. They had soon extended the string of forts well beyond the territory of the Hudson's Bay, and constituted such serious competition that by 1821 it seemed the better part of valour for the Bay to amalgamate with their rivals. The new company retained the HBC name, and incorporated the personnel and forts of both companies, although the layoffs were more severe in the Hudson's Bay Company.

The forts

At Rocky Mountain House the history of rivalry and amalgamation of the companies can be seen in the progression of ruins. This was clearly a strategic outpost during the fur trade years. You can see the pits in the ground, the only traces of the original fort built by James Bird for the HBC in 1799 (called Acton House after his home in England). Nearby are the remains of the North West Company Fort, called Rocky Mountain House, which was built by John MacDonald of Garth and operated from 1799 to 1821. In 1821 the amalgamation effected the abandonment of the North West fort.

A third fort was built in 1835, and burned in 1861. It had been abandoned due to starvation in the spring of 1861 and was burned by a group of Peigan who arrived at the fort intending to trade. The last fort was established in 1864 and abandoned in 1875. The ruins of the last two fort buildings can be seen as you wander along the interpretive trail. The large stone chimneys are reminders of the last fort.

Things to do

1. Visit the store close by the Interpretive Centre for an excellent collection of books on Alberta history, flowers and wildlife. Also available is a variety of wild teas.

2. Use your binoculars to observe the bison herd grazing in the paddock a little way from the fort site. Although the high demand for furs and buffalo tongues, combined with the technology of the repeating rifle, almost caused the buffalo to vanish from the plains, these buffalo are descendants of one of the last few herds. They were purchased by the Canadian government early in this century from a farmer in Montana, and placed in Elk Island National Park, near Edmonton. From there several were moved to the present location where they have flourished. They can be dangerous, so keep the fence and a safe distance between you and them.

Things to eat

Since this is a voyageur picnic, we will supply some useful recipes, and a few that are more likely to be of historical interest than stimulants to a present-day appetite.

Making pemmican was the method used by the Indians for preserving and storing buffalo meat. Voyageurs used pemmican extensively because of the high protein content and the ease of carrying. The pemmican was purchased from the Plains Indians and the pemmican trade was one of the reasons the fort at Rocky Mountain House stayed open for as long as it did.

In his journal in 1810 David Thompson made the following entry:

> . . . dried Provisions made of the meat and fat of the Bison under the name of Pemican, a wholesome, well tasted nutritious food, upon which all persons engaged in the Furr Trade mostly depend for their subsistence during the open season; it is made of the lean and fleshy parts of the Bison dried, smoked and pounded fine; in this state it is called Beat Meat: the fat of the Bison is of two qualities, called hard and soft; . . . the latter . . . when carefully melted resembles Butter in softness and sweetness. Pimmecan [sic] is made up in bags of ninety pounds weight, made of the parchment hide of the Bison with the hair on; slowly melted together, and at a low warmth poured on fifty pounds of Beat Meat, well mixed together, and closely packed in a bag of about thirty inches in length, by near twenty inches in breadth, and about four inches in thickness which made them flat, the best shape for storage and carriage . . . . I have dwelt on the above, as it [is] the staple food of all persons, and affords the most nourishment in the least space and weight, even the gluttonous french canadian [the voyageurs] that devours eight pounds of fresh meat every day is contented with one and a half pound p' day: it would be admirable provision for the Army and Navy. [*The Beaver* 295, 1964]

Pemmican

Select cuts of:
buffalo sinew
buffalo tallow
dried berries

Place hams, shoulders and sinews of buffalo in sun to dry for several days. When completely dry, pound until meat becomes a powder.

Melt the hard buffalo fat to form tallow, and pour into pounded meat powder. Mix well until meat is saturated. Add dried saskatoon berries or rose hips. Store in hide bags. (It is easier to store the pemmican bags if you knock them into square or rectangular shapes before the mixture has completely hardened.)

Buffalo were hunted not only for their hides, but for their tongues, which were considered a delicacy by nineteenth century American gourmets.

Buffalo Tongue

Start with about
10 pounds buffalo tongue

Wash the tongues, place in an earthenware bowl, and rub them well with 1/3 of the following mixture:
1 pound of coarse salt
1 Tbsp. saltpetre
1/2 pound brown sugar
Cover the bowl with cheesecloth.

Repeat the rubbing for two more days, using up all the mixture.

Leave the tongue in its own liquor for 6 more days, turning daily. Drain the tongues and smoke as follows:

Collect enough buffalo chips for a long slow fire; dry them.

Build a frame over a fire pit such that the rack is about 5 feet above the fire pit. Hang the salted tongues on the rack above the fire pit. Place the dried buffalo chips in the fire pit and light the fire. Smoke the tongues for four days over the smouldering fire.

Store until needed. When ready to serve, boil the tongues in water until the skin is loose. Cool, remove the skin, slice the tongue and arrange on platter.

The voyageurs would make a great pot of pea soup over their fire in the evening, and then place it in insulated wrappings to eat all the next day in the canoes. By the time they ate it, the consistency was more stew than soup. It provided a hearty, nourishing diet for the long journey from the mountain forts to Fort Garry and on to Fort William.

Voyageur Stew
(Serves 4 Voyageurs or 8-10 Picnickers)

1 pound salt pork
1 Tbsp. dry mustard
1 pound dry peas
8 cups cold water
1 Tbsp. coarse salt
1 clove garlic, minced
1 tin sweet corn kernels
1 tsp. summer savory, preferably fresh

Rub salt pork with the dry mustard. Cover and refrigerate for 12 hours. Cut into bite-sized pieces.

Sort, wash, and soak the peas in the cold water overnight.

In a soup kettle place all ingredients except the corn. Bring to a boil, and then reduce heat and simmer for about 5 hours. The stew consistency will be achieved by checking the mixture from time to time, and adding water to thin, or removing the lid to thicken. Fifteen minutes before serving, add the corn, stirring it into the mixture.

The explorers and fur traders often drank Labrador tea, and thus it is occasionally called Hudson's Bay Tea. The voyageurs also drank gallons of tea, and so, as we know, did the Mad Hatter.

Mad Hatter's Tea

Buy some of the locally picked tea in the shop on the museum grounds. You might find Labrador Tea, often used by the Indians, or raspberry tea, or even rose hip tea, with its high concentration of Vitamin C.

21 Bowden Olds

The Lone Pine Picnic

Once a major resting place on the Calgary-Edmonton Trail, the Lone Pine Stopping House is now just a memory.

How to get there

As near as we can ascertain, the Lone Pine Stopping House was just to the east of present-day Bowden, and so it is at the Bowden Rest Area that we situate our picnic. Bowden is 105 km (65 1/2 mi.) north of Calgary (40 km, or 25 mi., south of Red Deer) on Highway 2. To reach the picnic site, take the turnoff at Bowden and follow the signs to the rest area which you will find in an aspen grove directly to the west of the highway.

History

The Trail — known as the Calgary Trail to Edmontonians, the Edmonton Trail to Calgarians — predates the coming of the white man and was likely part of the great prehistoric migration corridor from Asia, over the Bering land bridge to Mexico. The Indians do not know how long it has existed; their legends say only that it is part of the Old North Trail that ran "north to the barren lands ... and south into the country inhabited by a people with dark skins, and long hair falling over their faces." Mexico?

The white man's recorded history of this place begins in 1873 when the Methodist missionary John MacDougall (son of George MacDougall. See Victoria Picnic) cut a cart path from the Fort at Edmonton to his new mission at Morley. Following the old Indian trails, MacDougall cut the trail due south from Edmonton, over the Red Deer River to the ancient Indian meeting place known to the Blackfoot as Minnie-Hay-Gwack-Pack-Waksut. This was the place where the Indians' Old North Trail intersected the trails to Blackfoot Crossing, to Rocky Mountain House, and to Morley. This is the place the white men called Lone Pine. Here MacDougall's cart road veered west to Morley on the Bow River (see Stoney Indian Picnic). Two years later in 1875, when the Mounties constructed Fort Calgary, the cart track was extended from Lone Pine to Calgary.

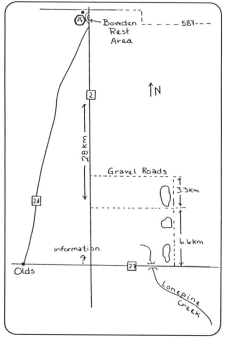

At this time Edmonton was the major settlement, but it was supplied only by the Carleton Trail which stretched 900 miles from Fort Garry (Winnipeg) to Fort Edmonton, and by the slow boats that moved up the North Saskatchewan. The way was long and the cost high. With the opening of the Calgary-Edmonton Trail an alternative and cheaper route became available. Goods could come by steamboat up the Missouri to Fort Benton in Montana, then by bull train along the Whoop-Up Trail (also the Bull Trail) to Fort Macleod, and then on to Calgary. Although official mail and supplies came through the Canadian route, and only private traders used the American link, the situation was such that in 1883 the mail moved faster from San Francisco to Edmonton than from Winnipeg to Edmonton. (Some things haven't changed much in 100 years!) On the trail however, the big heavy wagons kept sinking into the soft mud and so the great bull trains were soon replaced by the lighter Red River Cart on the Calgary-Edmonton Trail.

In 1883 the Canadian Pacific Railway reached Calgary and suddenly the trail became the main supply line to the north. The trail was improved, a regular stage coach run was started, and the Lone Pine Stopping House of John Langlois was a popular place for rest and refuge. The stopping houses were fairly rough and ready but they did have rules. A typical set of 1880 hotel rules might be as follows:

* Guests will be provided with breakfast and dinner but rustle their own lunch.
* Spiked boots and spurs must be removed before retiring.
* Dogs not allowed in bunks, but may sleep underneath.
* Towels changed weekly; insect powder for sale at the bar.
* Special rates to Gospel Grinders and the gambling profession.
* The bar will be open day and night. Every known fluid, except water, for sale. No mixed drinks will be served, except in the case of death in the family.

* Baths furnished free down at the river, but bathers must provide their own soap and towels.

* Guests are expected to rise at 6:00 a.m. as the sheets are needed for tablecloths.

In July of 1891 the tracks of the Calgary and Edmonton Railway Company reached South Edmonton (Strathcona) and the Calgary-Edmonton Trail's heyday was over.

Magic Picnic Spots:

We have chosen the Bowden rest area for the picnic site because a stopping place is a place of rest and refuge; after a hard day on the trail one is rarely looking for adventure. However, in our search for the original site, we did stumble into the incredibly beautiful valley of the Lone Pine Creek. Along its banks are many picnic spots, but a portable table or blanket is required. We reached the valley from Bowden by driving south on Highway 2 for 10 km (6 1/4 mi.) to Olds and turning left (east) on Highway 27. The valley is about 10 km along and there is a road beside it heading north. Follow the road, find a spot, and dream of Red River carts and Lone Pine.

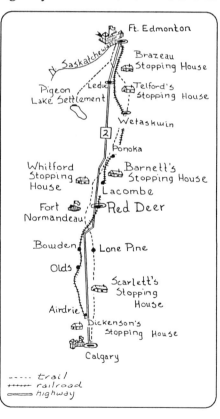

Things to do

1. Go to the Bowden Museum at the end of 20th Ave. in the town of Bowden.

2. Pitch horseshoes; they are provided at the Tourist Info Booth.

3. Go north 10 km (6 1/4 mi.) to Innisfail. The museum on the Agricultural Grounds is in a restored stopping house called "The Spruces" but usually known as "Half Way House."

Things to eat

An authentic Trail Picnic would include beans and bannock and other such rough eatables. However, these are included in other pioneer picnics so here, out of affection and loyalty to our publisher, we plan a Lone Pine Picnic with the following:

MENU

Pineapple Salad
Pin Wheels
Pinenut Balls
Pinenut Tarts
and to drink, a
Pina Colada

Pineapple Salad

(Serves 4)

Drain:
a tin of pineapple chunks

Place on top of:
a bed of lettuce

Cover the pineapple with:
slices of soft cream cheese

Dress with French Dressing (See Parkland Picnic.)

If the lettuce is washed and stored in plastic bags, and you remember the can opener, this salad is easily prepared at the picnic.

Pin Wheels

This is an interesting and attractive way to serve a small quantity of leftover meat.

Preheat oven to 450 °F.

Prepare a meat filling from leftover meat. This generally involves grinding the meat, sometimes adding some binder such as milk or a beaten egg, possibly some relish or chopped onion, and seasoning.

Make a biscuit dough. One of the pre-mixed varieties such as Bisquick is fine, or use your own recipe. Roll it very thin and in the shape of an oblong and brush it with soft butter. Spread the dough with the meat filling. Roll the dough loosely and plaster the end down with water. Cut the roll into 2 cm (3/4") pin wheels and bake in the oven for 20 minutes on slightly greased cookie pans. Refrigerate, and serve cold with chili sauce or catsup.

Pinenut Balls

Grind:
> *1 lb. pinenuts*

and mix with
> *1 cup sweetened condensed milk*
> *3 cups confectioners' sugar*

Shape into one inch balls and coat them with confectioners' sugar. Refrigerate until set.

Pinenut Tarts

(Makes 24)

Preheat oven to 350 °F

Beat together until fluffy:
> *1/4 lb. softened butter*
> *3 oz. cream cheese*
> *1 Tbsp. brandy*

Mix in:
> *1 1/4 cups all purpose flour*

until the dough is smooth. Shape into a roll and divide into 24 equal portions. Using your fingers press each portion into a shell in a muffin cup. Set aside.

In a large bowl, beat until light:
> *1 egg*

Beat in:
> *3/4 cup sugar*
> *1/4 tsp. salt*
> *1 Tbsp. melted butter*
> *1/2 tsp. vanilla*

Then stir in:
> *1 cup pine nuts.*

Spoon filling into shells. Bake for 30 minutes.

22 Tyrrell Museum Drumheller
A Petrified Picnic

The theme of the picnic is . . . OLD! The displays in the museum trace Alberta's history back 3.5 billion years.

How to get there

The Tyrrell Museum of Palaeontology is in Midland Provincial Park, 6 km (3 3/4 mi.) northwest of Drumheller on Highway 838. There are signs leading to the museum from most approaches to Drumheller. This picnic takes place in the picnic ground just beside the Tyrrell Museum. (Because of the mild weather in the region, this is a great spot for a winter picnic, too.)

The museum is open daily in the summer (from Victoria Day to Thanksgiving) between 9 a.m. and 9 p.m. Winter hours are 10 a.m. to 5 p.m., Tuesday to Sunday and all holiday Mondays. There is no admission charge, but donations are welcomed.

The museum

Albertosaurus (pronounced al-*bur*-toe-*sor*-us) was the somewhat unwieldy name given to the first significant dinosaur find in the province. It was discovered in 1884 by Joseph Burr Tyrrell, an

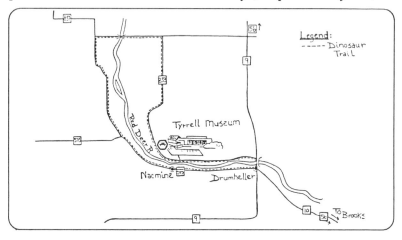

accomplished Canadian who, in his 99 years, was an explorer and map-maker, a mining consultant and miner, and a writer. He also made significant contributions to the fields of geography, botany, entomology, mammalogy and ornithology!

The museum makes the knowledge of the region's extensive history accessible to the general public, as well as to scholars. It is a centre for academic research in the field of palaeontology, and one of the well-equipped labs is separated from the museum by only a glass wall so that it is possible for visitors to watch the process of cleaning and identifying fossils.

Tracking the Dinosaur

Dinosaurs left footprints in sandy deltas which were then fossilized, later to astonish twentieth century observers with their size — and the size of the now-vanished creatures which must have made

---

HONEYBEES

The best known social bees of the super-family *Apoidea*, members of the order *Hymenoptera*, are the honeybees. These insects are the most widely studied social bee, and their social structures and nesting habits are well-documented. Humans enjoy the honey and the beeswax produced by honeybees from plant nectar. Indirectly, we also benefit from the pollination of fruit and seed crops achieved by the bees during their pollen-collecting activity.

Honeybees are easily recognizable by their yellow and black colouration, their large hind appendages, and their honey stomachs which accommodate nectar collection and storage. Winnie-the-Pooh noticed another distinctive feature:

"'That buzzing noise means something. You don't get a buzzing noise like that, just buzzing and buzzing, without its meaning something. If there's a buzzing-noise, somebody's making a buzzing noise, and the only reason for making a buzzing-noise that I know of is because you're a bee.'

"Then he thought another long time, and said: 'And the only reason for being a bee that I know of is making honey.' And then he got up and said: 'And the only reason for making honey is so as I can eat it.'" [A.A. Milne]

There is a common myth that a bee can only sting once and then it dies. Although this is not true of all bees, the worker bee has a barbed sting, and when removed it usually tears apart the bee's body, and kills it. Bees are slow, and are usually not aggressive unless they or their hives are threatened.

them. Impressions of the skin of dinosaurs in substances which have been preserved by the elements have also been found, even though the skin has long since turned to dust. And finally, discoveries have been made of bones and plates — the hard parts of the skeletons — which have excited palaeontologists and amateur archaeologists alike.

The age of the dinosaurs (the name means "terrible lizard") lasted about 140 million years — from 190 to 64 million years ago, give or take a few million years, during the Mesozoic era. At first the creatures were small, but they became very large as they adapted to their environment, and surprisingly diverse. Some had large protective plates like armour, some had extremely long necks, and some could swim. Most of them were vegetarian, which was sensible as they lived in a lush tropical environment in what is now Alberta.

No one knows why the dinosaurs became extinct, but the museum has a fascinating video which suggests some of the theories. Was there a huge catastrophe — a giant meteorite? Did the radiation from such a meteorite make the dinosaurs sterile? Or did the climate change over so short a time that the dinosaurs were unable to adapt? Whatever the reason, these impressive creatures became extinct some 64 million years ago.

Things to do

1. Follow the several self-guiding trails, reading the signs as you go, and learn about the geology of the badlands.

2. Spend some time (and perhaps some money) in the museum book shop. There is a fascinating collection of books — both academic and non — about dinosaurs, and enough dinosaur-derived kitsch to make a dinosaur blush!

3. Drive the 48 km (30 mi.) circular Dinosaur Trail. This drive begins and ends in Drumheller. The sites are well marked, but a brochure can be picked up at the museum which provides a map and more detailed explanation of the many interesting spots you will visit along the way. At the half-way mark you will cross the Red Deer River on one of the last cable ferries left in Alberta. You will also see lots of hoodoos, those peculiar formations of sandstone. You will visit a coal mining museum, and see many breath-taking views of the spectacular landscape of the Red Deer River Valley.

Things to eat

The theme of this picnic, as we said before, is old. The dinosaur fossils are old — even Mr. Tyrrell lived to be 99 years of age. So we suggest that you begin this picnic with a ripe old cheese on melba toast. Hard-boiled dinosaur eggs are a must. You will see some of them on display — but they are not for public consumption. If you can't find dinosaur eggs, chicken eggs are an acceptable substitute.

We suggest that you include any leftovers that you have in your fridge on this picnic — dinosaur bones are, after all, just B-I-I-I-G leftovers. We usually have rice and a few ribs left over from the last Chinese dinner, and there is always fruit cake in the freezer left over from Christmas. We'll supply recipes, in case you have to create your own leftovers. Since this is a provincial park, alcoholic beverages are forbidden, but we suggest that you savour a snifter of fine *old* brandy when you get home.

Hard-Boiled Dinosaur Eggs

Follow the same technique as for chicken eggs, only boil for much longer. Cool and bring to the picnic, along with some mayonnaise, salt and pepper.

Spareribs seem appropriate for this picnic, since there are so many bones lying around the area.

Garlic Spareribs

(Serves 4)

Make a marinade of:
   1/4 cup vinegar
   1/4 cup soy sauce
   1/2 cup honey
   3 cloves garlic, crushed

Cut 5 pounds pork spareribs into 2-inch pieces, cover with marinade and store in refrigerator overnight.

Remove the ribs, saving the marinade, and place in a shallow baking dish. Bake at 450 °F for 30 minutes. Pour off excess fat.

Combine marinade with:
   1 cup tomato sauce
   2 tsp. salt
And simmer on top of the stove for 10 minutes. Pour sauce over ribs, covering pan loosely with aluminum foil, and bake at 350 °F for one hour, basting occasionally. Cool and eat cold at picnic.

Rice Salad

(Serves 4-6)

3 cups chilled cooked rice
1 medium onion, diced
1 green pepper, diced
1 small can pimento, chopped
1 cup fresh peas
1 cup mayonnaise
salt to taste

Mix well, garnish with parsley. Keep chilled until serving.

23 Rosebud Drumheller
A Dramatic Picnic

Although a picnic can be held in Rosebud anytime from spring through autumn, we suggest that your picnic coincide with the dramatic presentation in the outdoor theatre. The production is more than an interpretive event: it is the product of the unique Rosebud School of the Arts, which is the heart of the community.

How to get there

This picnic takes place in the heart of the hamlet of Rosebud, population approximately 48. The town is about 45 minutes south of Drumheller: take Highway 9, and then Secondary 840.

Rosebud is very small. Once you have found the street with the big old Mercantile building on it, you have found the main street.

There are a variety of places to picnic. One is in front of the museum where you may spread your blanket or set up your portable table on the grass. A second is reached by going to the foot of the street to what was once the old hotel — and is now the welcome and information centre — where you can eat at one of the tables on the porch (or inside if it's raining), looking out over the Rosebud River valley. A third choice is to use one of the picnic tables in front of the old Opera House.

The community

On this picnic there is plenty of food, for the tummy and for the soul. A play is part of the afternoon's entertainment, but there are many other opportunities to enrich your aesthetic self. The tradition of culture has long been a driving force in Rosebud. In the years when it was predominantly a farming community, its surrounding beauty attracted artists such

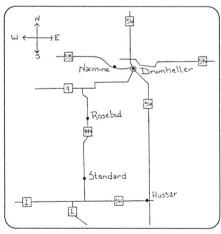

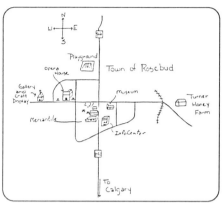

as A.Y. Jackson and Harold Glyde. Glyde's canvas of the main street, featuring the Mercantile, is part of the University of Alberta collection. Artists such as Royal Sproule, and Agnes Beynon Biggs — whose paintings of wild flowers are treasured by many Canadian museums and private owners — continue to live and work near the hamlet.

On the surface of this community are a number of attractions for the casual picnicker, such as a museum in the old Chinese Laundry, an art gallery in the old United Church (built in 1928), a craft display in the Mercantile, and an outdoor theatre beside the Mercantile on sunny afternoons. Future plans to enhance the cultural facilities include an old store, a commercial bank, and a trading company fronting a new theatre. Houses appropriate to the period are to be constructed as student residences. Visiting Rosebud now and again over the next few years should reveal rapid changes as the new/old community develops.

But our readers are not casual picnickers and will want to know about the currents beneath the surface of this highly motivated community. The town is being renovated — and parts of it rebuilt in keeping with the 1900-1920 period — by a dedicated young community of people. The hamlet is the home of an arts school which is organized on the old mediaeval European guild system. Behind the placid facades of the old prairie buildings, stage sets are being built, historical research is being done, actors are practising their lines in preparation for the afternoon's performance, and menus are being planned for the dinner theatre performance.

Ideally, communities are groups of people who choose to live near one another, and they often work together to maintain the environment in such a way that it sustains the lives of the people, plants and animals. There is room for individuality within a community. A community provides a safe place for each person to develop to full potential — for happiness and for creativity. It is a complete environment. Few such communities seem to exist anymore, and we associate them with the rural past. The enriched quality of life in such a community is sorely missed, however, and here and there are groups of people who are revitalizing the spirit of community and making it work in the present.

In Rosebud the community, though small, has a role for every resident. The focus of this community is art. Art is an everyday occurrence, and creativity an accepted form of communication. The ancient Guild system with its master-apprentice concept has been resurrected here as a teaching method, and the technique has Royal Assent from the Lieutenant Governor of Alberta. The hamlet produces three original plays a year, and the plays you will see here are the product of the four-year guild program where students develop skills and experience in every aspect of producing plays and mounting other artistic endeavours.

Things to do

1. After your picnic lunch, wander through the museum and then walk a block or so to the Akokiniskway Gallery and craft display in the old United Church. (See map.) There is also a craft display in the Mercantile building. All these things open at about 2 p.m. to coordinate with the theatre schedule, so take your time.

2. Attend the play at 4 p.m. in the garden next to the Mercantile. There is no charge, but donations are gratefully accepted. All plays are designed for family entertainment, and the summer play is usually written around some intriguing event of Rosebud's history. If you want more information about the title and content of the current play, call 677-2221.

3. Just across the railway tracks is the Turner honey farm. Alberta honey is internationally famous, and you will likely want to take

The town of Rosebud, circa 1920-21.

some home with you. The Turner family welcomes visitors, although an advance phone call to 677-2330 is appreciated. This family enterprise produces 100,000 pounds of honey annually. Be sure to try some of the new product — honeyfruit. Part of the tour of the farm includes a look at a most instructive glass bee hive which shows how honey is really made.

4. In the final days of the terrible competition for rapidly diminishing resources which set the Blackfoot against the Cree, one of the historic battles took place on what is now called Indian Battle Hill. It is now a place for contemplation of the beautiful prairie valley which it commands. Ask directions from someone in the village.

5. Stay on for the dinner theatre performance. Reservations are a must, since most performances are fully booked in advance. In 1987 alone over 11,000 guests attended the Rosebud Dinner Theatre. This event takes place on an indoor stage in the old Opera House, and the 150 people who attend are seated for dinner in various interesting rooms and alcoves. The atmosphere is informal, and the food is excellent.

6. As you drive through this part of the prairie, watch the skies for peregrine falcons. Several of the few pairs remaining in Alberta make their nests near Rosebud.

Things to eat

Creativity, artistry, extravagant drama: the quintessence of dramatic expression is the Italian grand opera, and so . . . this is an operatic picnic.

THE OVERTURE IS:

Antipasto

This translates rather easily from the Italian as "what you eat before the pasta." Traditionally it is a platter spread with little nibbles and nice tastes. Some items are suggested here — select the ones that please your group:

marinated mushrooms
slices of prosciutto
sliced tomatoes with herbs
anchovies
olives
pickled beets
gherkins
caviar

melon balls
green pepper slices
fontina cheese (or gruyere, emmental or cheddar as substitutes)

Serve the antipasto with a basket of thinly sliced Italian bread, or buns.

AND NOW ... THE OPERA PROPER ... STARRING —

Pasta Primadonna

(Serves 10-12)

A light Chorus of pasta and vegetables which can be served hot or cold.
Prepare ahead, and bring along to the picnic.

4 cups broccoli florets
1 cup baby peas
12 stalks asparagus, diagonally sliced (optional)
1 cup diagonally sliced celery
2 cups diagonally sliced zucchini
2 Tbsp. vegetable oil
12 cherry tomatoes, cut in half
2 tsp. minced garlic
1/2 cup pine nuts
1/4 cup chopped parsley
salt and pepper
1/3 cup butter
1 cup whipping cream
1/2 cup grated Parmesan cheese
2 Tbsp. dried basil or 1/3 cup fresh, finely chopped
10 large mushrooms, quartered
1 lb. vermicelli noodles

Blanch broccoli, peas and asparagus in boiling salted water just until
crisp, about 1 to 2 minutes. Rinse under cold water and drain. Set aside
with celery and zucchini.

In skillet heat oil. Sauté tomatoes, garlic, pine nuts and parsley for a few
seconds. Season with salt and pepper to taste. Remove from heat. In large
heavy casserole, melt butter. Stir in cream, Parmesan cheese, basil and
mushrooms. Heat through, stirring occasionally.

In large pot of boiling salted water, cook vermicelli until tender but firm,
about 4 to 6 minutes. Drain well. Add pasta to cheese-cream mixture in
casserole. Toss to coat. Add tomato mixture and vegetables. Reheat and
toss lightly. Taste and adjust seasoning. Makes 4 to 6 servings.

If you are serving the dish cold, skip the last reheat step; instead, toss
lightly, taste and adjust the seasoning, and keep chilled until you are
ready to serve.

ACCOMPANIMENT:

We suggest a duet of rose hip tea and honey, or

Chilled mineral water and Chianti (Italians dilute their red wine)

GRAN FINALE:

Make this classical virtuoso cookie a couple of days ahead. It will make 2 or 3 dozen pieces.

Torta Fregolotti

1 cup almonds
2 2/3 cups all-purpose flour
1 cup sugar
Pinch of salt
1 tsp. grated lemon peel
1 cup (1/2 lb.) plus 2 Tbsp. butter or margarine, softened
2 Tbsp. lemon juice
1 Tbsp. brandy or water

In a blender or food processor, whirl almonds until finely ground. In a bowl, combine ground almonds, flour, sugar, salt, and lemon peel. With a pastry blender or 2 knives, cut butter into flour mixture until it resembles coarse crumbs. Sprinkle with lemon juice and brandy and mix lightly with a fork until blended.

Spread mixture (it should be crumbly) in a greased and floured 12-inch pizza pan (do not press into pan). Bake in a 350 °F oven for 50 to 60 minutes or until browned. Let cool on a rack.

When thoroughly cooled, wrap well and let stand for at least a day. To serve, break into chunks.

CALGARY AND AREA

24 Heritage Park Calgary

A Steamboat Picnic

The SS Moyie at Heritage Park is a half-scale replica of the original lake steamboat, and serves as a fine place for a ride and a picnic on a sunny day in Calgary.

How to get there

Heritage Park is in southwest Calgary, on a peninsula jutting into the Glenmore Reservoir. It can be reached by driving west on Heritage Drive, which ends at the Park, or by coming south off the Glenmore Trail at 14 St. SW, and turning west into the Park at Heritage Drive. In the park, you can choose among several suitable sites depending upon your time and inclination.

Site 1 is on board the SS Moyie. It is great to munch your lunch on the tranquil waters of the Glenmore Reservoir. However, this is a brief picnic as the ride is only about 20 minutes long. The Moyie is reached by walking clear across the Park, or by taking the train from the Midnapore Station (near entrance) to the Shepard Station (by boat dock).

Site 2 is at the picnic tables in the park. There are some in the woods beside the Prince House, some more directly across the street near the Didsbury Bandstand, and three directly behind Gledhill's Drug Store; these have a great view of the unique two-storey outhouse.

Site 3 is your choice of a site along the nature trail by the reservoir. This trail is not used much, and if you are lucky you may find some saskatoon berries waiting for you.

S.S. Moyie — The Last of the Steamships

Heritage Park was originally intended to be a children's amusement park. However it quickly developed into a historical village
representing pre-1915 western Canada. As such it has assembled an
eclectic and informative collection of structures and reproductions.
One of the most interesting, from a historical perspective, is the SS
Moyie, a half-scale reproduction of the last of the steamships.

For a century the whistle of a steamboat was a familiar and
welcome sound on the rivers and lakes of Western Canada. The first
was the Hudson's Bay Company's Beaver, launched on May 2, 1835
at Blackwall on the Thames River. The Beaver left England in September of 1835 and arrived at Fort Vancouver on April 10, 1836. In May,
1836, it made its first voyage up the Pacific coast, thus ushering in the
era of the steamship in Western Canada. The end of the era came on
April 27, 1957, when the CPR sternwheeler SS Moyie made her last
run on Kootenay Lake and then was beached at the town of Kaslo in
British Columbia. During that 120-year period, over three hundred
steamships plied the rivers and lakes, and were the main means of
transportation to many parts of western Canada.

The original Moyie was built by the Bertram Iron Works in
Toronto. The ship was then disassembled into over one thousand
pieces and shipped by rail to Nelson, B.C., where it was reassembled.
The first voyage of the Moyie took place on December 7, 1898, when
she inaugurated the Kootenay Landing-Nelson passenger run along

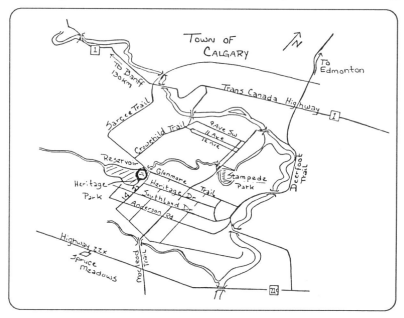

The S. S. Moyie at Heritage Park

the Kootenay Lake, thereby completing the southern railway link across the continent. She continued to sail on Kootenay Lake for the next 59 years.

The original Moyie weighed 728.9 tons gross, and was 161.7 feet long and 30 feet wide. The fact that the Moyie only drew 3 feet of water when loaded caused her to be retained in service when other newer steamers were being scrapped. She was able to get close enough to shore that freight could be unloaded at small settlements where no dock was available.

When the Moyie was through and about to be abandoned, the Kaslo Historical Society arranged to purchase her from the CPR for one dollar. She now sits in a berth in Kaslo where she functions as a Tourist Information Office, a museum, and a reminder of a more leisurely and elegant era.

Things to do

Heritage Park is designed as a collection of "things to do," and brochures listing them are given out at the gate. The list below reflects some of our personal favorites.

1. Enjoy a real ice cream cone at the Vulcan Ice Cream Parlor.

2. Chew some old-fashioned stick candy at the Claresholm General Store.

3. Ride the SS Moyie.

4. See the two-storey outhouse.

5. See the Dingman Discovery Rig (especially if you intend to go on our Turner Valley Picnic).

6. Catch the show at the Canmore Opera House — but watch out: The Opera House is haunted by the ghost of Sam Livingston. Old Sam usually only appears to the cast and then only during rehearsals; he sits in the darkened theatre and snorts and giggles in appreciation. The cast has noticed that if Sam doesn't appear at a rehearsal the show is generally not well received. It has been reported that he occasionally attends a regular performance, so watch out for him.

7. Watch for the "Picnic in the Park" program. The park staff inaugurated this program, which they hope to keep. It includes races and prizes for parents and kids, including a grand prize draw of a "Loaded Picnic Basket." The Basket comes complete with chicken, juice, potato salad, dishes, a complete apple pie: and you get to keep the basket. Phone 255-1182 for details.

Things to eat

There are several variations on picnics that can be held in the park. One is to take advantage of the picnic take-out service offered by the Wainwright Hotel Dining Room. There you will be provided with a picnic basket for two, complete with plates, cutlery, and linen napkins. Phone 255-1182 for prices and contents, and book ahead, as their supply is limited.

The Alberta Bakery makes incredible sourdough bread. Sometimes our children feel it is sufficient just to get a loaf and tear at it. However, a little pre-planning, and a stop at a delicatessen en route, can produce a delightful picnic. The pre-planning consists of bringing a basket (or box or bag) in which you have paper plates and napkins, a bread knife, several spreading knives, mustard, relish, pickles, some leaves of washed lettuce in a plastic bag and a Thermos of iced tea. Bring along some sliced meats and cheeses from the deli, and sourdough bread from the bakery, and you are ready to create gourmet sandwiches in the park.

For over-achievers in the crowd, we supply a recipe for sourdough starter and sourdough bread.

Sourdough Starter

We offer the recipe, but if you can find someone who will share his or her starter, so much the better!

 2 cups flour
 2 cups warm water
 1 packet dry granular yeast

Mix well and keep in warm place overnight, out of drafts. In the morning the mixture should be bubbly and frothing, and is now called a "sponge." Take a half-cup of the sponge and place it in a jar with a tight cover. Store in the refrigerator; this is your sourdough starter for next time. Once you have made your starter, you should never have to repeat this process again. We have heard of present-day miners who claim to be using starter that dates from before the turn of the century. A bit of starter even makes a nice gift, along with recipes for what to do with it.

In order to preserve your own supply of starter, feed it each time before you use it with 1 cup flour and 1 cup warm water. Do this weekly to keep starter fresh.

Sourdough Bread

To make the bread, begin the night before by placing 1/2 cup starter in a mixing bowl. Add:
 2 cups warm water
 2 cups flour

Cover with a cloth and set in a warm place overnight.

In the morning set aside 1/2 of the starter for the next time. Into the remaining sponge sift:
 4 cups flour
 2 Tbsp. sugar
 1 tsp. salt

Add:
 2 Tbsp. oil
And mix well.

Add enough additional flour to make a soft dough, and knead for 10-15 minutes.

Place in a greased bread pan, cover, and set aside in a warm place to rise. This should take about 2 hours.

Place in 375 °F oven and bake for 50-60 minutes.

25 Scotchman's Hill
Calgary
A Scotchman's Stampede Picnic

The World Championship Chuckwagon Races are the premier event at that Show of Shows, the Calgary Stampede. People around the world, some of whom cannot tell Alberta from Oregon, have heard about the Calgary Stampede and know that cowboys wear white hats.

The Picnic

A penny saved is a penny earned.

This is a very special picnic and takes place at a very special time and place. The special time is the early evening during the Calgary Stampede. The special place is Scotchman's Hill, a high bank on the southeast side of the Elbow River that directly overlooks the Stampede Grounds and the Chuckwagon Track. This location provides one of the best viewing spots for the races and, since it is free, it is excellent value for the money. We feel that in these materialistic times

it is good to know that there are still some pleasures that can be appreciated without financial expenditure. Thus, with a true sense of Scottish Frugality, we conceived the following Stampede Picnic.

The picnic preparation must begin early, in keeping with the proverb:

Early to bed, early to rise
Makes Jock healthy and wealthy and wise.

Of course, the reason for getting up early is because this is the time when the chuckwagons are giving out the free stampede breakfast of pancakes. You have only to wander downtown to find the munificent benefactors on busy corners. If you get there early, you can not only eat your fill, but you can get back in line for a third helping which you can use for your picnic. The conveniently located waste receptacles will provide you with a copy of a newspaper in which to wrap your picnic pancakes.

Now, we realize that free coffee is also served at the breakfasts but we could not determine an economical way to keep it warm all day and so, in keeping with Grandfather's adage:

Waste not; want not

we recommend only taking as much coffee as you can conveniently drink with breakfast. The picnic coffee problem can be solved later. A number of gasoline service stations, notably the Turbo ones, give free coffee with a gas fill-up. Wait until some motorist has a fill-up and doesn't take the free coffee. We have found that if approached these kind souls are happy to part with their coffee privilege, thus permitting coffee to be picked up nearer the time and place of the picnic. On the other hand, you may not want to leave this to chance. In that case, select your coffee benefactor early in the day, then tell the station operator you'll take a "rain check." After all:

A bird in the hand is worth two in the bush.

Seating can be a problem at this picnic. It is all right if you are one of the early arrivals, and can sit on the ground with your legs dangling over the cliff. However, if you are late you may find that all those seats are taken and that your vision is blocked by people in lawn chairs. We suggest that you borrow a lawn chair for the evening — a friend will probably let you have one since evening is not a good time for sitting on the lawn anyway.

The location of the Scotchman's Hill is shown on the accompanying map. If you live nearby, the evening is a great time for a stroll. If

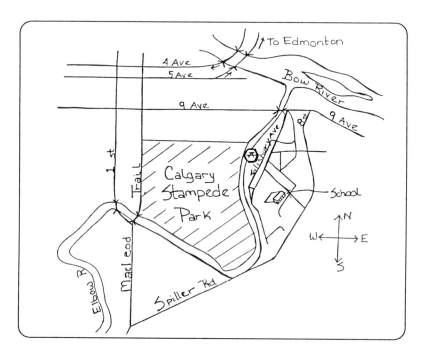

you live farther afield, Stampede time is one of fellowship and goodwill, and it is easy to obtain a ride by hitchhiking, and a person in a kilt with an armful of cold pancakes and a lawn chair is bound to be picked up quickly!

Things to do

Check the Daily Events Schedule (copies are free) to find out when the Special Days are. Usually there will be:

1. A Sneak-A-Peek Thursday with *free* admission to the grounds from 6 p.m. until midnight.

2. Family Fun Day with *free* admission to the grounds until 9 a.m. and a *free* Grandstand Show from 8 a.m. to 10 a.m.

3. Western Heritage Day, with *free* admission to Scots over 65, Kid's Day with *free* admission to Scots under 12; and Teen Day, with *free* admission to Scots Teenagers.

4. At 11 p.m. watch the sky for the *free* fireworks display.

26 Spruce Meadows Calgary

A Remittance Man's Picnic

The Southern family constructed Spruce Meadows to provide a World Class Show Jumping Facility for young Canadian riders. In the period since its first tournament in 1976, Spruce Meadows has continuously increased in both prestige and prize money offered, and in 1988 the prizes for its three major tournaments totalled over $1.6 million. The Masters tournament, with over $930,000 in prize money, is the richest show jumping tournament in the world.

How to get there

Spruce Meadows is located 4 km southwest of Calgary. It is reached by driving south on Highway 2 (the Macleod Trail), and turning west on Highway 22. The way is clearly marked with signs.

The facility contains restaurants, cocktail and coffee lounges, and fast food bars, although these generally operate only during tournaments. For those who want to watch the horses performing, there is a nice stretch of green grass in front of the stands where one can sprawl and eat. However, for a full-blown picnic, the appropriate spot is Amoco Park, a public park at the entrance to Spruce Meadows that has a fountain, reflecting pools, trees, and picnic tables.

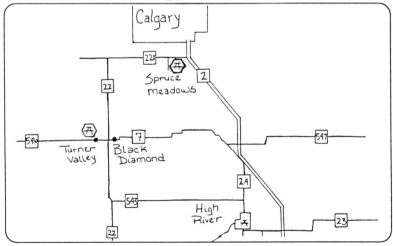

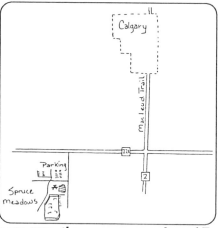

Imported elegance

Although the West may be the home of the cowboy, and horses were a natural and necessary part of the environment, the elegance of the show jumpers is an English or European import. Watching these beautiful animals and their correctly attired riders reminded us of an earlier import from across the pond, the remittance men.

In the early days of the West, especially in the Calgary area, there were a number of Englishmen of refined breeding and eccentric or erratic manners. The stereotypical remittance man was a perdition-bent son of a peer, who was sent off to Canada with a handshake, a sigh of relief, and sufficient funds to invest in a ranch. The ranch money was invariably invested in either a High River or Calgary bar, but it seems that father was more than willing to keep sending the monthly allowance (remittance) rather than face the prospect of having young Percy or Albert come home to embarrass the family in England. To Bob Edwards, the publisher of the Calgary *Eye Opener* around the turn of the century, they were a continuous source of amusement and delight. He made up a mythical remittance man, Albert Buzzard-Cholomondely (pronounced "Chumly," of course), son of Sir John Buzzard-Cholomondely of Skookingham (pronounced "Skookum," we think...) Hall, Skookingham, England. The pages of the *Eye Opener* would often include letters from Bertie to his parents which went something like the following:

The Ranch
P.O.Box 123
High River, North-West Territories

Dearest Papa,
    I do apologize for not having written for some time. Work here has been extremely arduous, to the extent that at the end of the day's labours I would collapse into bed, unable even to hold a glass, let alone a pen. The one thousand pounds you sent me to invest in a farm is being judiciously spent and although I have not exactly acquired the title yet, I expect to in the near future. To assist me in my endeavours I have made the acquaintance of four stalwart fellows: Hi Walker, Joe Seagram, Johnny Walker, and J. Dewar. They are

ensuring that I am seen in the right places, and move in the right circles. Unfortunately, their tastes are perhaps a little extravagant, and I am finding it a trifle difficult to manage on my present allowance.

Rising Star, my darling new wife, has suggested that maybe if we and the children came to England for a few months this summer we could more adequately explain our distressful financial situation. Furthermore it would provide you with the opportunity to meet your grandchildren. I think it a jolly idea since Rising Star's father, Standing Buffalo, who would of course accompany us, would be intrigued by the Great Hall at Skookingham; and perhaps you and I could manage some grouse shooting.

However, in case you should think that this suggestion smacks of indolence, I should tell you of the tremendous opportunity here to invest in Klondyke gold mines. (Such an activity would involve me totally and so would make a trip to England impossible this summer.) Unfortunately, I would need an additional 700 pounds to invest.

Do give my love to Mumsy and Cousin Felicity.

Your affectionate and obedient son

BERTIE

Needless to say, Bertie and his co-exiles always got their remittance; it has even been suggested that their contribution to the fledgling western economy, in the form of keeping money in circulation, was substantial.

Things to do

1. Watch the horses jump. Even when there are no tournaments or exhibitions there are often riders practising and training.

2. Tour the stables. See the elegant surroundings in which the handsome show jumpers live.

3. Drive to the Prince of Wales Teahouse on the EP ranch for an elegant tea of scones and jam. EP stands for Edward Prince and the ranch was formerly the property of Edward, Prince of Wales, who abdicated from the throne of England for Wallis Simpson, the "woman he loved." The trip is quite a long one and more justly belongs with the High River Picnic (which is where the directions are). However, it is mentioned here because it is just the kind of thing a Remittance Man would enjoy.

Things to eat

The Remittance Man's picnic is, naturally, a formal tea. This means that the bone china, a fine lace table cloth and a sterling silver tea service, preferably a British heirloom, are essential. The important thing to remember in a formal tea is that appearance is everything.

MENU

A tray of Watercress Sandwiches, Open Tomato Sandwiches and Open Cucumber Sandwiches;
Puff pastry shells filled with Chicken à la King and garnished with parsley;
Orange and Lemon Ice;
White cake with white icing
Earl Grey tea

Earl Grey Tea

Since the tea is the most important part of the repast, we shall consider its preparation first. The reader is reminded of the important rules of tea making:

> The water must be at a rolling boil
> Always bring the pot to the water
> Always put the milk in the cup first
> Remember to use the tea cozy

Although it goes without saying, we feel we should mention that in proper circles, tea bags are never used. In any case, they are unnecessary because any proper tea service includes a tea strainer and a slop bowl. Prior to preparation the pot should be scalded with boiling water, and then pre-heated by allowing hot water to remain in it a brief time. Into the pre-heated pot put
    1 teaspoon of tea leaves
for each
    5 to 6 ounces of water.

Allow the tea to steep not less than 3 nor more than 5 minutes. Then stir the brew to circulate the essential oils throughout, strain and pour.

The tea should be poured by the wife of the highest ranking male.

Watercress Sandwiches

The key to successful Watercress Sandwiches is the thinness of the butter and the blandness of the bread. The usual sandwich loaf made with white enriched flour and sliced thinly is adequate. After trimming off the crusts, the remainder of each slice should be divided into four equal pieces. These should be buttered thinly and a single sprig of watercress placed between two pieces.

Open Tomato or Cucumber Sandwiches

Cut small rounds of bread and butter them lightly. Place onto each round, so that it is almost completely covered, a round of tomato or a large round of peeled cucumber. Decorate each round with a dab of mayonnaise. Note the cucumber, tomato and bread should be packed separately and only assembled at the picnic ground immediately prior to eating them. This is to avoid the dreaded picnic plague of Soggy Tomato Sandwiches.

Lemon and Orange Ice

Heat to a boil:
   2 tsp. grated orange rind
   2 cups sugar
   4 cups water
   1/4 tsp. salt
and simmer for about 5 minutes.

   Chill the mixture and add:
   2 cups fresh orange juice
   1/4 cup lemon juice
   and churn-freeze the mixture in an ice cream churn.

Chicken à la King

(Serves 4-6)

Dice:
   1 cup cooked chicken
   1/2 cup tinned mushrooms
   1/4 cup tinned pimento

Melt:
   3 Tbsp. butter
and blend in
   3 Tbsp. flour.

Add while stirring:
   1 1/2 cups chicken stock
and when the sauce is smooth and boiling add the chicken, mushrooms and pimento.

Reduce the heat and add:
   the yolk of one egg
Stir until it has thickened slightly.

This can be prepared at home and reheated at the picnic table in a sterling silver chafing dish. Ladle onto puff pastries that you have previously purchased at the bakery.

White Cake

Preheat oven to 375 °F. Have all ingredients at room temperature.

Sift before measuring:
   1 3/4 cups white enriched flour
Resift with:
   1 cup sugar

Add:
   1/2 cup melted butter   2 eggs
   1/2 cup milk   1/2 tsp. salt
   2 tsp. double acting baking powder   1 tsp. vanilla

Beat vigorously for 3 to 4 minutes. Bake in a greased pan for 30 minutes. Put on a rack to cool.

White Icing

Sift two cups icing sugar into a bowl. Add gradually to 1/4 lb. soft butter and beat until creamy. Add 2 tsp. vanilla. If icing is too thin, add more sugar; if too thick, add a little cream. Spread on a warm cake.

27 Stoney Indian Park Morley

A Stoney Indian Picnic

Oh give me a home
Where the buffalo roam . . .

Once the Indians hunted buffalo here. Now they raise them, and
you can picnic on buffalo stew while watching the buffalo graze
against a backdrop of the Rocky Mountains.

How to get there

Stoney Indian Park is on the Stoney Indian Reserve between
Calgary and Banff. Although it is a campground, picnickers are more
than welcome ($3 per car) and there are many spectacular spots along
the hill overlooking the buffalo paddock. The best ones are campsites
2, 8 and 10 (see map), but if these are full, there are many others of
comparable beauty. All told, the campground occupies 2,200 acres.

The park is reached from Calgary by driving towards Banff on
Highway 1, and switching onto 1A northwest at Morley opposite the
Chief Chiniki Restaurant. Continue west on 1A, watching for the
Texaco station and camp store on your left. The turn-off into the
campground is just east of the store. Alternatively, drive east from
Banff along Highway 1. You can shift to 1A just east of Canmore, or
at Seebe. Proceed east, passing the Nakoda Lodge, till you come to the
Texaco station, and turn right. See map.

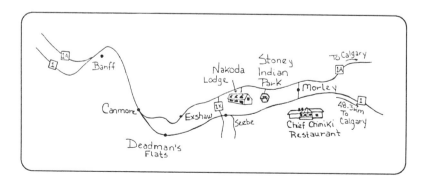

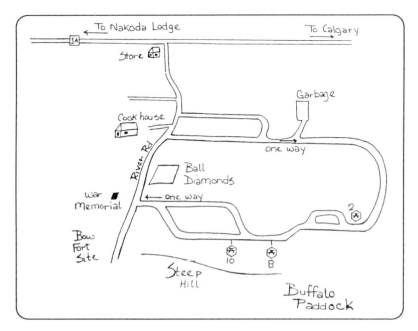

(Please note: The park site is available for large group picnics, and can accommodate up to 500 people. For advance bookings and catered buffalo roast picnics contact park managers, Lawrence and Sherryl Falt, P.O. Box 310, Morley, Alberta or telephone [403] 881-3766)

The Stoney Indians

There are three bands of Stoneys, the Bear's Paw, the Chiniki and the Wesley Bands, which today have a total population of 2,300 people. They are descendants of the Dakota Sioux who once lived in the upper Missouri River region. The smallpox epidemics of the mid-1600s killed thousands of the Dakota Sioux. The ancestors of the three bands now in Alberta migrated west to escape the smallpox and established hunting grounds in an area extending from the Brazeau River in the north to Chief Mountain in Montana to the south. The present reserve lands are a minute fraction of the traditional hunting area, and comprise only about one-eighth of the land Chief Chiniki understood that he was getting under the terms of Treaty #7 in 1877. Stoney is the European name for the Nakoda people.

Although in our language we always referred to ourselves as "Na-ko-da" (meaning "people"), today we are known everywhere as the Stoney Indians. The name "Stoney" Indians was first given to us by the early white explorers because of our method of making broth.

In order to make broth a fire is first made and some round stones placed in the fire so they would become very hot. Nearby, a small hollow was dug in the ground and lined with rawhide to form a bowl. Food, such as pieces of meat and vegetables, was placed in the bowl and water added; the hot stones were then taken from the fire and placed into the broth to cook it. The stones would not burn holes into the rawhide, but only make the water very hot. Early explorers from Europe noticed our clever way of making soup, and remembered us as the "Stone" people. That is why today we are called the Stoney Indians [Peter M. Jonker. "Stoney History Notes." 1983. Chiniki Band of the Stoney Tribe, Morley, Alberta].

The buffalo

Reports of early explorers describe herds of buffalo so large that the mass of movement reached as far as the eye could see. Later, in the mid-nineteenth century, trains crossing the western states were delayed for several hours when a herd was crossing the tracks.

The buffalo was fundamental to the economy of the Plains Indians for food, clothing and shelter. The rapidly increasing demand for hides in Europe and the States combined with the availability of guns to diminish these vast herds in a few decades. The legendary Buffalo Bill Cody was among those who slaughtered

buffalo for profit. He was under contract to the Kansas Pacific Railway when it was being built, and killed 4,820 buffalo in just 18 months to feed the work crews. Other entrepreneurs guided tourists across the prairies on trains, letting them shoot the buffalo from the windows with repeating rifles for sport. For a while nearly everyone in the West was hunting, eating, buying or selling buffalo, Indians and whites alike.

Concern was expressed by American leaders of the day, and the likely extinction of the buffalo was considered by some to be a clever strategy to force the Indian people into submission — and subjugation.

Buffalo range now only in protected areas; here they are protected by the Stoney Indians.

Things to eat

The quick-as-a-wink picnic

Just before you turn off Highway #1, take advantage of the take-out service at Chief Chiniki's Restaurant and pick up some buffalo stew, bread and salad, or a few buffalo burgers to take along to the picnic spot.

A Stoney Picnic

Rawhide and hot stones are a bit difficult to obtain on short notice, and so we suggest the equivalent which is an old-fashioned Dutch oven (a staple piece of equipment in the chuck wagons on the ranches for almost a century) which cooks in a pit with hot coals or stones on the lid. Traditionalists may choose to heat stones in a fire and put them inside the Dutch oven, in which case the pit is not necessary. Here is a recipe to feed a herd of hungry buffalo hunters.

Stoney Stew

(Serves 6)

4 pounds buffalo meat cut into small cubes
3 onions
3 carrots
3 potatoes
3 Tbsp. flour
2 pints water
1 small tin tomato paste

1 pint beer
1 (at least) clove of garlic
bay leaves
parsley, thyme, salt and pepper, and spices of your choice, to taste

Combine flour and seasonings in a bag and shake meat to cover. Brown the meat in hot oil in your Dutch oven, over a fire, or gas or propane stove. Chop onions and sauté with the meat. Add liquids, garlic, vegetables, and simmer for an hour or two in the pit or on the stove. Serves 6, but increase veggies for more people. Serve with bannock.

Bannock

(Serves 6)

3 cups flour
salt
1 tsp. baking powder
2 Tbsp. lard
3 cups cold water

Combine dry ingredients in a bowl. Make a well and pour the water in; mix into a dough and knead it; flatten out and place in heavy frying pan or the lid of your Dutch oven. Cook over the open fire or on the stove. You can also bake this in your home oven for about 40 minutes at about 400 °F; or you can roll the dough into a long thin strip and then coil it around a stick. Toast over the open fire.

Finish your meal with whatever berries are in season (wild strawberries at the end of June, saskatoons in late July) and campfire coffee.

28 Ribbon Creek Kananaskis
An Olympic Picnic

Kananaskis Country was pushed to the forefront of Alberta tourist areas during the 1988 Winter Olympics. This recent history overshadows the past importance of the region as a mining and logging district and a prisoner of war camp, as well as its beauty and richness as a wildlife habitat. Until ten years ago the interior of Kananaskis Country could only be reached by means of a forestry road, or by hikers and cross-country skiers. Kananaskis was the venue for the biathalon in the Winter Olympics of 1988, and is now the venue for our picnic.

How to get there

From the Banff-Calgary Highway #1 (the Trans-Canada) turn south on Highway 40, the Kananaskis Trail. The turnoff to Ribbon Creek and Nakiska is about 20 km (12 1/2 mi.) south, on your right on the west side.

The Olympics

The Winter Olympics took place in Calgary in February, 1988. Two of the sites were located in the Kananaskis: the downhill skiing events took place at Nakiska, and the cross-country events at the Canmore Nordic Centre. In association with the games a resort was also built near the Nakiska ski area, called Kananaskis Village. It currently includes three hotels, a gift shop and other tourist facilities.

History of the Kananaskis

Industrial development was late to arrive in the Kananaskis valleys because of the ruggedness of the terrain. Early explorers such as Sinclair, Palliser and Sullivan all sought a way through the mountains in this region. None of the passes has ever been developed as a major transport route.

The Ribbon Creek area has long been exploited as a source of resources of one sort or another. Native people hunted here for centuries; the fur traders and trappers travelled through it in search of plentiful sources of pelts; the surveyors came in the early part of

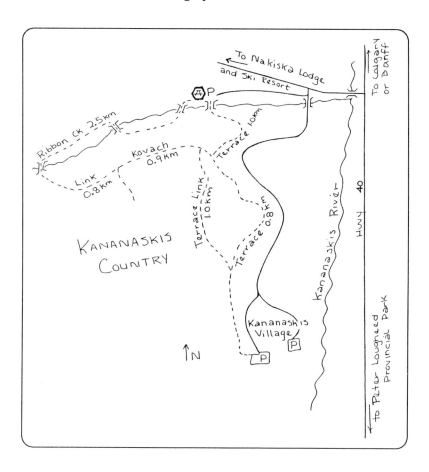

this century, and the creek became a source of hydraulic power. Logging began as early as 1883 in the Kananaskis, but the Ribbon Creek area was not seriously logged until the 1940s. Over this period logging advanced from horse-drawn vehicles and crosscut saws to trucks and power saws. A number of saw mills have operated in the region to turn the harvested trees into lumber. The miners came when coal was discovered on Mount Allan.

Only recently has the focus turned from exploitation to preservation of the resources of the Kananaskis area. The region is now an important centre for forestry research. Long-term reclamation experiments are being carried on, and much of the environmental scarring of the mining and logging era has been erased from the landscape.

The Biathalon Picnic

The 1988 Olympic Biathalon took place near Canmore in Ka-nanaskis. It was a double-skill sport, cross-country skiing and rifle shooting. We feel that a biathalon picnic should therefore require two sporting events from each participant. Although we do not advocate the rifle-ski combination, you could substitute a camera for the rifle. Since the area is rich in recreational facilities we will provide a list from which everyone on your picnic can choose two "events," not counting the warm-up, of course! You may wish to check at the Barrier Lake Information Centre — you passed it on Highway 40 coming south — for detailed information about trail conditions.

WARM-UP

1. Stretches: Standing, reach as high as you can above your head, arms extended. Slowly bend at the waist and reach down as close to the ground as you can get. Repeat this routine 8 times.

2. Spread feet shoulder-width apart, and do 8 deep knee bends in a slow, flowing, sustained fashion.

3. Do 12 jumping jacks.

4. Do 12 push-ups.

Repeat steps 2, 3 and 4 several more times, according to your own ability.

Now you are ready to begin your biathalon sports.

IN THE SUMMER

Walking: Along the Ribbon Creek Trail.

Running: A half-hour run on the Ribbon Creek Trail, or a 7 km (4 1/3 mi.) circuit along the Terrace Trail, and looping back through the Ribbon Creek Trail. Otherwise, there are about 47 km (29 mi.) of trails of varying levels of difficulty in the Ribbon Creek area, ranging from 0.3 km (1/5 mi.) to 10.2 km (6 1/3 mi.). The trail guide is on a sign board just behind the picnic shelter.

Bicycling: The Evan Thomas Bicycle Trail begins at the edge of the parking lot and goes for 8 km (5 mi.).

Golf: The world class Kananaskis Country Golf Course is described as a public golf course with a private club atmosphere.

Fishing: Ribbon Creek Pond is a few minutes walk away from the picnic site. Head east — it's just before the entrance to the parking lot, and there are signs. The pools at Mount Lorette a few kilometres away are stocked with rainbow and eastern brook trout; they are accessible to the handicapped and equipped for shore fishing.

IN THE WINTER

Downhill skiing: Use the Olympic facilities at Nakiska Lodge.

Cross-country skiing: Try the Ribbon Creek Trail system.

Ice-fishing: At Wedge Pond (check brochure map).

Snow-shoeing: There are lots of trails. (Stay on them, to avoid the risk of avalanches.)

Ice skating: At Ribbon Creek Pond.

Other things to do

1. Drop in at the Colonel's Cabin interpretive site on your way back from the picnic (summer only). It is just off the Kananaskis Trail, and the road is well marked. The cabin was part of the German Prisoner of War Camp during the Second World War. One of the watch towers is back on the site, after a brief period of service as a fire tower on a nearby mountain. The old photographs and displays explain why several of the prisoners have returned to the valley.

2. Visit Nakiska, the site of the downhill ski events for the 1988 Olympics, and ride the Bronze Chair Lift for a splendid view of the facility.

3. Hunt for the Lost Lemon Mine — if you dare! It is thought to be somewhere on a ledge in Kananaskis Country.

The Legend of the Lost Lemon Mine

The place is cursed; but was it cursed even before Blackjack and Lemon discovered it in the spring of about 1870? Quite a few people have known the whereabouts of this rich Eldorado, but each took the secret to the grave. The legend begins with the discovery of the ledge by two men from Montana, Blackjack and Lemon. While they were camping near the discovery site they had a disagreement and Lemon murdered Blackjack in his sleep with an axe. By morning guilt had driven him insane; he returned to Montana and confessed his deed to a priest. For the rest of his life he experienced periods of insanity. The priest staked Lemon for another attempt to find the lost mine, but upon approaching the site Lemon again became insane and the expedition was forced to give up. Lemon never recovered.

Hints about the location of the mine have passed from man to man by word of mouth, and many prospectors have wandered these creeks above High River. One died mysteriously of drunkenness on his way back to the region; another became desperately ill on the trail and had to give up his search. One, who had known Lemon, actually found the site, or so he said in the message which preceded him down the mountain. Upon his arrival, however, he was too ill to speak, and he died that night without revealing the secret of the Lost Lemon Mine.

The Indians allegedly knew the secret, and believed that their god, Wacondah, cursed the gold. The night that Lemon killed his partner, two braves had followed them along the trail, and witnessed the murder. They returned to their chief with their report, and the chief swore them to secrecy, since he didn't want the territory to be inundated by white miners. The secret was kept, and all evidence was subsequently scattered. After the priest sent a later expedition to the site to bury Blackjack, the Indians scattered the stones of the grave in such a way that the spot could not be identified. The chief even ordered that the Indian trails in the area be avoided, and they were quickly overgrown by the mountain forest. So vanished the path to the Lost Lemon Mine.

It could be that one of the trails that the forestry department has re-opened in the past few years is actually the old trail to the ledge; it is supposed to be in the southwestern part of Kananaskis Country, between Mist Mountain to the north and K-Country border to the south, bounded by the headwaters of the Highwood and Oldman Rivers. Watch carefully for an outcrop of pure gold. If you find it, perhaps you should just keep it a secret.

Things to eat

While you are exercising, here are some suggestion for high energy snacks:
Trail mix snack
Gatorade
Semi-sweet Baker's chocolate squares

This is an Olympic picnic — and so we have Greek food, of course.

MENU

Pita Bread
Houmus
Greek Salad
Lamb Shishkabobs
Baklava

Houmus

(Serves 6-8)

1 tin cooked garbanzo beans
1/3 cup lemon juice
2-3 large cloves of garlic
1/3 cup tahini
1 tsp. sea salt
2 Tbsp. olive oil

Do not drain the beans. Empty can into blender along with other ingredients and blend until smooth. Chill for 2 hours before serving. Garnish with parsley.

Lamb Shishkabobs

Buy 1/2 pound lamb per person. Cut lamb into 1-inch cubes and soak in marinade in refrigerator overnight.

Prepare the following marinade:
3/4 cup dry red wine
1/4 cup lemon juice
3 Tbsp. olive oil
1 tsp. salt

fresh ground pepper
2 garlic cloves, minced
1 onion, minced
1 bay leaf
2 Tbsp. oregano

At the picnic thread the lamb onto skewers, alternating with chunks of green pepper, cherry tomatoes, and mushroom caps.

Broil on your portable barbecue, turning as needed. Baste with the marinade several times during broiling.

Greek Salad

(Serves 6)

Mix together in a bowl:
   1 head romaine lettuce
   1/2 Spanish onion, thinly sliced and separated into rings
   1 green pepper cut into small triangles
   4 tomatoes, quartered
   1 cucumber, peeled and cut into chunks
   1/2 pound feta cheese, crumbled

And dress with:
   2 cloves garlic, minced
   1 Tbsp. wine vinegar
   1/4 tsp. salt
   1/2 cup olive oil
   pinch of tarragon
   dash of black pepper

Toss the salad and sprinkle liberally with calamata olives — the black ones.

Baklava and pita bread can be purchased at the Greek bakery, or at most large grocery stores — check the frozen foods section.

The appropriate beverage is retsina wine. Drink it if you like. We don't.

SOUTHERN ALBERTA

29 Hell's Half Acre Turner Valley
A Prosperous Picnic

This place smells, but the smell is of money and of progress. The odour is not unpleasant, but there is just enough of a trace of hydrogen sulfide — you know, the rotten egg smell — to remind you that this is the place where the Alberta Oil Industry really began. Dingman No. 1, blowing in at 4,000,000 cubic feet of gas per day; Hell's Half Acre where the gas that could not be sold was flared and burned with such an intensity it was visible all the way to Calgary, over 50 kilometres away; Royalties No. 1 which produced 850 barrels a day of light crude oil from 1936 until 1949: these are the legends of the boom that was determined to happen.

How to get there

Turner Valley is 50 km (31 mi.) from the Calgary city limits. The most direct route is Highway 22 which starts in a westerly direction from the south city limit. The selected picnic site is in the town of Turner Valley at the Hell's Half Acre Campground. The campground is located at the corner of Main Street between Edgar and Royal Avenues, directly behind the swimming pool.

This place is important and every Albertan should visit it, to smell the sulfide, and see the well-heads and the flare pit, because this is where the engine that propelled Alberta into a "have" province really began. The crops and cows are important, but it is oil and gas that have made Alberta, and it is here in this swamp that it all started.

The boom that could not be stopped

The Turner Valley Oil Boom, characterized by bizarre luck, major fires, and under-financed companies — and occurring during World War I and then during the 1930s world depression — seems almost a boom that occurred despite its supporters' best efforts.

That there was gas near the south fork of the Sheep River on Michael Stoos's property was obvious to anyone who passed that way. It leaked through the fissures of the rock in sufficient concentrations that it could be lit at the surface.

A syndicate, the Calgary Petroleum Products Company, was put together by Okotoks rancher, William Stewart Herron, and it included A.W. Dingman, R.B. Bennett (a future prime minister), W.H. McLaws, A. Judson Sayre, Sir James A. Lougheed, William Pearce, T.J. Skinner, Colonel Price Jones, O.P. Chaplin, O.G. Devenish, and A.E. Cross. The group's first well, Dingman No. 1, was "spudded in" on January 25, 1913, and on May 14, 1914, at a depth of 2,718 feet, it blew in at a rate of 4 million cubic feet of wet gas a day. The naphtha (natural gasoline) recovered from this gas, although somewhat sulphurous, was pure enough to fuel automobiles without any refinement.

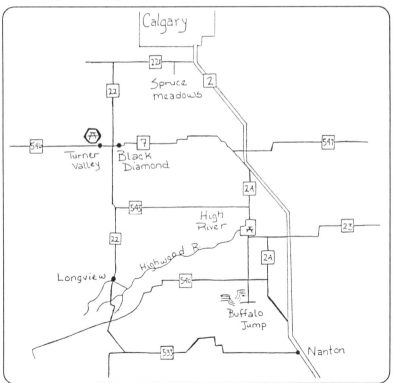

Looking north towards town of Turner Valley, circa 1930.

Within a few days of the strike over 500 oil companies were established in Calgary. Speculative and sometimes fraudulent companies sprang into existence as investors raced to catch the great Canadian oil boom. In the words of historian Tony Cashman, the 1914 oil boom "produced a little oil, a considerable amount of natural gas, and an enormous quantity of hot air." Speculation fever prompted the *Calgary Herald* to publish the following list of regulations for oil boom talk in the Palliser Hotel lobby:

* No dry holes will be tolerated in this lobby.
* All wells brought in must be in the thousand barrel class or larger.
* No wells shall be drilled before 6 a.m. or after 3 p.m. Operations at that time are apt to disturb paying guests in the midst of beautiful dreams of vast wealth and permanent gushers.

In any case, the boom was short-lived as three months later, on August 4, 1914, the first world war began, completely dislocating Canada's industrial development. Natural gasoline was not a priority item for Canada's unmechanized army and little drilling was carried on during the war, although the original syndicate did bring in two more wells, Dingman Nos. 2 and 3.

In 1920 the Calgary Petroleum Products Plant burned to the ground and the company found itself in financial difficulties. Negotiations with Imperial Oil Company produced a successor company called the Royalite Oil Company, which took over the three wells and renamed them Royalite Nos. 1, 2, and 3.

In September of 1922 Royalite No. 4 was spudded in. However, by the time the well had gone to a depth of 3,500 feet without a significant strike, the Company decided to abandon it and a cease-drilling order was sent to the rig. The chief driller on the rig, on receiving the order, decided to let the workers finish out the shift before shutting things down. Ten feet further into the limestone the rig met a sudden heave of gas pressure. It blew, and it was two months before all the fires were extinguished! When the well was tamed, it produced over 20 million cubic feet of wet gas and 500-600 barrels of naphtha per day. The second Turner Valley boom was on.

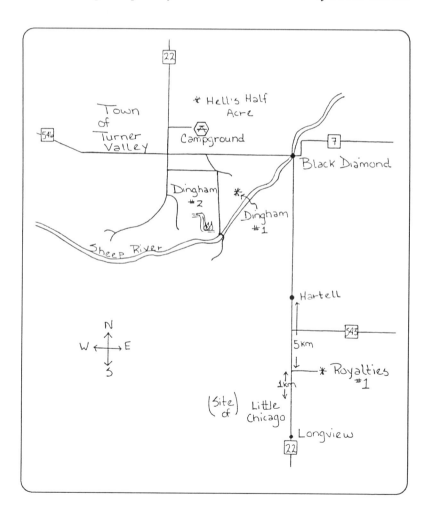

The gas contained hydrogen sulfide, and so in 1925 a scrubbing plant was built to remove the sulphur. The company had no method of storage for the gas that they could not sell and surplus gas, as much as 22 million cubic feet per day, was flared in a coulee that came to be known as Hell's Half Acre. The flares burned with such intensity that the coulee light was visible from Calgary and the rocks were seared into beautiful colours.

The boom triggered by Royalite No. 4, like the earlier boom from Dingman No. 1, was derailed by external events. In 1930, when Turner Valley had grown into a large settlement, the Great Depression began.

It was the crude oil well, Royalties No. 1, that triggered the last and most sustained Turner Valley boom. For years only gas wells were discovered around the area of the current town of Turner Valley. A Calgarian, R. A. Brown, believed that crude oil might exist at greater depths on the south of the gas field. The well was spudded in during 1934. Seven times the drilling was stopped because the backers ran out of money, and each time the determined Brown found more backers and got it started again. On June 16, 1936, at a depth of 6,828 feet, the well struck an oil pool that flowed at 850 barrels per day, and would eventually produce over 700,000 barrels of light crude.

Word of the discovery spread quickly, and soon the town of Royalties, also known as Little Chicago, sprang into being. The now sleepy town of Longview was then known as Little New York and boasted four restaurants, a Roxy Theatre and two lumber yards. The Longview-Turner Valley area was the centre of oil activity for the province until the 1947 Leduc oil strike shifted the focus to the north.

Things to do

The thing to do in Turner Valley is to visit the sites of the historic wells.

1. Dingman No. 2, is on the bench on the north bank of the Sheep River, just before the bridge. The easiest way to find it is to drive to the bridge and from there you will see the burning flare. This is the result of gas seepage from Dingman No. 2 which is located directly above the flare.

2. Dingman No. 1 lies inside the boundaries of the Western Decalta gas plant and is not accessible to the public. It is, however, amidst the structures and pipes directly across the road from Dingman No. 2.

3. Royalite No. 4 is just north of the town on the east side of Highway 22. Only a commemorative sign exists to mark the spot.

4. Hell's Half Acre is directly north of the picnic spot at Hell's Half Acre Campground.

5. Royalties No. 1 is about 5 km (3 mi.) south of the present town of Hartell, a few hundred feet east of the highway. A sign and a well-head remain to mark this historic spot.

6. Little Chicago (Royalties) stretched along the rise of land on the west of Highway 22 about one kilometre north and south of the Royalties well. Nothing remains today.

Things to eat

The legend goes that in an attempt to secure funding for his proposed oil company, William Herron invited R. B. Bennett and A. W. Dingman to go on a fishing trip on the Sheep River. When they were in the gas seepage area, Herron touched a match to a fissure in the rock. When a flame appeared, Herron produced a frying pan and proceeded to cook eggs for his astonished visitors.

Such a legend should immediately suggest that we devise a picnic around fried eggs. But this is such a mundane dish — and this place is a place of prosperity and development. Thus our menu leans more to the conventional prosperity picnic.

MENU

Rena's Ribs
A Big Pot of Baked Beans
Crusty Rolls and butter
Vegetable Salad
Ice Cream and Apple Pie

The Potato Salad Recipe is found with the Victoria (Church) Picnic; the Apple Pie with the Cave and Basin (CPR) Picnic.

Rena's Ribs

Allow 1 pound spareribs per person. Precook your ribs by parboiling them for 2 minutes. Preheat oven to 500 °F (260 °C). Place the ribs on the rack of a covered roaster. Reduce heat to 350 °F (190 °C) and bake for one hour.

Prepare the sauce at home, too.
Mix together in a pot and simmer:
   1 cup tomato ketchup
   1/4 cup cider vinegar
   1 tsp. dry mustard
   1 tsp. Worcestershire sauce
   1 tsp. paprika
   1 clove garlic, crushed
   1/2 cup brown sugar

Bring your portable barbecue to this picnic — the one with the lid.

Pour sauce over the cooked ribs, place in barbecue and cook for about 30 minutes with low heat — sauce will be bubbly.

Baked Beans

(Serves 6-8)

Soak overnight
   2 cups dried Great Northern beans

Rinse and drain in the morning. Cover with cold water and boil for 15 minutes. Drain, reserving the liquid.

Add to the beans:
   1 tin stewed tomatoes
   1 tsp. dry mustard
   1 medium onion, chopped
   1 Tbsp. brown sugar
   2 Tbsp. molasses
   oregano, marjoram, basil, and rosemary to taste

Place the resulting mixture in a earthenware bean pot or crock. Stir in
   1/2 pound salt pork or bacon in chunks
and bake in a slow oven for 4 to 6 hours. Use the reserved fluid to keep the beans from drying out.

Alternatively, if you lack a crock or oven, the beans can be cooked on the top of the stove in a large pot, stirring occasionally and using the reserved fluid to keep them moist.

The beans can be reheated at the picnic over the barbecue.

Vegetable Salad
(Serves 4-6)

2 tins whole kernel corn, drained
2 avocadoes, peeled and diced
6 hard-boiled eggs, diced
2 Tbsp. chopped onion

Prepare a dressing as follows:
1 cup mayonnaise
1 Tbsp. lemon juice
1/2 tsp. chili powder
1/4 tsp. ground cumin

Pour over the salad and toss just before serving.

30 George Lane Memorial Park
High River
A Picnic For Johnny Chinook

CHINOOK: A warm, dry, gusty, westerly wind which comes from the Rockies and which, in winter, can raise air temperatures by as much as 25 °C (45 °F) in a single hour. The wind was named after the Chinook tribe because it seemed to originate in their territory. The area between Calgary and Pincher Creek will receive 30 to 35 chinook days each winter. A characteristic of the chinook wind is that the clouds form a beautiful low arch, a chinook arch, in the western sky.

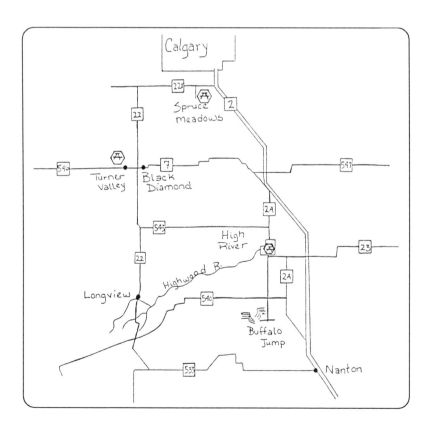

How to get there

High River is 56 km (35 mi.) south of Calgary on Highway 2, hereabouts called the Macleod Trail. The picnic site is in the George Lane Memorial Park, a picnic and camp ground on the banks of the Highwood River on the edge of the town.

Folklore and legends

Myths, tall tales, and legends exist for every part of the province, but it is here in Chinook Country, where the Macleod Trail crosses the Highwood River, that the tales are uniquely Albertan, for it is here that the warm wind blows. Johnny Chinook — a creation of author Robert Gard — is the narrator of tales, the muse of the mountains, the person who rides the wind and performs practical jokes. Some of these tales follow.

This story takes place during the year of the big snowfall — one of the biggest in history, which covered all the town to such a depth that all that stuck out of the snow was the

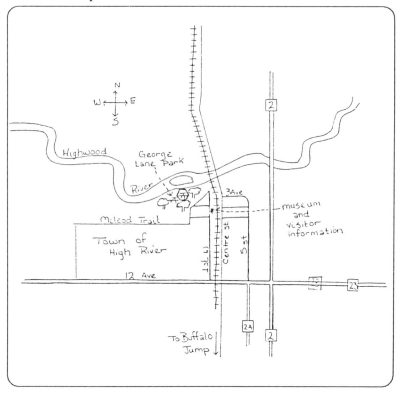

steeple of St. Benedict's. The people would come to church, tie their horses to the steeple, and go down through a snow tunnel to the door.

One day during this big snow Johnny had to go to Vulcan. He harnessed his horse, hitched her to the sleigh, and set off to the east. He was only about half way there when he heard a rustling noise but he knew what it was. It was a Chinook stealing up behind him. He whipped the horse, but the Chinook kept gaining on him, melting the snow as it came.

"Boys," says Johnny, "'Twas all I could do to keep the front runners on the snow! Those back runners were raising one hell of a dust storm."

And it was just chance that let Johnny complete his journey that day. The heat from the wind was such that Johnny undid his buffalo coat and started to take it off. Well, he had it partly off with his arms outstretched when the wind caught it like a sail. Now Johnny's feet were caught beneath the sleigh seat so instead of being blown off, Johnny carried the sleigh, horse, and himself along before the wind. They moved so fast that he established a High River-Vulcan land speed record that stands to this day.

And the people in the church had a terrible shock when they came outside. The snow was all gone and there were their horses dangling down from the steeple like bells.

According to Indian legend, the chinook is a beautiful princess, the blind daughter of the Great Southwind. She lives in Castle Mountain, twenty miles west of Banff, but sometimes, in the winter, she steals out of her hiding place in the castle and blows through the mountain passes down onto the frozen prairie. It is part of her magic that brings a temporary spring to the flatlands.

A "true" High River story concerns the former Methodist Church, now the Church of the Nazarene at 117-4 Ave. East. It seems that a gramophone salesman arrived in town and convinced the Methodist minister to give his Gramophone Choir a tryout. As the salesman explained, all church troubles were traceable to the choir. If a minister eloped, it was sure to be with a member of the choir, and so on.

However, the salesman also had records that were other than ecclesiastical, and the night before the service some of the local cowboys got the salesman drunk and switched his records around. Thus, on Sunday morning, when the

The Medicine Tree Arch

congregation was expecting, "Nearer My God To Thee," they were treated to an up-tempo rendition of "Just Because She Made Goo-Goo Eyes." The church did not purchase the gramophone.

High River has taken as it's official inisgnia the "Medicine Tree." Near the Highwood River two cottonwoods stood, joined by a single branch, thus forming the letter H. The Indians held that the tree possessed magic powers and gave it the name, "Medicine Tree." The tree was a convenient landmark and was a meeting point for traders. The tree blew down some time ago but the H was preserved and is exhibited in the George Lane Park.

Things to do

1. Visit the Museum of the High Wood. The town has established its museum in the abandoned CPR railway station.

2. Take a tour of High River. In the Tourist Information Caboose, next to the Museum, you can obtain an Alberta Culture booklet entitled "A Walking Tour of High River." The tour directs you past interesting and historic sites including the boyhood home of former prime minister Joe Clark, and the Church of the Nazarene.

3. View the buffalo jump. Proceed south out of High River on Centre Street. This becomes a section road and the first stop sign is Highway 540. Proceed south straight across the 540 and the buffalo jump is in the field to the right, west of the road. For the best view, take the first road to the right and drive into the valley.

4. Take Tea at the EP Ranch. In 1919, HRH The Prince Edward Albert Christian George Andrew Patrick David, Prince of Wales, purchased the Bedingfeld Ranch and renamed it the EP ranch for Edward Prince. The Prince owned the ranch for 43 years, selling it in 1962 to Jim Cartwright. The original ranch house built for the Prince of Wales has been restored and is now operated as a Tea House. Phone 395-2418 to check on menus and opening times.

Things to eat

High River is where the disparate landscape of Alberta comes together. It has the beauty of the plains, with the backdrop of the mountains. It is ranching country, but the oil fields of Turner Valley are just over the horizon. It has the long cold winters, and the hot dry summers, and it has the chinooks. Thus it is only fitting that the High

PRONGHORN ANTELOPE

Delicate and lightfooted, pronghorn antelope are among the fastest animals on earth. They have been clocked at speeds of up to 72 km/h, and they are usually seen for only a few seconds as they dash away from people and cars.

Pronghorn antelope are also referred to as prairie antelope, as they inhabit the grasslands of Alberta, Saskatchewan, and Manitoba. They are curious animals, and because of their curiosity and boldness they are easy targets for hunters. The antelope's hide is soft and supple; hence its popularity with hunters and with the earlier Plains Indians.

The Indians began hunting with guns in the mid-1700s, and the coincidental influx of homesteaders and fur traders to the prairies took their toll. By the late 1800s the pronghorns were nearly extinct. The protective measures taken when the species became endangered have brought the population up to 4,000, but they are now found only in the Southern Brooks Plains, and are no longer spread all across the central and northern plains of North America. You may be lucky enough to see them grazing in the dry grasslands of the south. We came across a herd just outside of Cypress Hills Provincial Park.

River Picnic be the truly Alberta indigenous meal, the one that started the cowboys on the trail, the Western Breakfast:

a small but thick steak
two fried eggs
hashed brown potatoes
toast
coffee

A Small Thick Steak

Marinades, exotic herbs, and fancy sauces are not for the cowboy. He liked plain beef, and lots of it. Unfortunately, he also liked it well done, which we suspect is more a result of the difficulty of control over an open fire than a true expression of taste. In any case, we suggest you purchase a whole, or a large portion of a filet. This is not really as expensive as it seems when you consider that there is no waste. Cut into rounds of about 1 1/2 to 2 inches in thickness. Brush with butter, and barbecue (grill) 10 minutes a side for rare, or 25 minutes per side for well done.

Fried Eggs

Heat pan to medium heat, add bacon grease or shortening, break in two eggs, fry at medium temperature. Easy to say but not so easy to do with a tin frying pan and a raging inferno. If your picnickers can't wait for the nice bed of coals to form, and you want to get the eggs cooked, try the following: place a greased heavy cast iron frying-pan on the fire, and heat until the oil spits at a drop of water. Remove the pan from the fire and place on the ground beside. Break eggs into the pan and cook. The cast iron retains enough heat to fry the eggs thoroughly.

Hashed Brown Potatoes

(Serves 4)

For this you must have a bed of coals or a propane barbecue to maintain a low to medium heat.

Heat in a cast iron skillet:
  5 Tbsp. bacon grease or oil

Add to the pan
  5 medium potatoes, peeled and diced   *1 medium onion, chopped*
  2 Tbsp. chopped parsley   *1/2 tsp. salt*
  1/2 tsp. black pepper

Spread the potato mixture and press it into the pan. Sauté slowly, and when the bottom is brown, stir the mixture up again and press it down. Keep it from sticking; add more grease if the pan becomes too hot.

31 Blairmore Crowsnest Pass
The Rum Runner's Picnic

This picnic takes place in Blairmore: a quiet little town since the mine closed in 1957, and the new highway bypassed the town by a crucial few hundred feet to the north. Such circumstances caused many people to move on to other towns, and to other jobs at other mines.

There are two phases of Blairmore's history which influence this picnic — one is the coal mining period at the turn of the century, and the other is the prohibition period in the 1920s. Blairmore was a centre for illegal rum running through Southern Alberta to Montana.

There are no facilities at this suggested picnic place — just an empty field filled with the bustle of phantom mining trains, trucks, buildings — and coal miners. Bring a thick blanket to sit on, or a portable picnic table if you wish.

How to get there

There are three exits from Highway #3 into Blairmore; take any of them, and continue along to 121 Street. Turn north, and follow the road until it ends, on 22nd Avenue, by an old mine bridge. Park here, and cross the bridge over the Crowsnest River — there is a footpath on the left side of the bridge. It is quite safe for people, but blocked to cars. Refer to the map and the photograph, which shows the view of the old Western Canadian Collieries from our picnic flat below. Select a grassy place in the field across the bridge, but make sure it is a place where you can see the gracious old grey mining building above you, the only survivor of the Greenhill Mine, part of the great Western Canadian Collieries.

You can perhaps imagine the activity of years gone by. The flats were covered with buildings, all of them black with layered coal dust. The steam engine, which now rests across from the post office, once moved loaded hopper cars from the mine along the spur to the main CPR line. The spur from the main CPR line ran just beneath the mine buildings. You can wander across the flats and see where the spur line must have run. There is even a pile of old rails rusting, forgotten, among the weeds.

History of the Crowsnest region

The Crowsnest Pass is one of the three major passes through the Rocky Mountains: the last to be discovered by the Europeans, although it had been used for centuries by the Blackfoot and Cree. The Canadian Pacific Railway completed construction through the pass in 1898, making the exploitation of the coal resources feasible for the developers. Soon the capitalist entrepreneurs arrived on the trains, as did immigrants from Slovakia, Wales, and many other places. Towns sprang up every mile or two through the pass, each connected with a mine along the railway line. The major ones were Bellevue, Blairmore, Coleman, Sentinel, Frank and Hillcrest. The economic bases of these towns were precarious, each dependent upon the fortunes — or failures — of the nearby mines.

Blairmore was renamed in honour of the Minister of Railways, A.G. Blair (a name which certainly has a nicer ring to it than "Tenth Siding," the original name).

The coal years

At first Blairmore was a supply depot for some of the other towns in the pass, but in 1907 Western Canadian Collieries established their management offices in town, making Blairmore an important administrative centre. Coal seams south of the town were mined, but they

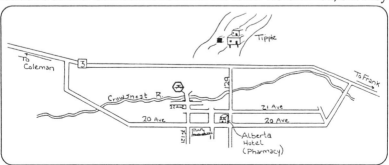

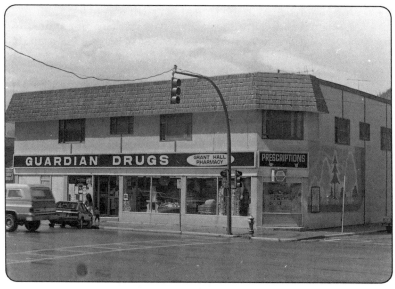

Old Alberta Hotel in Blairmore

were faulted so the mine was closed, and another opened on the present picnic site. The Greenhill Mine began to operate in 1913, and continued as the main source of employment and income for the residents of Blairmore until 1957.

There is a big move afoot to clean up the Crowsnest Pass, and the mining process itself, and you will see occasional signs along the highways in the region proclaiming "the cleanest mine." The slag heap is being hauled away. Large trucks ran back and forth in the distance, one climbing the hill every two or three minutes as we watched lazily from our picnic spot. They climbed to the highway, carrying the traces of the mine away to a landfill site somewhere else. This activity adds an authenticity to our phantom mine — one feels a sense of wonder at the size of the past operation which could keep so many trucks going so many years later.

The prosperous mining industry of Blairmore did compete for a very short time with the illicit rum trading industry: which paid much better, as long as you didn't get caught.

The Rum Runners

Prohibition lasted in Alberta from 1916 until 1923, and at first liquor was smuggled from B.C. and the United States into Alberta. In 1917, B.C. passed an act that severely limited availability of liquor, and the direction of smuggling reversed. British Columbia was supplied from the U.S.A. from illegal stills in the Crowsnest Pass. In

1920 prohibition began in the United States; it was to last until 1933. In 1923, when it ended in Alberta, the coast was clear for smuggling liquor over the border. There was a code of ethics, even among smugglers; some of them were habitual criminals or opportunists, but the more famous were otherwise respectable, upstanding men of the community, running reputable businesses as well as undercover smuggling businesses.

The story of the rum runners in Blairmore centres around Emilio Picariello, who was born in Sicily and moved to Blairmore in 1911. He was a bright and imaginative entrepreneur, and tried his hand at many things over the years. He bought the Alberta Hotel on the main street of Blairmore in 1918, and a few months later was the agent in the Crowsnest Pass for a Lethbridge brewery. He was soon operating a successful bootlegging business, running liquor through the pass into Southern Alberta. Frank Anderson, in his book, *The Rum Runners*, describes the operations;

> Preparatory to opening his sideline, Mr. Pick excavated a small room off the basement and from this room he extended a tunnel a short distance out under the roadway. The entrance to this side room was usually covered with burlap sacking, and in front of this rough curtain were several large barrels in which were stored empty 40-ounce bottles. A favourite device for bringing in liquor was to load trucks with flour. The outer layers of sacks contained flour — in case of a search — but behind this innocent wall were burlap sacks containing bottles of illicit booze. The trucks were able to drive right under the building to deposit their dual loads. The liquor was concealed in the tunnel and the flour was distributed to needy families in the town.
>
> One of Mr. Pick's prized possessions was a player piano which stood in the hotel lounge. When played loudly, as it usually was, it served to drown out the noise of the activity in the basement.

There was much ambiguity surrounding the liquor laws and their enforcement during these years. Although Mr. Pick was clearly breaking the law, he also ran a legitimate business, and did his smuggling in a way that the police could choose to ignore. In fact, he had established a reputation for paying high prices for the many empty bottles he always needed, and even the department of the Attorney General of Alberta sold him regular shipments of bottles for 40 cents a dozen. The kids in town could earn their spending money by washing bottles for cash.

Mr. Pick was executed in 1923 for murder, under questionable judicial circumstances, but his memory remains strong in Blairmore.

He held picnics for the community once a year, the only time that some of the people ever had pop and other treats during the Depression. When his safe was cleared out after his death, many letters from local police and government officials were found — requesting liquor for their weddings and their parties.

Things to do

1. A Prohibition Promenade. Stories about the rum runners in the Crowsnest are now legend, material for plays and movies. The Alberta Hotel in Blairmore was the base from which one of the most revered operators ran his business. The Alberta Hotel is now Grant Hall Pharmacy (now Guardian Drugs) — especially appropriate, because during prohibition a surprising number of diseases were suddenly treated with prescriptions for liquor. In fact, during the Depression demand for certain patent medicines and flavouring extracts grew so rapidly, because they contained a high alcoholic content, that these items were soon removed from grocery stores by law and could only be obtained in the drugstore with a prescription.

As you stand outside the store you can imagine the big trucks arriving to deliver their loads of flour which concealed the cargo of liquor from the stills in Fernie. You can almost see Mr. Pick's four big McLaughlins — the fastest cars of the time — silently driving off into the night across little known trails in the fields towards the border.

Bailey Bridge and Tipple

2. Ask at the Chamber of Commerce office for the Alberta Culture booklet, *Historical Driving Tour: Blairmore, Crowsnest Pass*, and then walk around town and see some of the historic old houses, reflecting the nationality of their original owners, and the wealth and architectural imagination of the times.

3. Walk along the main street to the mining memorial, just across from the post office. The steam engine which used to run on the spur line into Greenhill Mine is there, all painted up and shining as a reminder of much busier days. Standing just in front of the steam engine is a wooden statue of a miner, an axe carving by ex-miner, Don Shannon. The tree from which the carving was made was 300 years old, and 4 feet in diameter. Mr. Shannon, now a local artist, worked many years in Greenhill Mine, and figures that he is personally responsible for a good bit of the slag heap. He also observed that he, like the community, continues to bear traces of the now vanished mine — he has the coal miner's disease, pneumoconiosis.

4. Visit the Crowsnest Museum in Coleman to see fascinating mining memorabilia and to learn about the community.

Things to eat

Soon after Mr. Pick and his family arrived in Canada from Sicily he moved to Fernie. In 1911 he began work in a macaroni factory. The friends he made there became his suppliers and contacts for the rum trade. A tireless and imaginative entrepreneur, Mr. Pick also made and sold ice cream in the streets of Fernie — he was once producing 400 gallons a day — and he started the ice cream parlor in Blairmore.

Macaroni - Cheese Salad

(Serves 4-6)

Cook in boiling water for 7 minutes:
   1 1/2 cups shell macaroni

Drain and cool. Combine with:
   1 cup chopped celery
   1 cup shredded carrots
   1/4 cup chopped onion

In a separate bowl beat together:

1 tin cheddar cheese soup	*1/4 cup salad oil*
2 tsp. vinegar	*1 tsp. sugar*
1 tsp. prepared mustard	*1 tsp. Worcestershire sauce*
salt and pepper to taste	

Pour over mixture and toss. Chill in refrigerator.

Pepperoni Salad

(Serves 6-8)

In a large salad bowl, combine:
   1 head lettuce, torn into pieces
   2 tomatoes, cut into wedges
   1 cup mozzarella cheese, cubed
   1 tin drained garbanzo beans
   1/2 lb. thin sliced pepperoni
   1/4 cup sliced green onion
Pour Italian salad dressing over, sprinkle with salt and pepper, toss.

Italian Salad Dressing

Combine:
   1 cup salad oil   1/4 cup vinegar
   1 tsp. crushed garlic   1 tsp. salt
   1/2 tsp. white pepper   1/2 tsp. celery salt
   1/4 tsp. cayenne   1/4 tsp. dry mustard
Shake or beat well, refrigerate.

Raspberry Rum Trifle

A delightful use for old cake and a great way to smuggle rum into a meal.

Place in a deep dish:
   Remains of yellow, sponge or layer cake

Sprinkle with:
   1/4 cup dark rum

Spread over the pieces:
   2 cups raspberries

Prepare a custard (we tend to purchase Birds Custard Powder and just follow instructions on the packet) and pour it over the cake. Stir the resulting mixture.

Garnish with whipped cream.

The Lemon Cure

For each person, combine:
   1 stick cinnamon
   1 tsp. honey
   pinch of ground cloves
   2 1/2 ounces Lemon Hart Demarara rum
   juice of 1/2 lemon
   1 cup boiling water
Store in a Thermos for transport to picnic site.

32 Cameron Creek
Waterton Park
The Kootenai Brown Picnic

Waterton/Glacier is an International Peace Park on the Canada-United States border. The drive south from Pincher Creek, across slightly rolling prairie does not prepare you for the surprise when you suddenly reach "The Shining Mountains" of Waterton Park. This is the place where the prairies meet the mountains — with no transition at all! This picnic combines the natural beauty of the present with the ghosts of the past. A visit to the site of Oil City is an essential part of this outing — it is just a bit farther along the road from the picnic site.

How to get there

Drive south from Pincher Creek on Highway 6 for 48 km (30 mi.) to the park gate. Continue along to the Information Centre, where you can pick up any brochures. To reach the picnic site, drive 1 km

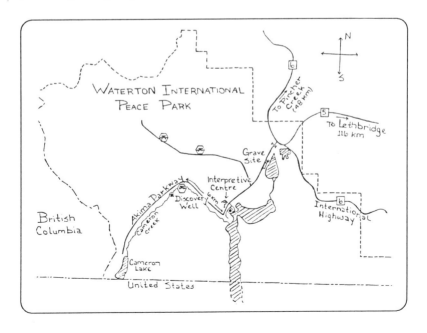

farther and turn right onto the Akamina Parkway. You will come to the picnic site in 6.2 km (4 mi.). It is in a beautiful spot on the edge of Cameron Creek.

The wildflowers

There are more varieties of wildflowers here than in Jasper and Banff combined! Even the roadsides are brilliant with colour from the yellow of black-eyed Susans and the radiant reds of Indian paint-brush and fireweed. There are over 800 different flowering plants in the park, and over 1200 species of plants altogether. The mountain hollyhock and the slender bog orchid are among the hundred or more rare flowering plants which can be found nowhere else in Alberta. Some of the plants are believed to have originated here and survived the last glaciation: the alpine poppy is one of these.

The story

The story of Waterton is really the story of one man, an astonishing man whom everyone called Kootenai Brown because of his fluency in the language of these Indians, and his extensive experience in trading with them. He was born in 1839, and died in 1916. He is buried on the flats by Lower Waterton Lake, where he lies between his two wives, Olive Lyonnaise and Blue Flash of Lightning. Born in England, Brown came to the Waterton district when he was in his late twenties. He had already served with the British colonial forces in India, had been a miner in the northern gold rush, worked as a freighter up the Fraser Canyon and a law officer at Barkerville. He built his first cabin in the Waterton district in 1877, and rarely strayed far for the rest of his life except to ride with the Rocky Mountain Rangers during the Métis uprisings of 1885, patrolling the area between the Red Deer River and the American border.

Kootenai Brown's legacy is the park itself. He founded it, lived in it, and promoted it, until it became a wildlife preserve and finally a national park. Fittingly, he was appointed the first Game Guardian and Fisheries Inspector when the area was designated as Kootenai Lakes Forest Reserve in 1895.

As an experienced miner, Kootenai Brown thought there might be oil in the Waterton hills, and (so the story goes) he invited the local Indians to sample a drink of molasses and kerosene so that if they ever ran into that taste again they would tell him where they'd found it. This system led to the discovery of oil at Seepage Creek, later called Oil Creek, and now known as Cameron Creek. The oil had been used for centuries for its curative powers by the Indians. By soaking it up from the creek with burlap sacks and wringing it out, Brown had enough to oil his wagon. He also supplied the local ranchers for a few years, until investors decided to try drilling. The Rocky Mountain Development Company Limited was incorporated in February, 1901, and drilling began near Oil City. Six months later the promoters estimated that the well would come in at 300 barrels a day, and the excitement began. There were delays at the beginning with equipment breaking down, but even when these were corrected, the flow became erratic, then dwindled to just a trickle. Efforts were made over the next twenty years to find another well-site in the area, but the search led farther afield, and ultimately to the Turner Valley deposit in 1914 (see Turner Valley picnic).

Oil City

To visit the site of the oil rig, continue along the Cameron Lake Road (Akamina Parkway) for 1.6 km (1 mi.) to the historical marker. The flowers in this meadow are wonderful and they flank the site of the first successful oil well in Western Canada. The drill is still in place, and is part of the attractive monument by the creek. If you

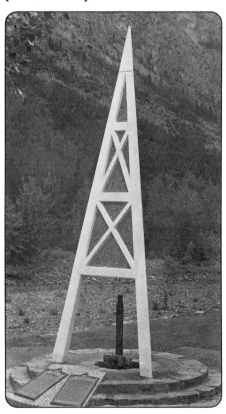

continue along the parkway for 1.3 km (almost a mile) you will come to the site of the city itself. Park well off the road and follow the short path to the town-site. The foundation of the hotel remains to help us to imagine the carefully-surveyed town which was meant to extend for twenty blocks. Land was bought and sold, but this foundation was all that was built of the town — the hotel was never completed, because the boom went bust. The few buildings at the discovery site sat where the parking lot is now. The well, opened in 1902, was closed for good by 1906: it had produced millions of dreams, but only 8,000 gallons of oil.

Things to do

At the picnic site:

1. Wade in the fresh waters of the creek and admire the pretty, brightly-coloured stones on the bottom.

2. See how many different varieties of flowers you can identify. (Don't pick them — leave them for others to enjoy.)

3. Watch for bighorn sheep and the large-eared mule deer which inhabit the area. Watch also for bears.

4. Visit the Oil City site.

Before or after the picnic, you can:

1. Have tea at the Prince of Wales Hotel in Waterton Village, directly across from the Information Centre. The hotel was opened in 1927 by the Great Northern Railway. The hotel was built to serve the bus tours operated by the railway from Montana to Jasper.

2. Hunt for the ferret. Some local naturalists have recently reported black-footed ferret sightings in the park, which is astonishing as the creatures have been believed extinct since 1937.

3. Take the Bear's Hump Hike, a guided tour that lasts about 2 hours and is designed for those who wish they knew more about mountain hiking, but are timid. You will learn all you need to know about mountain safety and bears, as well as about some of the more exciting aspects of hiking in Waterton. The walk starts from the Information Centre; check here for times. Once you have done this, you will be ready to strike out on your own into the back country.

4. The Cameron Lake Trail is an easy, but fascinating 3 km (2 mi.) hike. Cameron Lake is at the end of the Akamina Parkway.

5. Take an international boat ride on Upper Waterton Lake. The boat, which leaves from the dock in the townsite, travels to the American end of the lake.

Things to eat

Stop at the Waterton Bakery in the townsite and buy a selection of the best sausage rolls we have ever encountered. The cheese bread sticks are great snacks to keep people from eating the car upholstery on the way up to the picnic site. The croissants too are perfect. You can buy juice and milk here, as well as ice cream cones. Alternatively, for something a little more elaborate, we have the Bengal Lancers' menu, since Kootenai Brown served briefly in the British Colonial Forces in India.

(Note: there is a water source at the picnic site, but the water should be boiled before drinking.)

MENU

**Moghul Chicken
Potato and Pea Curry
Cucumber Raita
Trifle**

Moghul Chicken

(Serves 4)

This chicken can be cooked ahead at home, since it is delicious cold, or at the picnic.

Cut a broiler chicken into serving-sized pieces.

Prepare a marinade of:
*1 cup yogurt
1/2 inch fresh ginger, grated
2 cloves garlic, crushed
1/2 tsp. cardamon
1/2 tsp. chili powder
1/2 tsp. cinnamon
1/4 cup lemon juice*

Marinate chicken pieces in the mixture in the fridge over night.

Either bake in 375°F oven for 45 minutes and chill; or barbecue at the picnic site.

Potato and Pea Curry

(Serves 4-6)

Peel and dice 5 potatoes.

Heat in a pot:
  3 Tbsp. oil

Add:
  1 tsp. salt   *1 tsp. cumin seed*
  1 tsp. turmeric   *1 tsp. ground coriander*
  1 tsp. mustard seeds   *1/2 tsp. cayenne pepper*

Add potatoes. Stirring constantly, cook until the potatoes are evenly covered with the spices, and slightly crisp (5-10 minutes). Then cover the potatoes with water and simmer for 30 minutes.

Add
  1 cup yogurt
  2 cups frozen peas
And continue cooking for another 5 minutes.

Serve hot or cold.

Cucumber Raita

(Serves 6)

Peel 1 cucumber. Cut in half lengthwise and remove seeds. Slice very thinly.

In another bowl mix together:
  3 Tbsp. grated onion   *2 cups yogurt*
  1/4 tsp. ground cumin   *1/8 tsp. cayenne*
  salt   *dash of coriander*

Stir in cucumber and chill thoroughly.

For dessert we suggest a trifle, in keeping with British tradition.

Trifle

Begin with the remains of a stale cake. Place in a bowl and drizzle with rum or sherry. Cover this soggy cake with 1/2 cup jam or sweetened fruit if available. (Fudge it with tinned fruit cocktail, if necessary.)

Make a trip to your provisioner, and purchase a tin of Bird's Custard. No other brand will do — it was imported to India. Follow instructions to the letter, and when complete, pour the custard over the soggy cake. Cool and serve with a side pitcher of double cream.

33 Fort Macleod Lethbridge
An Unexpected Picnic

This picnic is planned around the last minute, unexpected guests — desirable or not — for whom outpost police wives had to be prepared. It was not uncommon for their husbands to return with prisoners who needed to be fed.

How to get there

Fort Macleod is just 42 km (26 mi.) west of Lethbridge on Highway 3, or 135 km (84 mi.) south of Calgary on Highway 2. The Fort-Museum is on Highway 2/3, which passes through the centre of the town.

The fort is short of picnic sites. There is a picnic table in the back right-hand corner as you enter the square in the centre of the fort. You are welcome to eat there, if you prefer. But we like to spread our blanket between the fort itself and the Stevens Building, which is set up as the old general store. There is a patch of grass between the buildings, and you can sit on the river bank.

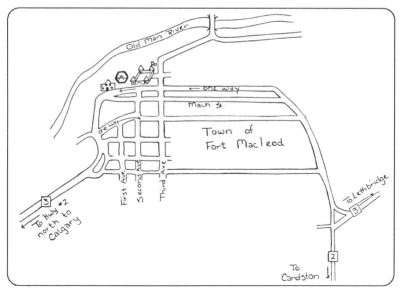

History

The creation of the North-West Mounted Police was long overdue when, on April 28, 1873, at the suggestion of Colonel Robertson-Ross, Prime Minister John A. Macdonald proposed a bill to create a military force to police the western frontier of Canada. Since 1869 there had been a serious need for law enforcement as the whiskey traders, wolfers and hide hunters pursued their own direct and brutal justice system, without controls.

Only one day after the proposal in Parliament a disastrous event occurred in the Cypress Hills in the North-West Territories (later Alberta and Saskatchewan) which was to underline the immediate need for justice in the West. A band of American wolfers attacked an innocent band of Assiniboine Indians in the hills to avenge the theft of their horses; thirty women, men and children were brutally murdered for a crime they did not commit. Although reports of brawls, fights and murders regularly reached Ottawa, this report was the final straw. Those who had concerns about the new bill were instantly persuaded by the horror of this frontier justice, and the bill passed quickly. Soon the North-West Mounted Police, dressed in their red serge uniforms, set out on the long trek to the wild west to quell the disorder and lawlessness. It was June of 1874.

The expedition of 275 officers and men was led by Lieutenant-Colonel G.A. French, with Major J.F. Macleod second in command. The expedition, which also included 339 horses, 142 oxen, 114 Red River carts, 73 wagons, 2 nine-pounder muzzle field guns, and 2 brass mortars, was said to have spread from between 1 1/2 and 5 miles as it crossed the grasslands and forded the swollen streams.

When the forces reached the Sweet Grass Hills they set up camp, and Colonel French and Major Macleod carried on south to Fort Benton to secure the supplies necessary to survive the winter. Here they also engaged the aid of the "half-breed" (Métis) guide, Jerry Potts. Potts had fought in the last great Indian battle at Lethbridge (see Fort Whoop-Up picnic) and had offered to direct the force to this infamous whiskey outpost. Indispensable as a guide, Potts also taught the green-horn Mounties the essential skills and techniques of survival in the West.

When the force finally arrived at Fort Whoop-Up, Macleod prepared for a battle, having been told that about 60 outlaws of various sorts operated their nefarious activities from the fort. But Potts insisted that the fort had long been empty because of the earlier rumours of the coming of the determined new police force. Macleod led his men bravely into the fort only to discover that Potts was correct. Macleod was met by the one man who remained as a resident of the fort, Dave Akers, who offered to sell the fort to Major Macleod for $25,000, but would not accept the policemen's counter-offer of only $10,000.

Fort Whoop-Up was left with the Union Jack flying instead of the free traders' flag, and the force proceeded further up the Oldman River to an island. Here they built Fort Macleod, the first North-West Mounted Police outpost of the west.

Things to do

1. Tour the fort. The fort which you are visiting is a replica of the original but is not on the original site, as the police were forced to relocate to higher ground because of periodic flooding. The display illustrates the colourful and exciting history of the force as it grew from the North-West Mounted Police to the North-West Royal Mounted Police, and finally became today's Royal Canadian Mounted Police.

2. Attend a performance of the famous Musical Ride. There are four performances a day from July 15 to the end of August, and these take place in a riding ring adjacent to the fort. Ten local highschool students dressed in full North-West Mounted Police regalia — the red serge — appear on horseback carrying the lances which once were the Mounties' weapons, and now are used for show. The riders perform an impressive set of manoeuvres, including the charge and retreat. It is a stirring performance, adding authenticity to the old fort's atmosphere.

3. Visit Head-Smashed-In Buffalo Jump. The Fort Macleod Museum features an exhibition focussing on the Blackfoot people, Head-Smashed-In Buffalo Jump, and the technology of hunting and utilizing the buffalo. This exhibit is excellent preparation for a tour of the site itself, about 20 km (12 1/2 mi.) outside of Fort Macleod. (See Head-Smashed-In picnic for more details.)

The Red Serge Wives

Thus far we have spoken of Mounties, traders, outlaws and Indian people, but another exhibit caught our eye, and became the focus of this picnic. NWMP officers often brought their wives to the West, and there is a small display which portrays this little known chapter of Fort Macleod history. These women, often newly wed, transformed outpost cabins into homes, and even became an informal part of the law enforcement team in Canada's wild west. Aside from raising a family and keeping the house, they were also expected

to serve as matrons, accompanying female prisoners from the detachment jail (usually in the officer's home) to court or to the hospital. Homemaker, cook, wife, mother, and jail keeper — a tall order!

In a book available in the gift shop, *Red Serge Wives*, stories of the experiences of these women have been collected. Life for a frontier police wife was full of surprises. One woman opened the ice box to discover grisly packages on their way to a post mortem, and her husband asked, "Where else could I put them?" Another found a murderer ready to turn himself in at her door while everyone else was out hunting for him. This frightened woman at first refused to let the fugitive in, but it was a cold winter night, and so finally she opened the door and quickly directed him to the bed and blankets in the jail. She waited nearby, listening until she heard him begin to snore, then rushed to the door, slammed it shut and threw the lock. Her husband returned later, exhausted and discouraged from his fruitless search, and annoyed at his wife's suggestion that the prisoner was already in the jail!

What to eat

The cooking duties of the police wives were quite unpredictable; they never knew how many people to expect for meals, as overnight guests arrived without warning, and prisoners had to be fed. Ruby Cutting recalls, "Often I'd find myself alone at meal time, but more often there would be two or three prisoners or a visiting Justice of Peace to think of."

She quickly learned to keep a piece of boiled ham or bacon or headcheese ready in case extras showed up for a meal. She never forgot the first time the butcher gave her a pig's head. Following the directions in a book a friend had sent her, she good-naturedly cleaned and boiled "the great grinning thing" to make the headcheese. It was so popular with visiting Mounties that she ended up making it every two months!

Headcheese

You can buy this delicious cold meat at your deli, or make your own from this recipe adapted from *The Old World Kitchen*. Headcheese is made from the meat and skin of a pig's head, sometimes salted first, sometimes not. Other trimmings are often included such as the heart, trotters and tail, or even a piece of shin beef. Whatever the ingredients, they must be boiled with aromatics until all is soft and gelatinous. It is a most excellent dish.

Time: Start 3 days before; 30 minutes plus 4 hours cooking.

> 1 pig's head, complete with ears and tongue
> 3 to 4 bay leaves
> 1 tsp. salt
> 1 bunch of sage
> onion skins (the papery brown outside only)
> 1 tsp. peppercorns

You will need a large stewpan and a pudding basin or earthenware mold. If you want the headcheese to be a pretty pink, put it to pickle rubbed with 1/4 pound salt and 1/2 ounce saltpetre (from the drug store) for 48 hours before cooking.

Have the butcher split the head in two. Put it in a heavy saucepan just large enough to accommodate the meat, with the aromatics, salt, and onion skins (these serve to tint the jelly a pale gold — the onion itself is not used, as it encourages the jelly to ferment). Cover with cold water. Bring to a boil, and then turn down the heat and skim the froth off the liquid.

Simmer steadily for 4 hours, until the meat virtually drops off the bones. Take out all the solids and strain the stock back into the pan. Leave the stock to boil and reduce uncovered while you pick the meat off the bones. Chop all the pieces and pack them neatly into a pudding basin or earthenware mold.

When the stock is well reduced to about 2 cups, taste and adjust its seasoning and pour it over the meat. Allow it to cool, and put it in the refrigerator for 24 hours for the jelly to set solid. When you are ready to eat it, unmold by pouring hot water swiftly over the outside. It will unmold instantly and elegantly. Serve on a bed of watercress and parsley.

If you are going to eat it right away, stir plenty of chopped parsley and a little grated lemon rind into the jelly when it is cool but still liquid, before you pour it over the meat. For a sharper flavour, add a tablespoon of vinegar to the stock before its final reduction.

Headcheese will keep in the refrigerator for two weeks, but don't store it in the freezer or the jelly is likely to liquefy when you defrost it.

Serve plenty of strong English mustard with the cold headcheese. Accompany the headcheese with pickles, crusty rolls and potato salad.

Company Potato Salad

(serves 10)

Combine in a bowl:
> 10 medium cooked, diced potatoes
> 1 peeled, diced cucumber
> 1 medium onion, chopped (red, if possible)
> 1 green pepper, chopped
> 2 eggs, hard-boiled and coarsely chopped
> 1 small tin pimento, chopped
> 1 1/2 tsp. salt
> 3/4 tsp. celery seed
> 1/4 tsp. pepper
> 1 tsp. fresh summer savory
> 4 leaves fresh basil, snipped

Mix well and chill.

Prepare a dressing of:
> 1/2 cup whipping cream
> 1/2 cup mayonnaise
> 1/4 cup vinegar
> 1 Tbsp. prepared mustard

Shake well in sealed jar and carry to picnic site. Toss with potato mixture 1/2 hour before serving. Garnish with raw, unsalted shelled sunflower seeds and fresh, snipped parsley.

At the end of your picnic go into the general store and buy the biggest, best ice cream cone ever! They are inexpensive, and "small" is big, "medium" is large, and "large" is humungous!!!

34 Head-Smashed-In Buffalo Jump
Fort Macleod
An Indian Picnic

Designated a UNESCO World Heritage Site in 1981, this is the best preserved jump in North America. It was in use for at least 5,700 years, until the last drive in the 1850s. By then the gun and the fur trade had virtually caused the buffalo to disappear from the plains, and from the centre of the lives of the Plains Indians. This is now a remarkable interpretive site. Plan to spend at least half a day exploring the centre and the surrounding fields; there is much to learn here.

How to get there

Just outside Fort Macleod, the site is 18 km (12 mi.) west of Highway 2 on secondary Highway 785, the Spring Point Road. The facility is open from 9 to 9, Victoria to Labour Day; 10 to 5 from Labour Day to the end of October. There is no admission charge but voluntary donations are suggested.

The picnic site we prefer is in a tipi ring on the plain below the sweeping majesty of the buffalo jump itself. There are no facilities, just the prairie. Full facilities are available in the Interpretive Centre.

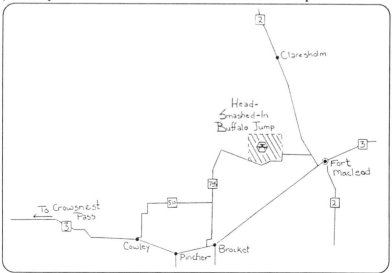

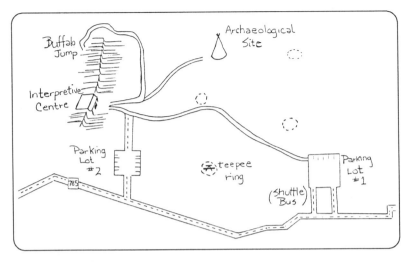

The buffalo

The animals which until recently roamed the plains in the thousands were the heart of the spiritual and economic life of the Plains Indians. The jump was used on specific occasions after a number of tribes had gathered — this type of hunting was a communal activity, and required many people: scouts, buffalo runners, butchers, dressers, and so on. Since every part of the buffalo was put to use, the number of different tasks and skills required was substantial. The actual processing of the animals took place immediately, at the bottom of the jump. The hides were cleaned and stretched to dry in the sun; the meat was cut into strips and dried on racks, then mixed with berries and fat tissues to make pemmican; the bones were crushed and boiled to extract the marrow and make bone grease; the hides were used for clothing and tipis; sinews made rope and bowstrings; the dung was dried for fuel. The products from the jump of a herd of several hundred buffalo would last a whole winter.

The noise of the thundering herd rushing over the cliff and falling to the plain below can only be imagined. It must have been a wondrous and terrifying sight. According to Peigan oral tradition, one day a boy was standing beside the jump at the bottom watching the great beasts fall, but he had misjudged his point of observation and became caught among them as they landed one upon the other. Later as the people were butchering the animals they came across the boy, crushed between two great buffalo, with his head smashed in; hence the name of this place, and a perpetual warning.

Because of their importance to the Indians the buffalo were revered as a gift from the Great Spirit. The drive to the jump was preceded by several days of ceremonies and purification. Before

dawn on the day of the jump the scouts, dressed in animal hides for camouflage, went out into the gathering basin and moved among the buffalo, gently nudging them in the direction of the rock-lined drive lanes leading to the cliff. When the animals had entered the lanes, a hundred or more other people would suddenly appear on the flanks and to the sides of the herd, shouting to frighten the buffalo into stampeding over the cliff. Those animals that did not die instantly were quickly dispatched with spears and clubs, for it was believed that survivors might warn the rest of the buffalo about the trap.

The Interpretive Centre

A remarkable piece of engineering, the centre is set into the cliff to the left of the jump site. Its grey colouring blends with the rocks, as does its step-like arrangement of blocks, aligned with the cliff slope. Viewed from a distance it adds to the overall beauty of the site. You enter the Interpretive Centre from the bottom of the cliff. The exhibits lead you slowly up through the building, and you finish on top, where the upper trail begins. Within the centre are fascinating displays, and well-informed staff to answer your questions. The film presentation in the theatre is worth seeing, and the cafeteria is a good place for a "prairie dog" or a "buffalo burger."

Tipi rings

As your eyes become used to the landscape you will notice several tipi rings in the fields below the jump. They are simply circles of rocks which once held down the sides of tipis. Some of the stones are half buried in the prairie turf now, but a few new ones are more easily spotted. Tipis were portable homes perfectly adapted to the life of the Plains Indians as hunters of the buffalo. The walls were made of buffalo hides mounted on three or four long poles. The bottom was anchored with pegs and stones. These homes were easily moved from camp to camp as the buffalo herds moved, and poles were replaced as necessary when the camp was near a wooded area.

At the time of a jump the plain in front of you would have been covered with tipis, as many tribes came together. Smoke would be curling up from many fires for treating the hides and meat. Several of these have been excavated by archaeologists to reveal details of life in years long past. A picnic here on the plain beneath the great cliff, in what was the centre of a Plains Indian family home in years gone by, was for us a memorable experience which we highly recommend.

Things to do

1. Follow along the Lower Trail from the Interpretive Centre to the bottom of the jump. Visit with the archaeologists as they excavate a dig. Learn how this is done, and what they expect to find.

2. Walk along the Upper Trail to the top of the buffalo jump. The view from here across the prairie is spectacular. A telescope is mounted to help you to enjoy the details of the vista. Look carefully at the edge of the cliff, just below the crest of the buffalo jump. If you watch you will see the many cliff swallows enter and leave their grey mud nests on the side of the rock. With the help of the telescope you may even catch sight of their hungry nestlings, and you may also notice yellow-bellied marmots sunning themselves on the rocks.

3. Spend some time — and perhaps some money — in the gift shop in the Interpretive Centre. The native jewellery is very attractive, and the book selection is excellent.

Things to eat

The menu is serviceberry soup, buffalo jerky (if you can't find a buffalo, substitute beef); buffalo chips (if you can't find a buffalo, substitute potato chips); dandelion salad (we know you can find these); and Indian grease bread with blueberry syrup and yogurt.

Serviceberry Soup

(Serves 6)
(Ruth Many Grey Horses, Blood Reserve)

Serviceberry is another name for saskatoon berries. There are different strains of the berry across the West, and names sometimes vary by region.

3 cups serviceberries, dried or fresh
9 cups water
flour

Wash the berries and place in a large pot. Cover them with water. Boil until berries break and water colours.

Remove from heat. Make a paste of flour and water. Slowly add the paste to the berry mixture. Stir until thickened. Add enough sugar to suit your taste. Pour into Thermos, and serve at picnic site.

Buffalo or Beef Jerky

In case (like us) you have often wondered, the word "jerky" comes from the word *charqui* which means dried beef. The product was prepared by Indians, voyageurs and traders by sun-drying the meat on racks. Occasionally they would light a fire to keep the bugs away.

Since the sun is unreliable and we have ovens, we will use this more consistent method to dry the meat.

Obtain beef; round steak is a good cut to use, because it has so little fat. Also, buffalo meat can be found at specialty butchers in most cities.

Carefully remove all fat, and season the meat with salt, pepper, oregano, basil, marjoram and thyme, pounding the seasoning into the meat.

Cut the meat into 1/2" strips along the grain. Spread on racks in your oven and put heat to about 120°F (as low as it will go). Leave the door partly open so moisture can escape. Turn strips over every four hours or so.

When done, the strips will be dry right through (16-24 hours), but flexible enough to bend without breaking. Store in the refrigerator or freezer in a paper (not plastic) bag.

To serve hand out pieces, and bite off chunks.

If you don't want to use the jerky for a while, it can be ground up and made into pemmican — see Rocky Mountain House picnic for recipe.

Buffalo Chips (the ones you can eat)

To make them yourself, peel lots of potatoes, and slice paper-thin. An automatic slicer or food processor is best for this. Soak in cold salted water for an hour, drain and dry in paper towelling. Deep fat fry a few at a time in very hot fat, very briefly, until golden brown. Let drain on paper towelling, cool, salt and serve.

Or, buy a box of potato chips.

Dandelion Green Salad

(Serves 4)

Combine:
One cup tender young dandelion leaves
1 apple, chopped
1 medium onion, thin sliced
2 carrots, grated

Dress with oil and vinegar, toss and serve.

Indian Grease Bread
(Sandra Eagle Child, Blood Reserve)

4 cups flour
3 tsp. baking powder
1 tsp. salt
1 1/2 cups water

Combine flour, baking powder and salt in bowl. Gradually add the water a little at a time. Knead dough until it does not stick to your hands. (If dough becomes too thick, add more water; if it is too thin, add more flour.) Place dough on floured surface. Shape into round balls, then flatten the balls and shape like a doughnut. Heat a large skillet containing at least half an inch of grease. Fry the dough for 5 minutes on each side or until brown. Serve hot or cool with jam or butter.

Blueberry Sauce

4 cups blueberry juice (about 7 cups berries)
2 cups sugar
2 cups corn syrup

Place 6 to 8 cups blueberries in a large kettle; crush with potato masher. Add 1/2 cup water. Heat mixture, mashing fruit as it cooks. Quickly bring to a full rolling boil, stirring constantly. Pour mixture into damp jelly bag; let drip. When cool enough to handle, squeeze out remaining juice by force. Discard pulp.

Make syrup by measuring 4 cups juice into kettle. Then stir in sugar and syrup. Bring to full rolling boil. Remove from heat, skim if necessary. Immediately pour into clean hot jars. Adjust lids; process in boiling water bath 10 minutes. Yield: 4 pints.

A final word: be sure to take lots of fluid to drink — the combination of jerky and potato chips builds up a thirst. Try cranberry juice and lots of cold water.

35 Fort Whoop-Up
Oldman River
A Fort Whoop-Up Picnic

Fort Whoop-Up, in Indian Battle Park on the banks of the Oldman River, is a concentrated collection of history and nature. Museums, the fort, an Indian village, a coal mine, a nature centre and a well-planned recreational area are the attractions of this picnic, so plan to while away at least half a day here. Although the theme of the picnic is the whiskey fort, the actual picnic site is in Indian Battle Park picnic ground.

How to get there

The park is on the southwest side of Lethbridge. It can be reached from Highway 3 (Crowsnest Trail) by turning south on Scenic Drive,

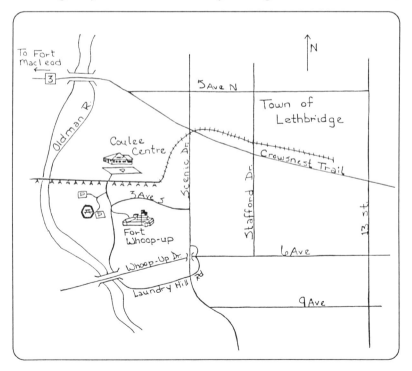

and then west on either 3rd Avenue South or Laundry Hill Drive. (Avoid Whoop-Up Drive, as it does not lead to the site.)

There are several picnic areas in the park, but we prefer a table near the Baroness Shelter, because it has a great story attached to it!

The Blackfoot Confederacy

In 1869 the Blackfoot Confederacy, which incorporated the Blackfoot, Peigan and Blood tribes, dominated the prairies. The strength, pride and courage of these peoples inspired fear in their longtime enemies, the Cree. But only a year later the Cree attacked and almost defeated their enemy. The Blackfoot were much weakened and only with reinforcement from their allies, the Blood and Peigan tribes, did they maintain a now-shaky dominance of the region. What had caused such a rapid demise of the so recently self-sufficient Blackfoot?

The decline of the Blackfoot began with disease brought by the white man, and was reinforced by the rapid drop in the numbers of buffalo. The smallpox epidemic, which reached the Blackfoot camp in the autumn of 1869, killed between 40 and 50 percent of the remaining people. Morale in the camp at the junction of the Oldman and St. Mary's Rivers was very low when the American traders arrived from Fort Benton in Montana.

The fort

In 1869, after whiskey trading had been declared illegal in America, traders Hamilton and Healy came along the Bull Trail and over the border into Canada where they built a fort near the Blackfoot camp. Officially known as Fort Hamilton, the place acquired its nickname from a casual comment made by a Mr. Wye when he was leaving for Fort Benton. He bade farewell, saying, "Don't let the Indians whoop you up." The allusion was to being "rounded up" by the Indians, but the meaning quickly changed. Fort Whoop-up was the first and most famous of the forty-four whiskey forts built in the next few years on the southern prairies.

Whoop-Up was temporary home to a number of disreputable enterprisers: the wolfers, the suppliers of buffalo products — hides, tongues and humps — and the whiskey traders. These people were motivated by the profits to be made from short-term projects, most of which exploited the Indians. Their enterprises, however, contributed to their own demise; wolves became scarce in the area, the buffalo vanished almost completely, and the Indians were so demoralized by the whiskey, disease and dietary changes instigated by the white man that they were no longer efficient hunters — and there were few buffalo to hunt, anyway.

The first fort lasted only a year — the Indian people burned it to the ground in the spring as soon as the traders left for the bush. When they returned, however, the traders built a stronger fort, and only the impending arrival of the North-West Mounted Police officers in 1874 could stop the insidious whiskey trade.

The traders exchanged one cup of whiskey, or "fire water" — an expression which accurately describes the taste — for each fur pelt. The Indians quickly became addicted to the fire water, and lost the incentive to hunt and trap. They would trade anything, including their own clothing and living supplies, to obtain the drink. The whiskey mixture was addictive because it was usually made with opium-based pain killers as well as with raw alcohol. Cayenne pepper, tobacco and lye often added to the "firey" taste. Recipes varied, but they were all strongly addictive, and in just one year, the health of the Indians deteriorated markedly, setting the stage for the Cree attack in 1870.

The battle

The Cree attacked at dawn; the noise of the attack aroused the nearby camps of the Peigan and Blood, which had not been noticed by the advance scouts of the Cree — a fatal error. The Cree were quickly outnumbered, encircled by the Blackfoot Confederacy, and almost 300 Cree were killed. The battle took place on the west side of the river — across from Indian Battle Park. This was the last major battle between Canadian Indian tribes; in 1871 a formal peace treaty was signed between the traditional enemies, The Cree and the Blackfoot. The final capitulation took place eight years later with the signing of Treaty Number Seven in 1877, confining their as-yet undetermined future to the borders of reserves, fractions of their range during the preceding centuries. The echoes of the war cries of these great peoples have died away on the plains, and now the shrieking whistles at Fort Whoop-Up are those of trains, not warriors. The gun shots still heard occasionally are blanks fired for tourists from an old cannon on the flats near the Indian village display.

The end of the whiskey traders

The whiskey era in the west was short-lived, but the damage was permanent. The federal government soon realized what was happening, and the North-West Mounted Police Force was created in 1874 to ride West and plant the British system of law in the lawless land. The impressive force marched their horses West (see the Fort Macleod picnic), but word of their travel preceded them to Fort Whoop-Up. By the time the Mounties arrived, only one man was left, affable Dave Akers, who tried to sell the fort to Major Macleod. The price was too high, and there was no justice to be meted out, since the outlaws had escaped. So the Mounties rode on and established their post at Fort Macleod. Fort Whoop-Up was left to age and collapse in time, after its brief moment in the historical spotlight.

Things to do

1. Visit the reconstructed fort, which is now an interpretive centre. Make sure you walk across the central square to the back corner of the fort, where the whiskey brewing room stands open to the air because of the large fire required for the preparation of the

brew. The cauldron is set up as it might have been, upon a tripod over an open fire.

2. Take the Whoop-Up train ride: a must! The interpreters will make you aware of the many features of the park, and regale you with amusing historical anecdotes. There is a small charge, but it is well worth it.

3. Visit the Helen Schuler Coulee Centre and Nature Reserve, located at the opposite end of Indian Battle Park from the fort.

4. Wander along some of the self-guiding nature trails, or the coal trail.

5. Admire the huge trestle bridge which spans the river valley in the middle of the park. The CPR High Level Bridge was built in 1907-09, and was then the longest and highest steel viaduct in the world. It is 95 m high (307 ft.) and 1,639 m across (5,327 ft.).

6. Follow the 1 kilometre walking trail which leads to the Galt Museum up on the hill, and learn more about the history and growth of the region.

And now, the story . . .

Once upon a time there was an aging baroness in England named Angela Bartlett Burdett-Coutts. She had inherited lots of money from her banker father. She had invested some of it in some coal mines in western Canada, but had never had any interest in going there. Since she was getting on in years, she began to worry about what would happen to her money when she died. She had not married and had no heirs, at least none that she wanted to leave all that money to. But she had a male secretary whom she liked, and since he was considerably younger than herself, she decided to adopt him and thus make him her heir. The government would not permit him to be adopted since at twenty-seven he was hardly a child, so the baroness married him. Married life must have agreed with her since she lived for another forty years. (When she did die in 1906, the baroness was the last person to be buried uncremated in Westminster Cathedral.)

The nearby picnic shelter is named after our baroness only indirectly; both shelters are named after the sternwheelers which carried coal from Coalbanks to Medicine Hat in the 1880s, the Alberta and the Baroness. The Baroness sternwheeler was, of course, named after our beneficent baroness. The Baroness shelter is not available to the general public but can be booked for group picnics. It has electricity as well as the wood stove. The Alberta Shelter, however, is available to the general public, in case it rains.

Things to eat

Here is the recipe you've been waiting for:

Whoop-up Wallop (Fire Water)

1 gallon of high wine (80% rum)
3 gallons of water (river water)
1 quart of alcohol
1 pound of rank black chewing tobacco
1 handful of red peppers
1 bottle of Jamaica ginger
1 quart of black molasses
painkiller medicine, if available
Castile soap or lye
water ad libitum

Mix well and boil until strength is drawn from tobacco and peppers. Add red ink for desirable colour. Serve hot.

Because the last time we were at the fort there was a pancake brunch for the public, we suggest that you do the same — have a sourdough flapjack brunch. Bring along sausages and maple syrup. Another treat that you might like to try on this picnic is rose hip preserve; put it on your pancakes!

Campfire Flapjacks

(Serves 4-6)

You will need to refer to the Calgary Heritage picnic for sourdough starter, if you don't have any on hand. Feed it, and use it to make the pancakes.

How to feed your sourdough
In a mixing bowl combine your 1/2 cup starter with 2 cups warm water and 2 cups flour. Beat well and set in warm place, free from drafts, to develop overnight. Cut off 1/2 cup for the next time and proceed with your recipe.

To the remaining sponge add:
1-2 eggs
1 tsp. soda

1 tsp. salt
1 tsp. sugar
2 Tbsp. oil

Blend together. Bake on a hot, greased griddle.

Rose hips are the most concentrated source of Vitamin C that nature offers, so we like to keep some around for our toast or pancakes, or to go with meats. The Indians in the area pounded rose hips into their pemmican.

Rose Hip Preserves

Three rose hips equal 1 orange in Vitamin C content, and cooking does not destroy the vitamin. Gather the hips after the first frost, or all winter long, from the bushes which in the summer flower with prairie roses. Dry the hips and store in tins if not using them immediately. Otherwise, remove the ends, cover them with water and simmer until they are soft, 8 - 10 minutes, then mash with a potato masher. Press the pulp through a colander to remove the seeds. To make jam, boil 2/3 of a cup of sugar to 1 cup of pulp. Store in small jars, as it doesn't keep well once opened. Keep opened jars in the refrigerator.

36 Nikka Yuko Japanese Garden Lethbridge
A Zen Picnic

This picnic takes place in a park, near the peaceful Japanese Garden in the heart of Lethbridge. The emphasis is on beauty, tasteful and restful arrangements of pleasing things which do not so much stimulate the mind as encourage internal peace.

How to get there

Henderson Park is in southeast Lethbridge, just off Mayor Magrath Drive. To get to the picnic spot turn east on North Parkside Drive and enter the park at the Kinsmen Picnic Ground.

The table we like is near the lake, just to the left of the shelter as you face the water. If you find the picnic ground too distracting, take a blanket and place it on the grass just beside the lake, so that you can see the Japanese Gardens in the distance across the water.

Zen

The Zen philosophy teaches meditation, peace, and concentration on only one thing at a time. It encourages intuitive rather than intellectual thinking. It is as much a part of Japanese society as the tea ceremony, judo, the *ikebana* art of flower arranging, landscape painting, and handwriting, all of which have deep religious significance.

To fully appreciate a garden or a meal within the Zen tradition, it should be approached as a single, unique experience, isolated from distractions. A meal should be pleasing to look at, with an interesting texture, and a taste which is pleasant but not over-powering. Each taste should be savoured individually; a vegetable dish should be prepared so that each piece is recognizable and adds to the effect of the whole. The meal should be eaten in a quiet place, with few distractions to interfere with the appreciation of the food. A view should be savoured for its colour, texture and total composition, an effect which is best achieved within the Japanese garden.

The Japanese heritage

The Japanese community in Lethbridge is the second largest in Canada. The first influx of Japanese people to the region occurred at

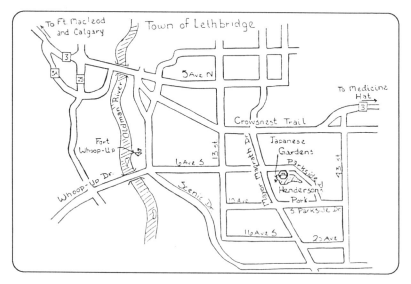

the turn of the century. Many were men who came to earn money to take back to Japan; some stayed and were later joined by their families. They settled mainly in B.C. but were never really integrated into mainstream society because of the racism of the dominant political group of the day. When World War II was declared the Japanese Canadians were classed as "enemy aliens," their property seized under the War Measures Act, and 22,000 people were forced to live in camps and ghost towns for the duration of the war.

Meanwhile, in the prairies the sugar beet farmers had lost their labour force to the army. They requested that some of the Japanese internees be assigned to assist them, and so several thousand Japanese people were moved to Lethbridge to work in the fields. (The Lethbridge camp was located where the exhibition grounds are now.) After four years of enforced residence many stayed on in the Lethbridge area after the war, and have since been joined by relatives and friends from Japan. The Japanese community in Lethbridge is now a driving force, and the inspiration behind the beautiful garden in Henderson Park.

The Nikka Yuko Japanese Garden

A walk through the garden is an integral part of this picnic. We recommend that you take this walk after your picnic, when your mind is free of the responsibility of the meal, and you are ready to rest and enjoy the serenity of the carefully designed environment. The ancient concept of the Japanese garden is the creation of a place which brings peace to both eye and spirit. This involves careful planning for colour, arrangement of plants, and overall design. You enter the garden through a pavilion, having removed your shoes according to Japanese custom. You will be welcomed by Japanese-Canadian interpretive guides who will explain the building to you, taking you past the tea room to the entrance to the garden. You are free to wander in the garden on your own, and to stay as long as you wish.

The garden is divided into five parts which are connected by a winding path: the dry garden, a mountain and waterfall, a stream, ponds and islands, and a prairie garden. Because Japanese plants are not adapted to the southern Alberta climate, Canadian plants have been used to create the desired effect. Japanese landscape architects have designed the pavilion, the bridges and the gates to resemble the Nikka Yuko Garden in Japan. Benches are placed here and there to permit restful enjoyment of the various vistas.

There is much symbolism here — the pagoda has five layers, each representing an element: earth, water, fire, wind and sky. The Japanese temple bell, with its deep, resonant sound, is the friendship bell, characterizing the relations between Canada and Japan. You will perhaps notice that there are no cultivated flowers in the garden to disturb the formal patterns of green. The attention to detail is impressive, and on close examination you will notice that the stream beds are lined with evenly sized, flat pebbles — these were carefully collected by members of the Japanese community and placed during a "pebble picnic" in the construction phase many years ago.

This is a mature garden, over twenty years old now. It reflects the centuries-old tradition of Japanese formal gardens, planned as landscape pictures which use naturally occurring components — trees,

shrubs, rocks — combined with artificially created streams and waterfalls. There is a harmony of the whole, a place to consider the Zen art of contemplating nature. The Zen philosophy has had a deep influence on gardening. An early book on garden design was written in the Kamakura period (1189-1392) by a Zen priest. This garden is an excellent representation of the Zen tenet of understatement. The effect should be implied, and the observer completes the picture with a personal interpretation.

A visitor to the garden, sharing a bench at the far end of the path, quietly observed that returning to the pavilion along the same path is not at all repetitious, but reveals an entirely new pattern. He had absorbed the meaning of the garden, and his quiet enjoyment spread along the bench to us.

Things to eat

Our Japanese picnic features sweet and sour tofu — one of our favourites — and sticky rice. Dessert is fresh fruit.

For those of you who have wondered how the Japanese cook their rice so that it sticks together to form mounds, and even hangs onto the chop sticks, here is a recipe adapted from *The Complete Book of Japanese Cooking*, by Elizabeth Lambert Ortiz with Mitsuko Endo.

Sticky Rice

(Serves 4)

1/2 kg rice
8 cm square of kombu (kelp)
1/2 L water
100 ml rice vinegar
25 ml sugar
10 ml salt

Thoroughly wash the rice in several changes of water until the water runs clear. Drain in a sieve for at least 1 hour. Clean the seaweed with a damp cloth and cut with kitchen shears into a 1 cm fringe. Disperse the seaweed in the rice. Add the water, cover, and bring to a boil over high heat, removing the seaweed just before the water boils. Reduce the heat to moderate and cook for 5 - 6 minutes, then reduce the heat to very low and cook for 15 minutes. Raise the heat to high for 10 seconds, and then let the rice stand off the heat for 10 minutes.

In a small saucepan, combine the rice vinegar, sugar and salt. Heat through, stirring to mix. Turn the rice out into a large, shallow dish. Pour the vinegar mixture, little by little, over the rice, mixing it with a shamoji (wooden spatula) or a fork, fanning it vigorously to make it glisten.

Sweet and Sour Tofu

(6 servings)

Cut into half-inch cubes:
16 ounces of tofu

Marinate in:
2 Tbsp. soy sauce
2 Tbsp. sherry

Cut into wedges:
1 large onion
2 green peppers
1 sweet red pepper

Cut into thin slices:
2 stalks celery
2 carrots

Stir fry in your wok over an even but hot fire for 3 - 5 minutes. Add a little oil as necessary.

Add:
1 tin pineapple chunks, drained
Continue stirring another 3-5 minutes.

Combine in a separate bowl:
2 Tbsp. honey
2 Tbsp. vinegar
1 cup stock
And add to the wok, along with the tofu and the marinade.

Dissolve:
2 Tbsp. corn starch in
1/4 cup water
And add to the vegetable mixture.

Heat, stirring until the sauce thickens. Just before serving add slivers of almonds.

For dessert, carefully cut a variety of fresh fruit into pieces and arrange attractively on a platter. Garnish with fresh mint leaves.

37 Dinosaur Provincial Park
Brooks
An Underwater Picnic

Seventy-five million years ago this land was a coastal plain where dinosaurs lurked in the swamps. Just 3 million years later the dinosaurs had vanished and the area was covered by a vast inland sea.

How to get there

The park is located 8 km (5 mi.) north and 48 km (30 mi.) northeast of Brooks — refer to the map. It is a two-hour drive from Drumheller. The final approach to the park entrance is a short gravel road at the end of Highway 551.

To reach the picnic site drive through the park entrance and, following the road, straight ahead into the picnic area. Do not take the sharp left over the bridge just yet — it leads into the campground and on to the Natural Preserve. Instead, drive around the picnic area to the left — it is a circular drive, so if you miss the first time, you'll get another chance. Follow the road to the second little parking lot which

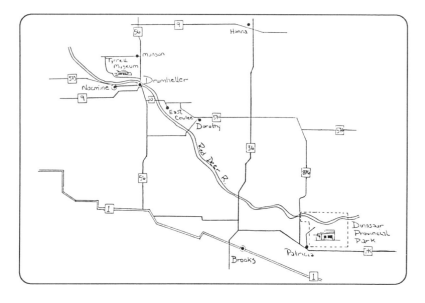

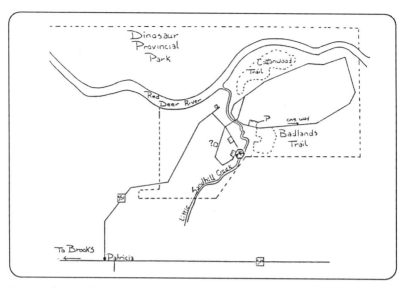

is past the confectionery. Park your car, and select a picnic table on the edge of the creek. There are two in particular with especially fine views of the valley and the hoodoos — you'll know which ones.

History

Seventy-five million years ago much of this region was a huge plain with marshy areas and rich deltas emptying into the sea. The drastic climatic change to the present makes this hard to imagine, but there really were ancestors of breadfruit and magnolias growing where now there is mostly cactus. The region was inhabited by many creatures: there were crocodiles, and turtles as big as umbrellas. Some of the fish were as much as ten metres long; there is a skeleton of a Xiphactinus on display in the Tyrrell Museum in Drumheller, with the skeleton of slightly smaller fish that he choked on — little wonder!

You are picnicking on the coastal lowlands of a great inland sea which covered most of what is now central Saskatchewan and Alberta.

There are many different fossils. Clams and oysters abounded — their fossilized shells are easily identified in the rocks. Ammonites, animals related to the modern squid, became extinct at the end of the Cretaceous Period. There were frogs and salamanders among the reeds. This last flooding of Alberta took place about 72 million years ago.

Things to do

1. Visit the Tyrrell Museum Field Station: a must. Allow an hour or more for this, as the display is excellent, and there is much to learn. The station is situated on the approach to the park entrance. It is just off the road to the right as you arrive, and is open daily from Victoria Day to Thanksgiving, and on weekends through the winter.

2. Follow one of the self-guiding trails. The brochures which explain the numbered points of interest are available at the park gate at the south end of the picnic ground. The "Badlands Trail" involves some steep hills, and the "Cottonwood Flats Trail" follows the edge of the Red Deer River, which is really only a small stream here.

3. Drive around the nature preserve by crossing over the bridge at the south end of the campground, then proceeding through the campground. Although the drive is only 3.5 km (2 mi.) long it can take an hour or so, and is well worth the trip. At the far end of the Preserve are several dinosaur skeletons in situ. The archaeological sites are protected by glass, but the skeletons have been partially excavated, and the digs are fascinating.

4. Take a Parks & Recreation guided tour of the restricted nature preserve. Phone Parks office for details 378-4342.

Miscellaneous information

It is illegal to remove any material or artifacts from the park. The reserve has been set up to provide public access to some of the protected sites. Please respect the irreplaceable nature of the things you are seeing, and leave them there.

Things to eat

This picnic takes place in a tropical sea environment—below the surface of history, as it were. We suggest that you select a menu from some of the following, and we will supply a few interesting recipes, like turtle soup and octopus salad, and "Fish in the Fern" casserole.

```
┌─────────────────────┐
│   ┌─────────────┐   │
│   │   M E N U   │   │
│   └─────────────┘   │
└─────────────────────┘
```

smoked oysters
shrimp cocktail
turtle soup
chilled garlic frogs legs
octopus salad
seafood salad
fiddlehead salad (ferns)
mineral water
seashell pasta salad
tinned salmon — especially the bones!
mangoes

Turtle Soup

(Serves 6)

1 pound turtle meat, cut into pieces
3 cups water
3 cups stock
bay leaf
1/2 tsp. thyme
2 cloves
1/4 tsp. ground allspice
1/4 tsp. freshly ground black pepper
1/2 tsp. salt
dash cayenne

Combine the above ingredients in a saucepan, bring to a boil, and let simmer for 30 minutes.

Sauté:
  2 *medium onions, chopped*

Purée in a blender:
  1 *cup peas*
  1 *cup corn kernels*
  1 *potato, diced*

Add to soup base and stir in:
  1 *Tbsp. flour*
  1 *tin tomatoes, drained (about 1 1/2 cups)*

Cook for 10 minutes, and add to soup, along with:
  1 *Tbsp. chopped parsley*
  2 *cloves garlic, minced*
  juice of 1 lemon
Simmer for at least 2 hours, or until the meat is tender.

Octopus Salad

(Serves 4-6)

Take 1 small octopus (about 2 pounds); remove mouth, anal portion and eyes; slip knife inside and remove and discard yellowish pouch and attached membranes. Clip and discard the tips of the tentacles. Wash well in running water to remove gelatinous portions.

Beat the octopus with the flat side of metal meat hammer for 15-20 minutes.

Wash thoroughly, drain, cut into bite-sized pieces and cook in a skillet until it becomes bright pink.

Make a marinade of:
  1/2 *cup olive oil*
  1/4 *cup white wine vinegar*
  2 *Tbsp. lemon juice*
  1 *Tbsp. minced parsley*
  1 *tsp. marjoram*
  salt and pepper

Pour over the octopus and store in a covered container in the refrigerator for 5 days, stirring occasionally.

To make the salad —

Finely chop into a bowl:
  1 *green pepper*
  4 *ripe tomatoes*
  1 *medium cucumber*
  1 *small, sweet onion*
Add the octopus and the marinade and toss.

Fiddlehead greens are tiny fern leaves which are picked early in the spring, although they are available in the frozen foods department of the supermarket at other times of the year. Although the ferns in New Brunswick (which is where Canadian fiddlehead greens come from these days) grow in the fields and woods, ferns used to grow beneath the water of the great inland prehistoric sea, and the fish swam among them. Thus:

Fish in the Fern Casserole

(Serves 4)

1 package frozen fiddleheads, steamed
7-ounce can tuna
1/2 cup mayonnaise (see Edmonton Legislature picnic)
1 tsp. curry powder
1 tin mushroom bits and pieces
1 cup sour cream or yogurt
1/2 cup bread crumbs
1/4 cup Parmesan cheese

Combine all ingredients except the bread crumbs and cheese in a casserole. Mix together the bread crumbs and cheese and sprinkle on top. Dot with butter, and bake at 350 °F for 30 minutes.

38 Taber Provincial Park
Taber

An Old-Fashioned Corn Roast

As you drive in this region be sure to notice the fields of sugar beets and corn, and the many irrigation canals. The lines of irrigation machinery snake across the fields, spreading green in an otherwise dry and yellow landscape. Taber corn is exported to all corners of the province, and you will see truckloads of it for sale on convenient lots in Alberta's towns and cities, from late July to mid-September. Corn roasts with Taber corn are part of the tradition in our family. To us it signifies the full richness of summer, even as we know it is about to end with the imminent first frost. This is, therefore, a corn picnic, with a touch of sweetness thrown in.

How to get there

To reach Taber Provincial Park drive to the west side of Taber on Highway 3, and turn north on Highway 864, which is also the road to the airport. Drive 5 km (3 1/4 mi.) north to the park gate which is on the east side of the road, just before the bridge. Turn left at the first opportunity inside the gate, and park in the first lot, beside the picnic

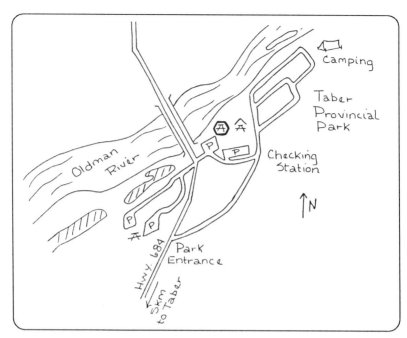

ground. Stay in the area southwest of the bridge by the river; the picnic ground on the west side is for group use only. The park is in a valley shaded by old cottonwood trees, a cool oasis in this otherwise arid central irrigation district.

The Central Irrigation District

Relics have been found which indicate that people have been inhabiting the Taber region for at least 11,000 years. This was the land of the buffalo for many centuries, and it was not far from here, on the banks of the Oldman River, that an archaeologist discovered a hammer-like tool embedded in a buffalo skull. After the buffalo vanished from the plains, cattle roamed the grasslands. Only in the last century have coal, and then oil, been discovered, and until very recently the nature of the land determined its use. Farming became possible only when the industrial revolution enabled farmers to dramatically affect the environment.

Among the first people to farm here were a group of Mormon settlers. In fact, the name "Taber" is derived from the word tabernacle, a fitting honour for these people who developed the first irrigation system and introduced sugar beet farming in the district.

Irrigation of the arid southern prairies was first undertaken in the 1890s, and at the beginning the initiative came from private individuals. The long straight ditches can be seen as you drive along the highways, over fifty miles of which were dug after the Mormon Church became a major canal contractor. The first company to invest in irrigation on a larger scale was the Canadian Pacific Railway. More recent irrigation techniques involve self-driven pivots of mammoth proportions, where wheels move large water pipes across the landscape. These capital-intensive projects irrigate vast areas of otherwise uncultivable farmland. Since 1958 the cost has been shared, with 86% contributed by the Alberta government and 14% by the districts. This is the most extensive irrigation program in Canada.

Corn

In a society in which most of the things we use and consume are processed beyond recognition, it is startling to realize that almost everything we use involves corn in some way. We refer you to the chapter on corn in Margaret Visser's remarkable book, *Much Depends on Dinner*, for a detailed discussion of the importance of corn to human society. She points out that it is almost impossible to buy anything in a North American supermarket which doesn't involve corn in one way or another. Animals are fed corn, so that all livestock, poultry, and even milk and eggs start out with corn. Frozen meat and fish are dusted with corn starch to prevent them from drying out. Canned foods are bathed in a corn-based liquid. Even most cartons and wrappings are partially created out of corn.

Things to do

1. Play scrub baseball on the grassy ball diamond across from the picnic area.

2. Fish from the banks of the Oldman River. The most common catch is goldeye, but you might pull in a walleye or whitefish for dinner.

3. Explore the self-guiding trails along the Oldman River in the park. In the right season you will see unusual migratory birds in the cottonwood trees — nighthawks, northern orioles and yellow warblers pass through here on their way to and from the north. There are about 130 different species of birds living in the park including white pelicans, a bald eagle, and a species of small brown bats.

4. Visit the Sandy Hills Stock Farm, an irrigation farm. Tours are available during the summer. Call the Taber Tourist Information Centre at 223-2265 for further details.

5. Visit the Empress Canning Factory where vegetables, spaghetti, and pork and beans are canned. Fruit juices are also packed here. However, if you want some Empress jam for your corn fritters,

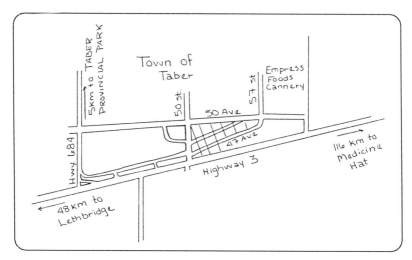

you will have to buy it at the Safeway store in town under one of the following brand names: Empress, Town House, Taste Tells and Belair. Tours of the canning factory are available year round — check at the Travel Information Centre, 223-2265, or call Empress Foods, 223-3566.

Things to eat

This picnic is corny but sweet! You should make the corn fritter batter ahead, and bring the Johnny Cake ready-made. Bring some Empress strawberry jam along for dipping them. The corn roast is all done at the site.

Campfire Roast Corn

Select as many choice ears of corn as you think you will need, and then a few more. Make sure they are really freshly picked, and that they are from Taber! Resist the force of habit — do *not* shuck the corn. Seal each ear in tin foil. There is enough moisture within the cob to steam it. Place the ears around the edge of the grill for about 15 minutes, turning one-third rotation every five minutes.

Corned Beef

Buy sliced from the deli or prepare at home (see Athabasca Landing picnic). Serve the meat with corn relish.

Corn Fritters

(Serves 4)

At home, grate 2 1/2 cups fresh Taber corn, and add :
  1 well-beaten egg yolk
  2 tsp. flour
  1/4 tsp. salt

Whip until stiff, but not dry
  1 egg white.
Fold it gently into the corn mixture, and store in a tight container —
keep chilled until you reach the picnic site.

At the picnic, while the corn is roasting at the edge of the fire, heat butter, margarine or oil in a heavy iron skillet, and place over the fire. Drop fritter batter into the pan and sauté until light and fluffy.

Serve the fritters with Empress strawberry jam, or . . . corn syrup, of course!

Johnny Cake

Corn bread can be made over an open fire, but it isn't as successful as when it is baked in the oven. Since your fire will be busy with fritters and corn cobs, we suggest that you prepare this at home.

Preheat oven to 450 °F.

  1 cup all-purpose flour
  1 cup yellow cornmeal
  2 tsp. baking powder
  1/2 tsp. baking soda
  1 tsp. salt or salt substitute
  1 cup milk
  2 1/2 tsp. lemon or lime juice
  1 egg, beaten
  2 Tbsp. lard, melted

Combine the flour, cornmeal, baking powder, baking soda and salt in a bowl. Mix the milk and lime or lemon juice and add to the dry ingredients, along with the egg and the lard. Mix well, but avoid beating. Pour into a heavy, well-greased 11 x 7 x 1 1/2-inch baking pan. Bake for 15 to 20 minutes. When it is cooked the top will be golden brown. Cool slightly and cut into squares. Cover and take on picnic. You may want to serve this with corn syrup — it's scrumptious!

If the picnic seems a bit corny, you can prepare celery and carrot sticks for a change in colour and taste — or even a fresh green salad.

39 Cypress Hills Medicine Hat
A Glacier Picnic

The Cypress Hills reaffirm the vastness of the prairie landscape, and the enduring effect of the powerful glaciers which passed by so long ago. The area has played an important historical role as a hunting range for various tribes of Indians, and as part of the route of the Bull Trail. Its ecological and geological importance supersedes the periodic impact of the human race.

How to get there

Cypress Hills Provincial Park is in the southeast corner of the province, 66 km (41 mi.) southeast of Medicine Hat. To get there, drive 32 km (20 mi.) east from Medicine Hat on Highway 1, turn south at the junction with Highway 41, and continue for 34 km (21 mi.) to the park gate.

The picnic site is at Reesor Lake Lookout, about 14.5 km (9 mi.) from the park visitor centre. The route is well marked. Please refer to the map. Once you park at the lookout, walk out along the ridge to the right for about 30 metres, to where the land curves back into the valley. Set your picnic blanket there, among the flowers.

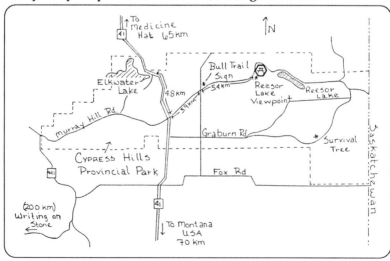

Geology

Knob, kettle and slump — these are words which explain what you see once you settle down on the grass at the lookout. The hills straddle the Alberta Saskatchewan border. They are about 40 million years old, compared with the 65 million years of the Rockies. Reesor Lookout is situated on a very high plateau which towers above the surrounding prairie at some 1,500 feet. The gradual approach of the highway doesn't prepare you for the sudden impact of the majestic view. The Cypress Hills are the highest land between the Rockies and Labrador — 4,000 to 4,500 feet above sea level.

You are standing on an island; 12,000 years ago the view from this plateau would be of a vast sea of ice — today the view is of a sea of grass.

The Cypress Hills are a pocket of unique sedimentary formations which are not found elsewhere in Canada. About 50 million years ago the region was the bed of a great river which flowed east from the Rockies. Reesor Lake sits in a large valley that would have carried meltwater from the retreating continental glacier of ten to twelve thousand years ago. The glaciers of the last ice age passed among the hills, but not over them; the top 300 feet or so of the hills have never been covered by glaciers. The valleys and depressions and lakes that you see below were the pathways of the receding glaciers. The "knobs" are the strangely shaped hills, some with part of the base eroded so that the top of the hill resembles a knob or door handle. "Kettles," also called "prairie mounds," are the smaller roundish potholes which are thought to have formed when pieces of stagnant glacial ice broke off and melted slowly, leaving a basin-like depression in the land. There are thousands of prairie mounds on the plains of southern Alberta, and especially in the Cypress Hills region.

The tops of the hills remain protected from erosion by a cover of "conglomerate." Precipitation passes quickly through this conglomerate to the layers below, which, over time will erode. A "slump" occurs when the lower layer has weakened to such an extent that the top layer collapses, sliding downhill. You can pick out the slumps because they tend to have little or no vegetation on top. The one slightly to the right in the middle distance is a good example; it is called Police Point Slump, and it collapsed in 1967.

Ecology

The picnic site is set high on the plateau overlooking a breathtaking view, and an astonishing variety of ecological zones. Sitting on the ridge it is possible for you to see miles of prairie stretching to the horizon. It is surprising to find stands of lodgepole pine on the prairie! The vegetation at the higher altitudes in the Cypress Hills is indeed the same as that in the Rocky Mountains because the two

regions were once connected by a narrow band of vegetation. As the glacier melted the prairie grasslands intervened, creating pockets of montane, or mountain-like vegetation, such as the Cypress Hills and the Sweetgrass Hills, far away from the Rockies. The anomalous mountain climate persists only at higher altitudes, and it is easy to spot these islands of alpine forest here and there as you look about.

The flowers at the picnic site are typical of the prairie and grassy hillsides, but are much smaller than on the prairie lowlands. Among those we recognized were the common harebell, the false dandelion, the tufted fleabane, gaillardia, purple vetch, the wild rose of Alberta and cinquefoil. There is such a profusion of flowers that you may find it useful to carry the book, *Wild Flowers of Alberta*.

Things to do

1. On your drive in or back from the Reesor Lake site, stop at the marker by the road which indicates the Bull Trail. Here you can actually see the ruts made by the freighter wagons as they passed from Fort Benton in Montana to Fort Whoop-Up with their contraband liquor, and then back with the tongues, humps and hides of buffalo (while the buffalo lasted). This trail was so heavily used that one hundred years have not succeeded in wearing away this path from the past. (For more information on the Bull Trail see the Fort Whoop-Up picnic.)

2. Drive to the "Survival Tree" in the southern part of the park. The driving tour takes about 2 1/2 hours. (Check with the park

information office to make sure that the road is open. It is sometimes closed if the fire hazard is high, or because of unsafe — muddy — road conditions.) The legend of the survival tree, a venerable old lodgepole pine, is that it has survived several severe forest fires, including the one in 1886 which cleared the park of trees. As well, its shelter saved the life of a local resident when he became lost in a snow storm.

3. Stop at Horseshoe Canyon Lookout. From here, in the evening, you can see the lights of Medicine Hat, so save this for your return trip, after the picnic. You can see another land slump here. It is an older one and the vegetation has begun to fill in the top, whereas Police Point Slump is still bald.

4. Fish for trout in the well-stocked Reesor Lake.

5. Request the mammal, bird and plant checklists at the park visitor centre, and see how many of these you can identify.

6. Take the guided van tour through the park. Tours depart from the Visitor Centre daily May to September. Check the schedule.

Things to eat

Because of the dryness of the grassland on the plateau, we advise that you bring only cold food; fires and even camp stoves are too dangerous up here, and are prohibited. Cold food is especially appropriate, anyway, in this post-glacial landscape!

Our menu begins with a Thermos of cold vichyssoise, and continues with a quiche, some sausage rolls with HP sauce, fresh finger vegetables with a dip, and for dessert a Glacier Special. If it weren't a provincial park we'd also recommend a fine white wine.

Vichyssoise

(makes 12 cups)

Chop:
  6 medium leeks
  2 medium onions
And sauté in 1/4 cup melted butter.

Peel and chop 8 medium potatoes.

Add the above vegetables to:
  8 cups chicken stock
And simmer covered for 15 minutes.

Purée the mixture in a blender.

Add:
   1 1/2 cups yogurt
   salt and white pepper

Refrigerate. Serve garnished with chopped chives.

Bring your own sausage rolls and HP sauce.

Quiche

(Serves 4-6)

Pastry for 1 pie shell (see Aunt Nell's Pie Crust recipe)
1/2 pound bacon, diced
1 cup Swiss cheese grated
4 eggs
1 1/2 cups milk
1/2 tsp. salt
1/8 tsp. pepper
1/8 tsp. nutmeg
1 tsp. chopped chives
1/2 tsp. dried summer savory — or fresh, if you have it.

Roll out pastry and line a 9-inch pie shell. Brush it with the white of 1 egg. Puncture well with fork tines.

Fry bacon until almost crisp, drain and place in bottom of pie shell. Top with grated cheese.

Beat eggs until frothy. Add remaining ingredients gradually, stirring all the while. Pour into pie shell. Bake for 35-40 minutes in a 375 °F oven. Chill and take to your picnic.

Glacier Special

Buy or make individual meringues, top with ice cream and garnish with chocolate bark.

40 Writing-On-Stone
Milk River
A Picnic Under Eight Flags

The Milk River runs south, to the Missouri River system and on to the Gulf of Mexico. The Milk River Ridge divides the north and south watersheds; north of here the rivers run into the Arctic Ocean. This quirk of geography is the reason why the land has been under eight different flags, and considered the property of five countries and one private company, since the seventeenth century. Even before the territorial claims, however, this region was inhabited, as evidenced by the petroglyphs and pictographs of a long-departed culture. This international picnic takes place in Writing-On-Stone Provincial Park.

How to get there

From Lethbridge drive southeast on Highway 4 to Milk River. From Milk River drive east on Highway 501 to the marked intersection. From here it is 8 km (5 mi.) on a gravel road to the park gate. The park is 43 km (27 mi.) from the town of Milk River.

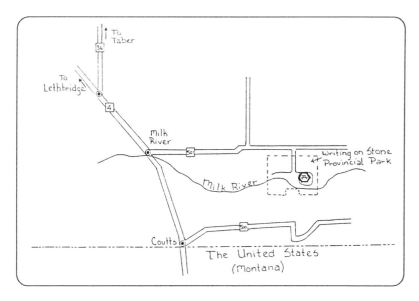

The picnic site is within the park, on the lush banks of the Milk River, a surprising oasis in this desert-like valley of hoodoos. The parking lot is next to the picnic ground. Pick the table with the best view of the hoodoos — it is close to the parking area.

The Milk River snakes along through this unearthly landscape, a narrow corridor of cottonwood shade. And speaking of snakes, there are lots of them around, although spotting one will be difficult because they are shy, and tend to avoid people.

The Hoodoos

The strange formations all about you are called hoodoos, and are actually sandstone formations between 82 and 84 million years old. They are capped by a firmly-packed ironstone layer which does not erode as quickly as the more porous base. The pillars of stone are created by centuries of erosion by wind and water.

The Petroglyphs

A "petroglyph" is a picture or pattern which has been carved, chipped or hammered into the rock face by human hands. A "pictograph" is a painting on a rock face, usually done with ochre or other natural substances. Both are sometimes referred to as rock art. Petroglyphs may have been painted after they were carved, but the colour has usually faded or washed away. Little is known about the people who carved these petroglyphs, but archaeologists estimate that they inhabited the valley for about 300 years, perhaps as recently as the 17th century, but likely much earlier. The pictures have been categorized according to style, and a progression has been suggested by scholars. The meaning and purpose of the symbols can still be explained only by conjecture. It is likely, based on what we know of the native peoples in the region in the last century, that the site had religious significance. The symbols, often depicting animals, may have been important components in hunting rituals. Because many of them are in hard-to-get-at places, niches and crevices in the cliffs by the river or hidden in coulees, they may have been part of an initiation rite which was experienced in isolation. Some of the more recent images reflect historical events after the arrival of the traders and settlers; there are drawings of carts and even a gallows with a human figure hanging from it.

History

The French

The first territorial claim on the region was made by the French explorer, La Salle, who claimed for King Louis XIV the lands drained by the entire Mississippi River system in 1682. He called the claim Louisiana.

The Spanish

Ninety years later, in 1762, the French — who had paid little attention to their distant holding — ceded it all to the Spanish Empire by the Treaty of San Idlefense.

Again the French — Encore les Francais

Spain, in turn, ceded the territory to the French Republic under Napoleon in 1800. Despite the best of intentions, Napoleon never managed to establish French control.

The United States

And so the territory was sold to the United States government of the day for $27 million, and the deal is known to students of history as "the Louisiana Purchase."

The Hudson's Bay Company

The new boundary of British North America was to be the 49th parallel, as far west as the Rocky Mountains, according to a formal agreement between the United States and the United Kingdom. This effectively cut the Milk River region off from the rest of the Missis-

GIARDIASIS

Commonly known as "beaver fever," giardiasis is an intestinal infection which causes fatigue, abdominal cramps and nausea. Giardiasis occurs all over the world, transmitted in unsanitary conditions, often through water sources. In Canada, as the nickname for the disease implies, the beaver is among the animal carriers of the disease. The excreta of these animals contaminate water in streams and rivers; the parasite is carried through the water systems, and humans pick it up from the water further downstream from the site of contamination. The disease is very contagious, and can be spread by unsuspecting persons before the symptoms even occur.

Avoidance of giardiasis is not difficult if you take the necessary precautions. Be sure to find out about drinking water before you drink. Local health authorities and parks staff can confirm whether the parasite is present in the local water. When in doubt, boil all drinking water for five minutes at 100 °C (212 °F) to kill the parasite.

sippi drainage lands, and it became part of the North-West Territories administered by the Hudson's Bay Company on behalf of the British Empire.

Canada

In 1867 the Dominion of Canada was formed, and in 1869 the lands under control of the Hudson's Bay Company were transferred to the federal government in Ottawa. The Hudson's Bay flag was taken down and replaced by that of the British Empire — the Union Jack. During the last years of the nineteenth century the North-West Mounted Police established a post in the area which operated for thirty years.

In 1945 the Union Jack was replaced by the Red Ensign, the result of a growing Canadian nationalism. In 1965 the Maple Leaf flag, of truly Canadian origin, was proclaimed the official flag of the Dominion of Canada, bringing to eight the number of flags which have flown over the Milk River district.

Things to do

1. Visit the petroglyphs in the protected area. Because of the combined effects of weathering and vandalism the portion of the park in which the petroglyphs are located can be visited only in the

company of an interpreter. Tours depart from the park naturalist's office every day at 2 p.m. and at various other times according to demand. Visitors with cars usually follow the park van to the interpretive sites; the van carries visitors without cars. The tours are run from May to September, and last approximately 1 1/2 hours. Free tickets are obtained from the park naturalist's office.

2. Wander through the hoodoos. The area nearest the picnic ground is available to the public year round. It is a fascinating place to explore, and a magical place to cross-country ski in the winter.

3. Canoe along the Milk River. You will undoubtedly see mule deer, yellow-bellied marmots, and a variety of other animals. The region is excellent for bird watchers.

Things to eat

Since this is an international picnic for reasons which you now thoroughly understand, even if you have already forgotten the dates, we will draw our menu from each of the nations which has controlled the land in the last two centuries.

MENU

France — French bread
Spain — gazpacho and country paella
United States — Coca Cola!
Canada — Hoodoo Salad (marinated mushrooms)

There are many different kinds of gazpacho, the cold vegetable soup favoured by Spaniards. Our favourite recipe comes from southern Spain, and includes bread crumbs. This can be made a day or two before, as chilling only increases the flavour of this wonderful soup. It is usually prepared with a hand grinder — we tend to use the blender, however, even though it produces a more finely textured soup.

Gazpacho

(serves 8)

3/4 kg tomatoes
1 cucumber, peeled and chopped
1 green pepper, chopped
100 g dry bread crumbs

1 clove garlic, peeled
1 medium onion, chopped
50 ml vinegar
7 ml olive oil
1 L water
salt

Reserve 1 tomato for garnish. Scald the rest of the tomatoes in boiling water for 1 minute, remove skins and slice into quarters. Sauté the green pepper, cucumber and onion until soft. Sprinkle the bread crumbs with the vinegar and let stand for a few minutes. In a blender or food chopper grind all the vegetables. Add the bread crumbs and the garlic, with a little of the water. Slowly add the oil, stirring well, and then the rest of the water. Chill well, and serve cold.

Paella

(serves 10)

The Spanish are consummate picnickers, and the paella is a uniquely Spanish dish. It has a rice base, but the ingredients vary according to the region, and the pocketbook of the cook. Inland you will likely have chicken or pork in your paella, and by the sea, fish. Our recipe is Andalucian, taught to us by a Madrilena who learned it from her Basque parents. Paella is usually prepared over an open fire, but the grill of your portable barbecue works just as well.

1 1/2 kg rice
saffron
2 medium onions, chopped
4 cloves garlic, chopped
2 green peppers, cut into small pieces
2 large red peppers, cut into small pieces
1 tin tomatoes
1 tin peas
1/2 kg shrimp, unshelled
1 kg baby clams
1 kg mussels
5 chicken stock cubes
1 cooked chicken, chopped into pieces
oil
white wine

Put the saffron to soak in 125 ml water.

Build the fire up and let it burn until you have a good bed of coals. Scrub the clams and mussels and soak in cold water for 1 hour. Remove the heads from the shrimp and wash in cold water.

Smooth the coals out and place the paella pan directly on them (if you don't have a paella pan, 2 large shallow frying pans will do. A wok won't — not enough bottom area). In the pan sauté the chicken pieces with the garlic in oil until they are brown, and set them aside. Sauté the chopped onions and peppers, and set aside.

In a separate pot boil the clams and shrimps until the clams open.

Add more oil to the paella pan and add the rice to the oil. Sauté the rice until it is transparent, 2 - 3 minutes. Take the pan off the fire. Add to the rice the chicken, tomatoes, peppers, onions, clams, shrimp, 5 chicken stock cubes, the saffron liquid, and more liquid (roughly twice the volume of the rice). The liquid that was used to boil the clams is good, but so is water, and so is dry white wine, or chicken stock — or any combination of the above. Rake the coals down so that there is a level place for the pan; return the pan to the fire, and let simmer for 20 minutes. Resist the temptation to stir or cover, but do add more liquid if it seems to be boiling off too quickly.

In a separate pot boil the mussels until they open.

When the paella is cooked (liquid gone), remove it from the fire. Cover with a cloth and let stand for 5 minutes. Split the mussel shells, and arrange them on the half-shell as garnish just before serving.

Hoodoo Salad

The mushrooms are reminiscent of the marvelous hoodoos which surround this Canadian picnic spot.

Select and clean 1 1/2 pounds medium sized fresh mushrooms.

Prepare marinade by mixing together:
1 cup vegetable oil
1/2 cup white wine vinegar
dash Worcestershire sauce
salt and pepper
1 clove garlic, crushed
dash Tabasco sauce

Pour over the mushrooms and refrigerate over night. Garnish with freshly chopped chives and serve your pickled hoodoos with toothpicks.

Loaves and Fishes *or*
Feeding the Multitude

This chapter is for that fortunate individual who has just been elected or appointed Social Convenor, or equivalent, of a group or club and is now responsible for the planning and conduct of the annual picnic.

Reunions, companies, unions, churches, communities, and lots of other groups hold picnics for their members and families. The planning required for such events is quite detailed, but with reasonable care you can indeed keep everything under control — except, of course, the weather.

In this chapter we will describe the generic large group picnic, covering a variety of concerns such as theme, supplies, games and activities, recipes for preparing large quantities of food, and we will provide an answer to that worrisome question, "how many potatoes in a potato salad for 100?" The chapter is mainly one long and involved checklist, with some games and recipes tacked on. You have undertaken an awesome and daunting task, one that would overcome a lesser individual, but we hope to provide enough suggestions that you may enjoy the afternoon and even volunteer to do it again!

☐ 1   What happened last year?

Did the picnickers enjoy themselves? Was the location OK? Who booked it and from whom. . . is she still in town? Was Mrs. Brown's Potato Salad the hit of the picnic, or the basis of the food fight that broke out? Will you be a hero by just repeating what was done before, or were many people dissatisfied? Organizations are often very bad at this type of history, but some conscientious digging can probably head off a lot of hurt feelings, and make the picnic fun for all.

☐ 2   The occasion

Picnics are often associated with an event, such as the completion of spring planting in rural communities, or a harvest festival. Certainly the fall bazaar or fair is still a common occurrence in many rural and urban communities alike. Work parties are another good reason for a picnic — it used to be barn-raising, but now it is sometimes garage-raising or developing the community ball field.

Picnics can be planned around a theme, although this is not at all necessary. Some suggestions to spark your imagination are as follows:

Canada Day	Summer solstice
Christmas in July	50th birthday
a wedding	retirement
end of school	end of summer

☐ 3   The group

The first step is to recognize the composition of the group since this will influence all the other factors: the food, the activities, the facilities, and so on. With old, established picnics this is fairly well understood, but with new groups, watch out. This may be the group of boys that you bowl with on Wednesday nights, but the picnic will include their families, too . . . . What do you know about them? What are the ages of their children? Do they like a primitive but beautiful site or are they happiest in an urban park? Do they have teenagers, or little kids, or is this an adult group (which, on a picnic, may be counted on to behave as a lot of aging adolescents)? This last group is especially hard to deal with as you can count on several bad sprains and possibly a broken bone or two as the picnickers try to convince their 40-year-old bodies that they can still play football like they did when they were 20. Even if it is the same group as last year, remember that a year has gone by, and while it may not have changed you or your friends much, the children might have metamorphosed from fun-seeking kids to very self-conscious teenagers.

☐ 4   The facilities: Where to hold the picnic

Municipal and provincial parks usually provide pleasant settings for large picnics, and some provide special places and facilities for large groups. Once you have selected a likely spot, visit the site and check to see that there is enough space for the activities you are planning, shelter in case of rain, sanitary facilities and a water source. If these are missing, portable toilets can be rented, and a water supply can be carried, but both of these arrangements require lead time and planning.

If you intend to serve alcoholic beverages, check first to make sure that this is legal in the site you have selected. The consumption of alcohol is usually forbidden in public parks, but sometimes you can obtain a permit, particularly if you are using a community hall as a base.

It is a good idea to notify the local police department about the event, as well. You may need assistance with traffic control, or help in dealing with unruly guests — or you may need nothing at all. This is just part of the ounce of prevention which beats a pound of cure.

If you are booking a park as the site of your picnic, you might wish to be weather-safe, and book an alternative venue, such as a community hall or church, in case of rain. Sometimes groups set up an alternate date, assuming that if the first day is rainy, the second won't be. The invitation or announcement might read, "Social services department picnic at Kinsmen Park on Saturday, July 6th, or, in case of rain-out, Saturday, July 13th." Make sure you book both dates with the parks department, or appropriate authority.

☐ 5   Equipment

You will need supplies for decorating the picnic site, such as balloons and streamers. In larger centres these can be found by checking the Yellow Pages under "balloons," "helium" or "giftwares." Helium machines can be rented for a nominal fee, and even outdoor sites look more festive when there are brightly coloured balloons flying from the trees and telephone poles.

You will need prizes for any contests or races — and make sure that you have plenty. We usually give at least three prizes for all children's contests, and, if possible, a prize to everyone. Ribbons for first, second, third, fourth, and so on, are usually available at the same place where you bought the balloons.

You will need to buy, borrow or make the equipment for any races or contests: barrels for barrel races, strong ties for three-legged races, bags (green garbage, perhaps) for the sack race, eggs for an egg toss, and so on.

Finally, there will be the cleanup afterward. Rakes, brooms, shovels, or maybe just a lot of garbage bags will be needed, and line up your work crew ahead of time.

☐ 6   First aid equipment

We have found it wise to bring a complete industrial first aid kit. These can be purchased from any industrial supply store, and come in a water-proof metal box.

Alternatively, you can put together a kit for yourself with a minimum of the following:

Band-aids of various sizes	sterile 2" and 4" gauze pads
low-allergy adhesive tape	skin disinfectant
lots of clean cotton balls	scissors
elastic bandage for sprains	sling
safety pins	burn ointment
insect repellant	

In any case, make sure that you have an adequate first aid kit at the picnic.

☐ 7   Activities

Games

Think back to the picnics of your childhood — what games did you play? I'll bet that you, like us, have trouble remembering the rules. Later in the chapter are the rules for some of the games we remember, but we have found that there are regional variations. Alter them to suit your own recollection.

Contests

Contests are fun, if they are not taken too seriously. Pies seem to offer the most versatility for contests: there are pie-baking contests, pie-throwing contests, and pie-eating contests. There are also barrel-rolling contests, where the contestants line up on their barrels (empty oil barrels are fine) at the starting line, and the prize goes to the person who reaches the finish line first without touching ground, or to the person who goes farthest. There are arm-wrestling contests. There are spelling bees. Prizes can also be given for the best decorated bike, the scariest costume, and the most lovable dog. If you are at a beach for your picnic, there could be a sand-castle building contest.

Searches

Treasure hunts of various sorts are lots of fun, and work well as team activities. Each team is given a list of things to find, and the winning team is the one which first collects everything on the list. Alternatively, quantities of a particular item, eggs, or specially wrapped candies, or tokens of some sort, can be secreted about the picnic site, and the prize can go to the team — or individual — who finds the most.

Team Sports
The old reliables, the baseball game, the touch football game, or for some groups, a rousing round of croquet always go better if someone remembers to bring the bats, balls, mallets, hoops, and base sacks. Delegate the responsibility to someone else.

Kite flying
If your picnic site has a big enough field, and no power wires nearby, you can ask people to bring their kites; alternatively, you can supply some. This only works in a big space, and only a few people can fly kites at the same time, since the strings easily become entangled. If the picnickers know and understand the rules for kite fighting, that is also an interesting pastime.

Balloon rides
Hot-air ballooning has become very popular in the last few years. Many balloon owners are willing to attend community events or private functions to provide balloon rides — for a fee. Some groups have even rented helicopters for the afternoon, and sold rides to the picnickers.

Guided hikes
If the picnic is in a rural setting, a park just outside town, or even some of the larger city parks, guided hikes for groups of picnickers can be a welcome diversion, especially for senior citizens. Identify someone in the group who has special knowledge of birds, plants, animals, or all three. Ask your guide in advance, so that he or she can brush up if necessary. Limit the hikes to no more than an hour — and perhaps less, depending on who you expect to participate.

Camp-fire sing-songs
Most effective after dark, sing-songs provide a quiet ending to an exciting afternoon. Everyone slows down and relaxes, little children fall asleep on blankets by the fire, and adults feel that sense of warmth and companionship which can only happen by a fire. Make sure that you provide at least one guitar or accordian player who has a wide repertoire appropriate to the ages of your group. Consider having song sheets available, if you think people will be able to see them. Alternatively, brain-storm with your accompanist in advance, and prepare a list of tunes for which most people already know the words, so that awkward silences and false starts will be avoided.

Fireworks
Fireworks have made a big come-back in the last few years, much to the chagrin of many parents. Nonetheless, they make a marvelous display when carefully selected and responsibly detonated.

☐ 8 Things to eat

Donations
There are many factories in most cities and larger towns which will be happy to donate some of their product for your picnic, in exchange for recognition in the announcement or invitation. Others will donate, but prefer to remain anonymous to stem the tide of subsequent requests. Some may prefer to give a small cash donation. Think about what you will need in the way of food, and then consider which companies are represented in your community. Most have a public relations officer to respond to such requests. It is certainly worth a try.

Supplies for food preparation
If you are using a community hall or equivalent as a base for your food preparation, arrange to visit the place to assess the number and capacity of mixing and serving bowls, pots and pans, and so on. If you are going to be working in a park, preparing hot dogs and hamburgers, make sure that you book enough barbecues and frying pans, or whatever else you will need. Nothing is worse than a bottleneck in the food production area when everyone is hungry. The easiest system is to select cold foods, and to have them prepared by individuals in their homes in advance. This is the ideal time for a pot-luck dinner, in true "picnickian" style, with everyone contributing to the feast. We have found that it isn't even necessary to direct people about what to bring — you will get several potato salads, but this is a popular dish anyway, and most of it will be eaten. You will also get some of the specialty salads that people like to make for such events, and the variety is endless. The most direction we have ever given is to request either a salad, casserole, dessert or bread. Usually the picnic organizers provide the beverages, in the form of juice or pop. Have water on hand for those who want it.

Most important, make sure you have enough. Err on the side of too much! To help you, we provide selected recipes.

Chicken Salad

(100 Servings)

8 qts. cooked chicken, cut into small pieces
8 cups chopped celery
2 Tbsp. salt
2 Tbsp. pepper
2 qts. mayonnaise or salad cream
6 green peppers, chopped
16 hard cooked eggs, sliced

Mix ingredients together, and keep well-chilled until serving time. It is best to prepare this the day of the picnic. You can maintain a safe temperature by placing the serving bowls in a tub of ice on the picnic table.

Salmon Loaf

(100 Servings)

Mix together:
20-1 lb. cans of salmon
6 qts. bread crumbs

Scald:
8 qts. milk

And mix with:
3 cups melted butter
5 1/2 cups flour
1 tsp. paprika
4 Tbsp. salt

Cook for 15 minutes.

Combine the sauce with the fish, blend together, and pour into greased loaf pans. Sprinkle with buttered bread crumbs and bake at 350 °F for 30 minutes.

Cole Slaw

(100 Servings)

Combine:
10 lbs. cabbage, shredded
3 lbs. carrots, shredded
3 lbs. celery, diced
1 pt. mayonnaise or salad cream

1 cup salad oil
1/2 cup vinegar
celery seed, salt and pepper to taste

Potato Salad

(100 Servings)

28 lbs. potatoes, cooked and diced   Dress with:
10 doz. hard cooked eggs, sliced   *2 cups salad oil*
2 cups onions, finely chopped   *1/2 cup vinegar*
5 sweet red peppers, chopped   *2 tsp. dry mustard.*
5 green peppers chopped   *1 qt. mayonnaise*
salt and pepper to taste

Mix ingredients together and chill well. As with the chicken salad, it is best to prepare this the day of the picnic, and to keep it chilled while serving.

Group Picnic Checklist

The following can be used as a rough guide, or as a plan of action, assigning committee members to each task and setting scheduled dates of completion.

Select date for picnic, and alternate date, if appropriate
Select site.
Visit site to check for:

water	ball diamond
toilets	games/races area
number of picnic tables	electricity
shelter	nearest telephone
cooking facilities	nearest hospital
fire wood	

Book site.
Get liquor permit, if needed.
Develop supply list:

prizes	plastic cutlery
ribbons	serviettes
safety pins	garbage bags
string	garbage buckets
rope	lawn chairs for seniors
tape	barbecues
fireworks	fuel
paper cups	pots and pans
paper plates	cooking implements

pot holders, oven mitts
first aid kit
water buckets
List food requirements:
    snacks
    main course
    salads
    buns or bread
List beverage requirements:
    drinks for little kids
    drinks for teenagers
    drinks for adults
    coffee, tea, cocoa, milk
    cups to drink from

felt pens and cardboard
    for signs

casseroles
desserts
cookies
pies

Games for Groups

Elves, Giants and Wizards
Materials: none
People: ten, to a large crowd

Directions:
Two roughly equal groups of people should be formed. They should then be taught the three basic positions of the game:
- an elf is little with two little horns on his head (so the person squats with hands behind head)
- a giant is huge (so the person puts arms way above the head and walks on tiptoe)
- wizards are sneaky fellows, always shooting rays of magic lightening out of their fingers. A wizard sort of person, therefore, looks sneaky and is always pointing his arms in the direction of the other groups.

To play the game, each group has a secret meeting and decides which of the three characters it will be. A first plan and a back-up plan should be chosen. Then the groups face each other, about five metres apart, on a large field. There should be designated safe zones at each end of the field since the participants are going to chase each other up and down the field.

Once facing each other, and conducted by the games' mistress or master, they all chant together three times in a row, "elves, giants, wizards" with the action for each word. After the third chant each group then chants its planned word. The result will be the two groups

yelling the same, or different characters. This seems pointless unless you know that:
    - elves can run under wizards' cloaks and pull the hair on their legs;
    - wizards can shoot magic rays that will destroy giants;
    - that giants can stomp on elves' heads.

Thus whenever the first planned word called out by each team is different, there will be a winner (a chaser) and a loser (who will get chased). For example, if one side calls elves, and the other wizards, the elves are the winners and get to chase the wizards. So also, wizards chase giants, and giants chase elves. Anyone tagged before getting to a safe zone has to join the other team. If the first planned word is the same for both teams, then each should immediately chant their back-up plan word.

Kick-the-Can
    Materials: one can
    People: four, to a crowd

    Directions
    This is a fast-paced game a lot like hide-and-go-seek. One person is chosen to be It. The can is kicked by someone and this is the signal for everyone except It to race off, within the prescribed boundary, and hide. It retrieves the can, takes it home, and then with closed eyes, counts slowly to 60 out loud. It then goes to find the others without letting anyone get home undetected. When a person is discovered It runs to the can and says, "1, 2, 3 on (name of person)." The person should be named correctly, but with a large group, when names may not be known by all participants, this rule can be relaxed. There will often be a race to the can, and hidden persons who get there first shout, "Home Free," and are safe. Once a lot of people are at the can, both caught and safe, the last people out can try to sneak home and "Kick the Can." This action would free all the people at home to run and hide again. If no-one kicks the can, then the first person caught is It for the next round. No on can be It more than twice in a row.

Dragon
    Materials: a blindfold, and a treasure (a shoe, a box, a coin, etc.)
    People: Seven or more

    Description:
    Millions and hundred of years ago, dragons roamed the earth .. . and these dragons had great treasures. It seems that not all the dragons died off; one still lives, and he is the richest dragon of all time. This dragon has been collecting money and jewels for centuries

and has caves full of treasure. He is a very ferocious dragon, but he is blind. However, because of this, his hearing is especially good. Is there anyone in the group who is stealthy enough to steal the dragon's treasure?

Select one person to be the dragon and blindfold that person. The dragon sits on the ground with his or her legs spread out. The treasure rests on the ground between the dragon's legs, but not touching the dragon. Have the group sit in a circle around the dragon. The leader will point to one person who will try to steal in and take the treasure. If the dragon hears something it will point at the sound, and the intruder will be zapped by magic dragon fire. The dragon can only point at sounds. The group should be very quiet, and only one person may try at a time to steal the treasure. Sometimes, the group can make rain noise by rubbing hands together. When the treasure is stolen, appoint a new dragon and continue.

References

Anderako, Mark 1985 *Historic Trails Alberta*. Edmonton: Lone Pine.
Anderson, Frank W. 1980 *The Rum Runners*. Surrey, B.C: Heritage House.
Athabasca Historical Society, David Gregory, and Athabasca University 1986 *Athabasca Landing: An illustrated history*. Athbasca, Alberta: Athabasca Historical Society.
Avis, Walter S., Editor-in-Chief 1973 *A Dictionary of Canadianisms*. Toronto: Gage.
Beaver, R. Pierce, Jan Bergman et al 1982 *Eerdmans' Handbook to the World's Great Religions*. Grand Rapids, Mich: Wm. B. Eerdmans.
Berton, Pierre and Janet Berton 1966 *The Centennial Food Guide*. *Toronto: Weekend Magazine*: McClelland and Stewart Limited.
Berton, Pierre 1971 *The Last Spike*. Toronto: McClelland and Stewart Limited.
Butler, James R. and Roland R. Maw 1985 *Fishing Canada's Mountain Parks*. Edmonton: Lone Pine Publishing.
Cameron, William Bleasdell 1977 *Blood Red the Sun*. (First published in 1926.) Edmonton: Hurtig.
The Canadian Encyclopedia 1985 Edmonton: Hurtig.
Canadian Living Magazine 1984 *The Great Canadian Cookbook*. Toronto: Telemedia.
Cashman, Tony 1979 *A Picture History of Alberta*. Edmonton: Hurtig Publishers.
Cashman, Tony 1971 *An Illustrated History of Western Canada*. Edmonton: Hurtig Publishers.
Centennial Book Committee 1985 *Red Serge Wives*. Edmonton: Lone Pine.
Craighead, John J., Frank C. Craighead, Jr. and Ray J. Davis 1963 *A Field Guide to Rocky Mountain Wildflowers*. Boston: Houghton Miflin Company.
Cormack, R.G.H. 1977 *Wild Flowers of Alberta*. Edmonton: Hurtig Publishers.
Daniells, Roy 1969 *Canadian Lives: Alexander Mackenzie and the North West*. Toronto: Oxford University Press.
Dempsey, Hugh, Ed. 1981 *The Best from Alberta History*. Saskatoon, Saskatchewan: Western Producer Prairie Books.
Dennis, Thelma B. 1986 *Albertans Built: Aspects of housing in rural Alberta to 1920*. Edmonton: Thelma Dennis.
Dodd, John and Gail Helgason 1986 *The Canadian Rockies Bicycling guide*. Edmonton: Lone Pine. 1987 *The Canadian Rockies Access Guide*. Second ed. Lone Pine Publishing.

Fairbairn, Garry 1984 *From Prairie Roots: The Remarkable Story of Saskatchewan Wheat Pool*. Saskatoon: Western Producer Praire Books.

Fort Edmonton Historical Foundation 1986 *Just Like Grandma Used to Make...Old Time Recipes from Fort Edmonton Park*.

Frideres, James S. 1983 *Native People in Canada: Contemporary conflicts*. 2nd. Ed. Scarborough: Prentice-Hall.

Frontier Publishing 1978 *The Ghost Towns Journal, Vol. 2: The Dead and Dying Ghost Towns of South-east Alberta*. Calgary: Frontier Publishing.

Fryer, Harold 1976 *Ghost Towns of Alberta*. Langley: Stagecoach Publishing Company. 1982 *Stops of Interest in Southern Alberta*. Frontier Series No. 33. Surrey, B.C: Heritage Publishing Company. 1982 *Stops of Interest in Central and Northern Alberta*. Frontier Series No. 34. Surrey, B.C: Heritage Publishing Company. 1984 *Frog Lake Massacre, 1885*. Frontier Series. Surrey, B.C: Heritage House.

Gard, Robert E. 1967 *Johnny Chinook: Tall tales and true from the Canadian West*. Japan: M.G. Hurtig.

George, Chief Dan 1974 *My Heart Soars*. Saanichton: Hanock House Publishers.

Getty, Ian A.L. and Antoine S. Lussier 1985 *As Long As the Sun Shines and Water Flows: A reader in Canadian Studies*. Vancouver: University of British Columbia Press.

Gilroy, Doug 1976 *Praire Birds in Color*. Saskatoon: Western Producer Praire Books.

Gilroy, Doug 1979 *Parkland Portraits: Some natural history of the prairie parklands*. Saskatoon: Western Producer Prairie Books.

Griffiths, Deirdre 1979 *Elk Island National Park: Island forest year*. Edmonton: University of Alberta Press.

Grunfeld, Frederic V. 1975 *Games of the World: How to play them*. Zurich: Swiss Committee for UNICEF.

Hamilton, Jacques 1978 *Our Alberta Heritage*. Calgary: Calgary Power.

Hancock, David and James Woodford 1973 *Birds of Alberta, Saskatchewan and Manitoba*. Don Mills: General Publishing Company.

Hardy, W.G., Ed. 1967 *Alberta: A natural history*. Edmonton: Hurtig.

Helgason, Gail 1987 *The First Albertans*. Edmonton: Lone Pine.

Hewitt, Jean 1971 *The New York Times Natural Foods Cookbook*. New York: New York Times Book Co.

Hill, Douglas 1967 *The Opening of the Canadian West*. Don Mills: Academic Press.

Hohn, E.O. 1983 *The Northern Naturalist*. Edmonton: Lone Pine.

Holmgren, Eric J. ed. 1975 *Alberta at the Turn of the Century*. Publication No. 2. Edmonton: Provincial Archives of Alberta.

Howard, Joseph Kinsey 1965 *Strange Empire*. Toronto: Swan.

Indian and Northern Affairs Canada 1984 *The Canadian Indian: The prairie provinces*. Ottawa: Indian and Northern Affairs Canada.

Jonker, Peter M. 1983 *Stoney History Notes*. Morley, Ab: Chiniki Band of the Stoney Tribe.

Kariel, Patricia 1987 *Hiking Alberta's David Thompson Country*. Edmonton: Lone Pine.

King, D.R. 1968 *Alberta Archaeology: A handbook for amateurs*. High River, Ab: D.R. King.

Kochanski, Mors L. 1987 *Northern Bushcraft*. Edmonton: Lone Pine Publishing.

Kroetsch, Robert 1968 *Alberta*. Toronto: MacMillan Company of Canada Limited.

Kucera, Richard E. 1972 *Probing the Athbasca Glacier*. Vancouver: U.B.C. Press.

Langshaw, Rick 1983 *Naturally: Medicinal herbs and edible plants of the Canadian Rockies*. Banff: Summerthought.

Lewis, Gwen 1957 *Buckskin Cookery, Vol. I - The Pioneer Section*. Williams Lake: Gwen Lewis. 1957 *Buckskin Cookery, Vol. II - The Hunting Section*. Williams Lake: Gwen Lewis.

Lister, Robert 1979 *The Birds and Birders of Beaverhills Lake*. Edmonton: Edmonton Bird Club.

Lower, J.A. 1973 *Canada: An outline history*. Toronto: McGraw-Hill Ryerson Limited.

Luard, Elizabeth 1987 *The Old World Kitchen*. Toronto: Bantam Books.

MacDonald, Janice E. 1983 *The Northwest Fort: Fort Edmonton*. Edmonton: Lone Pine. 1985 *Canoeing Alberta*. Edmonton: Lone Pine Publishing.

Macdonald, R.H., Ed. 1985 *Eyewitness to History: William Bleasdell Cameron, Frontier Journalist*. Saskatoon, Saskatchewan: Modern Press.

MacEwan, Grant 1975 *Calgary Cavalcade: From fort to fortune*. Saskatoon: Western Producer Book Service.

MacGregor, James C. 1977 *A History of Alberta*. Edmonton: Hurtig Publishers.

Mairesse, Michelle 1981 *Health Secrets of Medicinal Herbs*. New York: Arco Publishing.

Martin, C. Y. 1973 *The Saga of the Buffalo*. New York: Hart Publishing.

Maud, Ralph 1982 *A Guide to B.C. Indian Myth and Legend*. Vancouver: Talonbooks.

McCourt, Edward 1965 *The Road Across Canada*. Toronto: MacMillan of Canada.

McCowan, Dan 1955 *Upland Trails*. Toronto: The MacMillan Company of Canada.

McNaught, Kenneth 1976 *The Pelican History of Canada*. England: Penguin Books Limited.

Milne, A.A. 1976 *When We Were Very Young*. New York: Dell.
Montgomery, F.H. 1970 *Trees of Canada and the Northern United States*. Toronto: The Ryerson Press.
Neering, Rosemary 1974 *Settlement of the West*. Toronto: Fitzhenry and Whiteside.
Newman, Peter C. 1985 *Company of Adventurers*. Harmondsworth: Viking.
Oltman, Ruth 1985 *The Valley of Rumours...the Kananaskis*. Exshaw, Ab: The Ribbon Creek Publishing Company.
Parry, Caroline 1987 *Let's Celebrate! Canada's Special Days*. Toronto: Kids Can Press Limited.
Patton, Brian and Bart Robinson 1978 *The Canadian Rockies Trail Guide: A hiker's manual to the National Parks*. Canmore: Devil's Head Press.
Peters, James 1968 *A Guide to Understanding Canada*. Toronto: Guiness.
Pike, Warburton 1894 *The Barren Ground of Northern Canada*. London: Macmillan.
Place, Marian T. 1970 *Cariboo Gold: The story of the British Columbia Gold Rush*. New York: Holt, Rinehart and Winston.
Ramage, Norma and Jim Wilson 1985 *The Complete Guide to Kananaskis Country*. Edmonton: Lone Pine.
Regan, Charonne N.D. *Magic Goose Feathers*. Abilene, Alberta: Abilene Farms and Commons.
Root, John D., Johanna E. Jacks and Judith T. Johnson 1982 *Rocky Mountain Landmarks: A visitor's guide to Banff and Jasper Parks*. Edmonton: Hosford.
Savage, Brian and Marg Barry 1985 *Ski Alberta*. Edmonton: Lone Pine.
Shulakewych, Bohdan I., Ed. 1986 *Shadows of the Past*. Edmonton: St. Michael's Extended Care.
Snow, Chief John 1977 *These Mountains are our Sacred Places: The story of the Stoney People*. Toronto & Sarasota: Samuel Stevens.
Stenson, Fred 1985 *Rocky Mountain House National Historic Park*. Toronto: NC Press.
Tyrell, J.B., Ed. 1916 *David Thompson's Narrative of his Explorations in Western America 1784-1812*. Toronto: The Champlain Society.
Ukranian Women's Association of Canada 1984 *Ukrainian Daughters' Cookbook*. Toronto: Ukrainian Women's Association of Canada.
Visser, Margaret 1987 *Much Depends on Dinner*. Toronto: Mclelland and Stewart.
Walker, Marilyn 1984 *Harvesting the Northern Wild*. Yellowknife: Outcrop.
Wood, D.M., P.T. Dang and R.A. Ellis 1979 *The Insects and Arachnids of Canada, Part 6: The mosquitoes of Canada: Diptera:Culicidae*. Ottawa: Minister of Supply and Services.
Wood, Kerry 1957 *The Map-maker: The Story of David Thompson*. Toronto: MacMillan.

About the Authors

The search for the perfect picnic has been an all-consuming passion of the Gibson-Whittaker family. The search has been conducted on five continents and included mountaintops in India, riverbanks in Africa, castles and olive groves in Spain, and buffalo jumps and ghost towns in Canada. Nancy is a cultural anthropologist, gardener, management consultant, author and university lecturer. John is a cook, management consultant, author and professor of engineering management.

Nancy Gibson and John Whittaker

Photo Credits

John Whittaker
Cover, Maligne Canyon   p. 42, Saskatchewan Crossing p. 36, Pyramid Lake p. 48, Bon Accord p. 59, Dunvegan p. 64, Peace River p. 74, Slave Lake p. 81, Victoria Settlement p. 86, Frog Lake p. 92, 97, St. Paul p. 101, Vegreville p. 104, Edmonton Legislature Building p. 117, 119, Leduc #1 p. 124, Blackfoot Grazing Reserve p. 136, Spruce Meadows p. 183, Morley p. 187

Carolyn Whittaker
Ft. Edmonton p. 111, 113, Blairmore p. 213, 215, Waterton Park p. 220, 221, Fort MacLeod p. 227, Head-Smashed-In p. 232, Ft. Whoop-Up p. 238, 239. Lethbridge p. 245, Taber p. 254

From *Castorologia: Or the history and Traditions of the Canadian Beaver* by Horace T. Martin, London: Edward Stanford, 1892.
Rocky Mountain House: Modifications of the beaver hat p. 150

Provincial Archives of Alberta
Having lunch on the Athabasca. Photograph Collection A5498, p. 53
A stopping place. Photograph Collection A11451, p. 73
Wandering Spirit. E. Brown Collection B1716, p. 93
Imperial Leduc #1. H. Pollard Collection P2729, p. 123
Markerville Picnic. Photograph Collecion A2236, p. 146
Rosebud. Public Affairs collection A11528, p. 167
Turner Valley. H. Pollard Collection P1893, p. 199
Medicine Tree. Public Affairs Collection PA6908, p. 208
Loaves & Fishes: Picnic at Athabasca. Photograph Collection A11508, p. 272

Travel Alberta
Rocky Mountain House p. 151, Calgary-Scotsman p. 176, Kananaskis p. 192, Brooks p. 250, Cypress Hills p. 261, Milk River p. 266

Kaslo Historical Society
Calgary - S.S. Moyie p. 173

Recipe Index